ECLIPSES

About the Author

Celeste Teal (Arizona) has been a passionate student of astrology for nearly thirty years. A graduate of the West Coast College of Astrology, Westminster, CA, in basic and advanced courses, she attained professional certification in 1986. Teal is a member of the American Federation of Astrologers and the Arizona Society of Astrologers. Besides hosting her popular astrology Web site to teach students of all levels, called *The Moon Valley Astrologer*, she writes feature articles for popular astrology magazines, including *Dell Horoscope, American Astrology* (now called *Horoscope Guide*), and *Astrology: Your Daily Horoscope*. Celeste Teal has authored two previous books on astrological technique: *Predicting Events with Astrology* (1999) and *Identifying Planetary Triggers* (2000), published by Llewellyn.

ECLIPSES

Predicting World Events
& Personal Transformation

CELESTE TEAL

Llewellyn Publications
Woodbury, Minnesota

First Edition
First Printing, 2006

Series design and format by Donna Burch
Cover art © PhotoDisc
Cover design by Ellen Dahl
Llewellyn is a registered trademark of Llewellyn Worldwide, Ltd.

Chart wheels were produced by the Kepler program by permission of Cosmic Patterns Software, Inc. (www.AstroSoftware.com)

Library of Congress Cataloging-in-Publication Data

Teal, Celeste.
   Eclipses : predicting world events & personal transformation / Celeste Teal.—1st ed.
       p. cm. — (Special topics in astrology)
   Includes bibliographical references and index.
   ISBN-13: 978-0-7387-0771-6
   ISBN-10: 0-7387-0771-6
     1. Predictive astrology. 2. Eclipses. I. Title. II. Series.

   BF1720.5.T426 2006
   133.5'3—dc22   2005055176

Llewellyn Worldwide does not participate in, endorse, or have any authority or responsibility concerning private business transactions between our authors and the public.
   All mail addressed to the author is forwarded but the publisher cannot, unless specifically instructed by the author, give out an address or phone number.
   Any Internet references contained in this work are current at publication time, but the publisher cannot guarantee that a specific location will continue to be maintained. Please refer to the publisher's website for links to authors' websites and other sources.

Llewellyn Publications
A Division of Llewellyn Worldwide, Ltd.
2143 Wooddale Drive, Dept. 0-7387-0771-6
Woodbury, MN 55125-2989, U.S.A.
www.llewellyn.com

Printed in the United States of America

Other Books by Celeste Teal

Predicting Events with Astrology
(Llewellyn Publications, 1999)

Identifying Planetary Triggers
(Llewellyn Publications, 2000)

Acknowledgments

Getting this book completed has been a joy and a challenge. It has required time, research, patience, and a lot of support and encouragement from friends, family, and colleagues. I'd like to start by expressing my thanks to everyone at Llewellyn for their individual and group efforts on the book, from proofreaders, to Ellen Dahl in the art department, to Alison and Brett in publicity, to Drew in marketing, Jennifer in marketing/copywriting, and of course to Donna Burch for doing such a beautiful job of designing the book. A special thanks goes to my editor and fellow Sagittarius, Andrea Neff, for her keen eye to detail and for helping to make the final proofing session a pleasure. Special thanks are also in order to Stephanie Clement, who went beyond the call of duty as an acquisitions specialist and who has always been so encouraging. Their assistance is truly appreciated.

I want to express my gratitude to Judy Collins for those early tips in mundane astrology and for answering endless emails so promptly when I needed to double-check data. A big thank you goes to Ken Irving for supplying some critical data at the last minute. Acknowledgments also go to the many gifted astrologers, past and present, that I've learned from over the years, whose teachings have contributed to this book. The list is too long to mention everyone, but a few in particular are Maggie Hyde, Anthony Louis, Mohan Koparker, Michael O'Reilly, Bill Meridian, Bruce Scofield, Alan Oken, Robert Hand, Robert Schulman, Ronald C. Davison, Evangeline Adams, Joseph Goodavage, DeVore, Lewi, Raphael, Green, Carter, Cardan, Leo, Omarr, Vaughn, Sakoian, and Acker.

I am most especially grateful to my friends and family for their love, understanding, and support. In particular I have several Taurus individuals in my life that I don't know what I'd do without since they are like rocks of strength. Thank you to my Taurus husband and to my friend Linda, with birthdays on the same day and with their Sun on my Vertex, so they have truly been an essential part of my destiny. Thanks to Donna, my dear Scorpio friend who loves to Google, and to Aussie Sagittarius Cher, for their input and data searches. Thank you Candace for your input on the book cover design. You are amazingly gifted, and an inspiration for anyone with a Grand Cross in his or her horoscope.

To all of those individuals who contributed personal eclipse stories for the book, thank you so much! I know that readers will appreciate it too.

Contents

CHAPTER SIXTEEN—REAL PEOPLE & THEIR ECLIPSE STORIES . . . 129

Introduction

Throughout history, eclipses have been considered as very powerful phenomena. In ancient times, an eclipse was regarded as highly ominous for the lands over which it fell. People were terrified of a Solar eclipse, as the light of the Sun faded to darkness in the middle of the day. Noisy ceremonies and customs, complete with beating drums and shooting arrows, were performed to chase away the evil dragon that was believed to be swallowing the Sun. Equally rare, but viewed by more people and just as frightening to the ancients, were the Lunar eclipses, when the light of the Moon turned dark red.

The term *eclipse* comes from *ecliptic*, which is the apparent yearly path of the Sun through the celestial sphere as the earth orbits the Sun. During an eclipse, the earth, Sun, and Moon come into a straight line, so that with a Solar eclipse, the light of the Sun is temporarily blocked out as the Moon passes directly between the earth and Sun. During a Lunar eclipse, the Moon loses its reflected light from the Sun as the earth passes between the Sun and Moon.

The definition of eclipse is to dim; to hide or conceal; to render invisible by an elimination of light.

Early astrologers noted this particular symbolism as they applied it to the horoscopes of their leaders and countries. Also called a nativity or a natal chart, a horoscope is a picture of the heavens at the moment of birth. A slice of the celestial sphere, with the earth in the center, is turned from a horizontal to a vertical position, converting to the horoscope with the various planets against the backdrop of constellations. From the moment of birth, this horoscope maps all the major crossroads met in life. For an individual, the moment of birth, from which the horoscope is calculated, is the moment of the first independent breath. For a country, the birth map is calculated from the time of its independence or founding. Although astrology was developing in many parts of the world at the same time, the first horoscopes were known simply as the "Babylonian numbers."

In the early days, astronomy and astrology were undivided; actually, astrology was the first science from which astronomy eventually flourished. Astronomy, which is the science of the heavenly bodies and their positions, distances, and physical attributes, is simply that—a science. Astrology was considered a social science, more valuable due to its usefulness in planning activities according to the most auspicious alignments of the planets for a particular occasion. First utilized as a way to combine worship with science, priests were the acting astrologers, and religious and other ceremonies were set to take place in accordance with the stars. Because the Sun, Moon, and planetary bodies appeared to exert distinct influences that affected not just the fate of individuals but general conditions, they became objects of hope, fear, and worship and were assigned the names of mythical gods. Still, it was only the very influential who were privy to the services of an astrologer. Drawing up a horoscope was a time-consuming process saved for royals and select circumstances such as the "birth" of an eclipse.

Eclipses became noted for their significance preceding famine, prosperity, disease, war, and other broad-scale events. Astrologers plotted the effects of an eclipse well into the future, and noted them for reflecting conditions affecting the multitudes. While events affecting the "common people" were said to be shown by the Lunar eclipse, the Solar eclipse foreshadowed events affecting nobles, clergy, heads of state, and countries. The science of astrology was very well respected in those days, and leaders ran their countries according to the information provided by their astrologers.

Over the course of hundreds of years and throughout the world, great mathematicians and astronomers studied the heavens, attempting to find a scientific explanation of celestial phenomena and the movement of the planets. It was through the rare appearance of an eclipse that some of the most valuable discoveries were made. The first catalog of stars was drawn up utilizing an eclipse of the Sun, and it was observed that the stars do not sink below the horizon in the daytime but instead shine in the sky along with the Sun. It was also apparent during an eclipse that the size of the Moon and the size of the Sun appeared to be the same, leading to the judgment that their size must be proportional to their distances from earth. Utilizing the shadow cast over the Moon during a Lunar eclipse, the size of the Sun and Moon were estimated by Aristarchus of Alexandria, who realized that the Sun was much larger than the earth. Another scholar, Philolaus, had already made the suggestion that the Sun was the center of our planetary system, but it wasn't until much later that this idea took root.

As astrology continued in its development, eclipses continued to hold immense interest, and copious notes were made about them by many of the greatest minds. Several of these great minds originated in Egypt and included not only Aristarchus but also Claudius Ptolemaeus, better known as Ptolemy. He is still considered to be among the leading astronomers and mathematicians of all time, although his belief that the earth was the center of the universe in the second century AD went unchallenged until the sixteenth century.

In the meantime, in the year 640 AD, during the rapid Islamic expansion into the East, the substantial astrological library and school in Alexandria, Egypt, was completely destroyed by the armies of Caliph Omar. Texts and materials were burned with the reasoning that the books either disagreed with the teachings of Mohammad as given in the Koran or that they agreed with the teachings and were therefore unnecessary. Either way, their only possible fate was destruction, and so much of the ancient wisdom surrounding eclipses was lost and the guidelines applied to eclipses by the old mathematicians gone, save for a few manuscripts that were translated, copied by hand, and passed down. Of these, there has been confusion as to the authenticity of some of the material as well as contradictory principles purported to come from the same source.

One of these rules in particular, having to do with the duration of effect of an eclipse, left modern astrologers in a quandary, as several different equations exist and all supposedly come from the same highly reputable source, Ptolemy. The most often heard rule is that a Solar eclipse has an effect that lasts as long in years as the eclipse lasts in hours, which gives the average Solar eclipse a life span of about three and a half years. This means that at certain times within that period, events signified in the eclipse horoscope will occur, and that conditions symbolized by the eclipse continue.

The ancient rule regarding the Lunar eclipse is more obscure, but the most often heard rule applied to the Lunar eclipse is that it has an effect duration, or life span, of one month for every hour of the eclipse shadow, equaling up to about six months at most.

Although there are many astrologers who regard eclipses as having a lengthy duration of effect, it is probably because of the inconsistencies in the old rules regarding them that a few astrologers now study the effects of any eclipse for the brief period of only a few months.

If it weren't for the fact that I may never tire of astrology research, I might have done the same; however, with several studies going on at once, the duration of effect of an eclipse was a matter that came up frequently, and I could not get Lunar eclipses to fit the formula. They consistently showed effects lasting longer than a few months.

I should explain that when I entered the world of astrology, it was as a nonbeliever. The first time I opened an astrology book, in 1975, my intention was to discredit it and prove to a friend that it simply couldn't be believed. The book I opened happened to go beyond the usual Sun Sign descriptions, though, and you can't imagine my astonishment to find that there actually *was* something to it. The first thing I realized was that astrology was based on a mathematical science and couldn't be compared to other occult practices. Discovering that our lives really are somehow synchronized with the movement of the planets, astrology soon became a passion. I felt it must be a valuable tool that could help guide us in our lives. Since then, I've put astrology to the test, looking for the secret key to the big picture and hoping to eventually learn even half as much as the great astrologers of the past.

One particular area of my own studies that stood out as far as the quality of information it furnished was the eclipses. Over time, I developed a certain fascination for them as I marveled at their special connection to timely crossroads on our individual journeys, as they seemed to connect us with our spiritual purpose and pull us to our destiny. It became routine to monitor eclipses in personal horoscopes as I noted the fascinating rhythmic process they revealed.

The reason the answer to this question involving the duration of effect of an eclipse was important to me is because by early 2001, eclipses had come under my focus in a research project concerning global events.

Setting off with the intention of doing 200 years of research on the history of the United States, I wondered if the same set of eclipse principles I'd found reliable for reflecting timely junctures in private lives also applied to larger events.

It didn't take long to make some amazing discoveries.

One thing I found that was pretty startling was in connection to stock market crashes and recessions at previous times in American history. As I looked at three of the major crashes, they were timed according to the principles I was testing, and I was dismayed to see that serious conditions showed on the horizon, evidently an indication that events of great consequence would begin affecting the U.S. economy and stock market in 2001.

As a matter of fact, from my research up to that time, it appeared that we were entering a most critical period based on eclipses and similar patterns of notable events existing at previous times. By early September of 2001, I was still tabulating results of research from the early part of the twentieth century, but I'd marked September 8–13, 2001, as a dangerous period for the United States going by the data gathered.

Then came the events of September 11, underscoring the direst of cycles noted in my research and confirming the timing as synchronized with eclipse stimulation. Though I'd researched a lot of major events by this time, nothing of such magnitude had ever happened, so I was in shock as I realized the full meaning of those red-letter days. Understanding from my research that this was only the beginning of an important era, it was at this point that I felt compelled to write about the convincing parallels between eclipse patterns and events on earth in hopes that such information can be utilized constructively in the future by turning eclipse energy to our advantage. An eclipse involves a process of transformation and shows where change is necessary. In the largest sense, you could say it acts as a cosmic regulator that maintains balance on earth, though often producing a crisis to bring attention to a situation. Understanding these processes enables us to effect changes with more wisdom.

Eclipses even reveal our individual ties to these universal processes, where we fit in the big picture and where and when we make links with others, what I call our "cosmic connections" to people, space, and time. Oftentimes they point to imbalances in our personal lives, raise our consciousness to these, and enable a flow of cosmic energy that eventually results in more satisfying conditions.

In these pages, you'll learn of the mysterious power of an eclipse. Part 1 explains the eclipse itself, how it derives its power, how it holds a particular message, and what sets some eclipses above others in terms of power potential. Part 2 illustrates world events, past and present, and includes some speculation about the future. (Because this work was completed in 2003, with projections from that year, there are occasional references to events that have since occurred.) Part 3 shows you how to find personally important eclipses and what they mean for you. The appendix supplies all the tables and resources you'll need to track eclipses through 2015, and to learn how they may impact your life, your company or business, or the world at large.

The eclipse is a fabulous place to look when attempting to understand the big picture as well as our individual places in it. I hope this presentation will help establish a firmer grasp of eclipses and their functions, that it fills a gap in the currently available material on eclipses, and that it inspires more observation of the eclipses.

PART ONE

The Hidden Power
& Message of an Eclipse

CHAPTER ONE

The Mysterious Dragon's Head & Dragon's Tail

An eclipse introduces an era and begins a lengthy process as it relates to mankind's activities and evolving consciousness. Regardless of the part of the globe over which it can be seen, an eclipse can always be traced to one of the twelve signs of the celestial zodiac and one of the 30 degrees of that sign.

An astrological chart drawn up for the event of an eclipse gives a specific picture, through planetary symbols, of the overall circumstances and conditions affecting earth and its inhabitants. It shows where transformation and change are due to take place and to where our attention will be directed. The eclipse, charted this way, provides a cosmic telegram for the world, and the symbols can be assessed for strength, breadth, longevity, difficulty, or ease. The eclipse chart can then be traced to those individuals, nations, businesses,[1] or entities for which it holds special importance.

Beginning a cosmic process that requires a certain period of time to complete, just like any other entity, an eclipse has a birth, a rise to maturity, a decline, and then a death. Each eclipse initiates a theme or trend for a brief era of time, lasting from one to seven years but averaging about three and a half years. There are various features of an eclipse that determine the theme of the era, how long it will last, and the kinds of events or changes that are suggested, both for the world and for individuals.

The first of these variables and a most important factor depends on the presence and influence of the nearby Dragon's Head or Dragon's Tail when an eclipse occurs. Also called the North Lunar Node and South Lunar Node, respectively, these are the intersections of two orbits, and although invisible, they are the magical components that make an eclipse possible only about every six months, when a New Moon or a Full Moon aligns closely with either the North Lunar Node or the opposite South Lunar Node.[2]

Each month when we have a New Moon, it brings a one-month period of new beginnings and opportunities into a certain area of our lives, varying personally for each of us. This might be career, money, relationships, family, or another of the twelve areas of life symbolized by the twelve sectors in the astrological chart. When we have a Solar eclipse, it's like a super New Moon, with effects lasting for many months due to the magnetic properties of the Lunar Nodes, which draw upon the energy vibrations of nearby planetary bodies to a powerful degree. The North Lunar Node and the South Lunar Node act as portals through which cosmic energy flows, and these portals remain open during the entire span of the eclipse era, enabling new energy to stimulate conditions and bring about events at certain times within the eclipse era whenever another planet passes by the open Lunar portal. It is this nodal factor that heats an eclipse, and is the reason that an eclipse degree cools very slowly. If an eclipse touches upon a personal planet in an individual's astrological chart, it is of greater personal value and impact, also coinciding with more profound periods and eventful transformations in life. The planetary potential is magnified and sensitized to future transits.

The Lunar Nodes, or Dragon's Head and Tail, have long been associated with karmic workings, timing, and connections. Even the earliest astrologers were aware of the powerful energy flowing through the invisible Lunar Nodes during the time of an eclipse and attempted to convey this information to their heads of states. Unfortunately, some royals used the knowledge from their personal astrologers to manipulate the common people, warning them that a dragon would devour the Sun or Moon on a certain day, impressing and frightening the people at once when the eclipse did come to pass to put out the light of the Sun or Moon. Clearly, this did nothing to help the reputation of eclipses, but today the dragon lore lingers in the names given to the Lunar Nodes, which help to define their specific influence.

Traditionally, the Dragon's Head was considered a point of intake or gain, where benefits arrive more easily and without conscious effort. It has generally been considered to be luckier and more auspicious than the Dragon's Tail, which is equated with a point of loss or vulnerability, or where sacrifice is required. The Dragon's Head offers an inflowing rush of new energy, and the Dragon's Tail provides an extracting force, inviting the release of accumulated energy.

The particular magnetic attribute of each of these portals has its beneficial function. By understanding their differences, we have the opportunity to work with the universal forces and turn them to our advantage during the span of the eclipse process.

The energy of the Dragon's Head acts as an enticement toward participation in earthly matters and material acquisition. Even though the Dragon's Head eclipse offers new stimuli and often leads toward fresh opportunities of conquest, the rush of incoming energy may come as a surprise that is experienced at first as disruptive. And, because the Dragon's Head energy is an amplifier, when falling on a planet in the personal horoscope, this eclipse can unleash the greedy, materialistic, lustful, or less desirable traits of an individual, depending upon how spiritually guided and practically grounded the person is.

The Dragon's Tail acts as an attraction to timeless service and things everlasting. Through this vibration we are called upon to offer something back. It is payback time; time to balance the ledger. The energy of an eclipse with the influence of the Dragon's Tail may be exactly what is needed to complete a project that has previously consumed much time and effort. This eclipse has to do with giving back, serving selflessly, and practicing compassion. It may be the most difficult eclipse in many respects simply because we are more conditioned and encouraged to acquire than to give. When experienced negatively, it may bring about situations most symbolic of the traditional "eclipsed" symbolism. It can bring a distorted sense of powerlessness or low self-esteem, resulting in an uncharacteristic or desperate handling of situations that is to one's disadvantage.

For example, in 2001, prior to her insider trading scandal and fall from grace in 2003, entrepreneur and homemaking diva Martha Stewart experienced a powerful Dragon's Tail eclipse in her chart. It fell on her Moon, the planet representative of her public popularity, and opposite her progressed Jupiter, the planet representative of her financial wealth. It is likely that the insecurity and loss of control she felt at this eclipse contributed to some uncharacteristically poor judgment calls. But, from this example, one can see how the Dragon's Tail became equated with loss, vulnerability, and sacrifice.

Truly, the Dragon's Head and Tail form a continuous circle; they are connected to one another. If we visualize that the Dragon's Head breathes fire and the Dragon's Tail inhales smoke, we see how they portray karma and the laws of cause and effect. Whatever is put out at the Dragon's Head has its result, or effect, at the Dragon's Tail. One must take care not to misuse the power bestowed by the Dragon's Head eclipse because the effect of an eclipse with the influence of the Dragon's Tail is quite reliant on what has gone before.

Each eclipse has the influence of either the Dragon's Head or Dragon's Tail, and in any year we have about an equal number of them, equal shares of opportunities for give and take, equal amounts of incoming and outflowing energy.

Although there are additional features of an eclipse that may add to or take away from its strength and impact, the closer an eclipse aligns with the Dragon's Head or Tail, the more intense and profound the potential is for changes to occur in the months or years following the eclipse, both in the way of the world and for an individual whom the eclipse touches.[3]

As a guideline, it is generally recommended to avoid initiating major decisions or drastic life changes near the time of an eclipse. The state of flux and initial charge of energy coming into the atmosphere tend to destabilize new ventures. Perhaps it isn't strange at all that this may be exactly the time you feel most compelled to push forward into new territory or to overthrow an existing set of conditions, especially should an eclipse be significant for you personally. In fact, it is often exactly the energy of an eclipse that is needed to clear the cobwebs and make way for fresh experiences. Still, it is easy to make faulty choices now, increasing the possibility of problems and accidents, and it is difficult to get plans to solidify at this time.

Now that you know that an eclipse may magnify or distort a facet of your personality or character, you can contemplate whether what you are feeling seems inappropriate or unusual for you. Remember that everyone feels the effects of an eclipse to some extent, some more personally than others, so even if you feel quite certain and stable about changes you want to pursue, the person on the other end of your new arrangements may be unable to follow through.

Use table 1 in the appendix to find the date of the next eclipse, and then watch what is happening around you at that time to see what you detect. Sometimes events happening here offer a clue to situations that will require attention later on. Table 1 also identifies the presence and influence of the Dragon's Head or Tail at the time of the eclipse.

Eclipses usually come in pairs, so from ten days before the first eclipse until three days after the last, it is best to refrain from initiating grand new arrangements. That allows time for the eclipse energies to settle out some.

Because the Dragon's Head and Tail are always opposite one another, and moving slowly backward through the zodiac, we always have eclipses falling in signs of the zodiac that are opposite one another. An eclipse can occur only when the Sun joins the zodiac sign of either the Dragon's Head or Tail. For example, in 2005, eclipses occurred in the sign Aries and its opposite sign, Libra. By 2007, eclipses will take place in the opposite signs of Virgo and Pisces.

The Dragon's Head and Dragon's Tail take about nineteen years to make a full circuit of the zodiac, enabling a rhythmic sweep of eclipses that prevents stagnant or unhealthy situations anywhere on the globe or anywhere in our personal lives.

Every entity, from a person to an enterprise, also has a Dragon's Head and a Dragon's Tail occupying a place in the astrological chart. In part 2, you'll see how this energy manifests in world matters. You'll learn in part 3 of their revealing significance in your personal life.

In the coming chapter, you'll find out why the planetary Lord of an eclipse holds the key to its meaning and how that planet has dominion over earthly affairs.

---

1. The birth of a business is generally based upon its incorporation date and time, or the time of its official opening, when it is both an operating entity in the world and operating within legal boundaries. All new enterprises have a birth time, from a company to a Web site, which is dependent upon the moment at which it is up and functioning and able to receive visitors.

2. The Lunar Nodes are invisible points of intersection of two orbits that pierce the celestial sphere; in this case, the Moon's orbit with that of the ecliptic (the apparent yearly path of the Sun through the celestial sphere as the earth orbits the Sun), as the Moon circles the earth. Occurring twice a month, we have a pair of Lunar Nodes opposite one another.

3. A Solar eclipse can occur only when the New Moon forms within 18.50 degrees of one of the Lunar Nodes. A Lunar eclipse can occur only if the Full Moon forms within 12.25 degrees of the Lunar Nodes.

The motion of the Lunar Nodes is about 19 degrees per year backward through the zodiac. Usually, two Solar eclipses occur each year as the Sun moves into the zodiac sign occupied by either the North or South Node. Two weeks prior to and/or two weeks following a Solar eclipse, there may be a Lunar eclipse at the time of the Full Moon, all depending upon how close the Sun and Moon are to the Lunar Nodes. Sequential years show eclipses within neighboring degrees and frequently in the same sign of the zodiac.

CHAPTER TWO

The Lord of an Eclipse

In regard to worldly events and conditions, the zodiac sign of an eclipse, whether of the element of Fire, Earth, Air, or Water, was regarded by early astrologers as highly symbolic of the nature of events coming due. As such, an eclipse that took place in one of the three Fire signs was symbolic of wars and terrible slaughters; in Earth signs, of barrenness, scarcities, droughts, and earthquakes; in Air signs, of wind and storm; and in Water signs, of heavy rains and floods.

In fact, each eclipse is unique, just like people are, so it's not quite that simple to categorize them. All eclipses falling in the Fire element of the zodiac are not necessarily forerunners of terrible wars and bloody slaughters, although some might be. If an eclipse does foreshadow war, the planetary ruler of the zodiac sign where the eclipse fell should help identify the kind of war or the basis of the war. Each sign of the zodiac has a natural planetary ruler, which becomes Lord of an eclipse occurring in the sign it rules.

For example, in December of 2001, we had an eclipse that took place in the Fire sign Sagittarius. The planetary ruler of Sagittarius is Jupiter, which is associated with spiritual and religious beliefs, and further defined this eclipse as bringing the potential for holy wars. That the U.S. would be involved in this war was indicated by that eclipse falling in alignment with the planet Mars in the U.S. horoscope. Mars signifies the military, thus the U.S. initiated the war against terrorism following hostile actions taken against U.S. interests. Radical Islamic groups profess that they are fighting a holy war, which they call a jihad, and this eclipse occurred at the time of heavy bombing by the U.S. in Afghanistan. As this eclipse remained active, in March of 2003, when the eclipse was stimulated by passing planets, this war against terror, led by the U.S. and the Coalition of the Willing, spread to include taking out the oppressive regime in Iraq.

Another manifestation of this "holy war" eclipse was noted in the Catholic Church crisis, with scandals and lawsuits against priests for sexually abusive acts upon children in their care. There was also an increase in contention between those who are for or against gays in the priesthood, another expression of this "holy war."

Here, we will take a brief look at each of the four elements, the zodiac signs belonging to each, and the planetary rulers of the signs to see the general point of crisis that might most likely be signified by an eclipse in each sign. This is helpful in determining the overall message of an eclipse, most especially as it relates to worldly matters. An eclipse often signifies a fairly drastic change in direction in the matters indicated by sign, and the planetary ruler of the sign helps identify the people whose interests will be affected.

The Fire Signs

Aries, the first Fire sign, is ruled by the planet Mars, symbolic of offensive power and of a competitive, adventurous spirit. Aries and its ruler, Mars, are associated with heat, fire, war, fevers, pestilence, illness, accidents, weaponry, crime, controversies, and tumult. Mars signifies the police, the military, heroes, firefighters, surgeons, engineers, mechanics, agitators, and those who use sharp tools or instruments. It rules athletes and those of good physical coordination and strength. The energy associated with Mars is passionate, quick, aggressive, angry, infectious, and dangerous. Alternatively, it is pioneering and courageous and shows admirable initiative, positively linked to new enterprise and discoveries. Those engaged in Mars-ruled activities would find eclipses in Aries to be a precursor to changes and transitions that bring a focus to their skills.

Leo is the second Fire sign and is ruled by the Sun. Leo is associated with the internal will and the power to create. It brings an accent to royals, leaders, men of power, executive and governmental heads, and possible threats of death or the overthrow of such leaders.

The Sun is vital, strong, prideful, egotistic, and commanding. It rules gold and is of a positive and usually benevolent quality. All else revolves around the Sun. Central figures and those who are described by the Sun will find that eclipses in Leo may be especially meaningful as they make an impact on personal interests.

Sagittarius is the third Fire sign and is ruled by Jupiter. Sagittarius expresses qualities of aspiration and enthusiasm. It accents religion, distant travel, foreigners, publishing, philanthropy, propaganda, and higher education. Jupiter rules journalists and reporters and signifies clerics, the judiciary, world travelers, professors, and industrialists. Jupiter supports order, peace, and prosperity. It is associated with expansion and distant vision and is benevolent and acquisitive by nature, but is sometimes significant of overproduction. Those connected to Jupiter-ruled activities would find eclipses in Sagittarius to be quite significant of coming changes having a direct impact upon their interests.

The Fire signs are action-oriented and inspirationally motivated. Eclipses in Fire signs may produce sensational events, with dissension among men, excessive heat, lack of rain, fire, fevers, movements of armies, death or imprisonment of great men, religious disputes, and the destruction of cud-chewing animals.

The Earth Signs

Taurus is the first Earth sign and is ruled by the planet Venus. Taurus symbolizes fruitfulness, lushness, and productivity. It is associated with wages, bankers, property, textiles, builders, resources, and reserves, including paper money and coins. Venus signifies designers, interior decorators, dealers in art or ornamentation, musicians, theaters, and festivals. The energy attributed to Taurus is that of steady pressure. Bankers and others involved in Venus-ruled activities would find eclipses in Taurus to be especially meaningful, as they encourage a transitional period in related affairs.

Virgo is the second Earth sign and is ruled by Mercury. Virgo is associated with the goddess of fertility. It is associated with harvests, crops, food supply, natural resources, environmental factors, and public health. Those signified are farmers, growers, nutritionists, and health workers. The energy of Mercury as the ruler of Virgo emphasizes purity, practicality, detailed analysis, and the need for critical faculties. Those involved in activities falling under Virgo's domain will find that eclipses in Virgo bring an emphasis to their work and announce that transitions are in order.

Capricorn is the third Earth sign, ruled by Saturn. Capricorn, symbolized by the mountain-climbing goat ever in pursuit of wealth and position, is symbolic of changes shaped by the passage of time. It is associated with industry, business, organization, public buildings, national calamities, and scarcity. Saturn signifies elders, minor state executives, civil service employees, landowners, and various authorities. Saturn limits, disciplines, conserves, and restricts. Those involved in the business and organizational activities governed by Saturn will find that eclipses occurring in Capricorn are a prelude to important transitions.

An eclipse in an Earth sign may signify recessions, financial problems, trade and agricultural disturbances, drought, scarcity, famine, crops or fruits of the earth threatened, earthquakes, volcanic eruptions, or avalanches. Earth signs are motivated by practical concerns.

The Air Signs

Gemini is the first Air sign and is ruled by Mercury. It indicates the marketplace, trade, elementary education, transport, all forms of communication, and relations with neighboring countries. Mercury rules the media, periodicals, intelligence gathering, the press, and messengers, including mail workers. It also signifies youth, secretaries, merchants, teachers, travelers, gossips, and thieves. The energy of Mercury in Gemini is that of movement, versatility, and variability. Those engaged in Mercury-ruled activities would find that eclipses in Gemini bring an accent to their industry with transitions at hand.

The second Air sign is Libra, ruled by Venus. This sign is associated with balance, equilibrium, justice, cooperation, and reciprocation. Libra corresponds with social issues, courtship, and marriage. Venus rules young women, wives, and sweethearts. Venus is associated with preservers of the peace and those who cater to the pursuit of pleasure. A crisis erupting with an eclipse in Libra may involve division, abuse, and circumstances affecting public tranquility or jeopardizing morals. Counselors, social workers, and others involved in these Venus-ruled activities would find that eclipses in Libra bring a spotlight to the need for their special skills.

The third Air sign is Aquarius, ruled by Uranus. Aquarius promotes the humanitarian principles, in which knowledge and service are provided to all of humanity. Aquarius is associated with invention and technology, spacecraft and aeronautics, labor organizations, revolutions, strikes, riots, and explosions. Uranus is connected with electricians, rebels, astrologers, and eccentrics. The energy of Uranus is spasmodic, unexpected, and shocking, and often arrives at the speed of lightning. Computer technicians and others pursuing Uranus-ruled activities would find that eclipses in Aquarius are most relevant to their work and interests. Saturn is the co-ruler of Aquarius.

Eclipses in Air signs may signify sociological upheavals, uprisings, seditions, destructive storms, high winds or pandemics, party splits and defections, and changes in treaties and alliances. Some eclipses in Aquarius may denote earthquakes. The Air signs are intellectually motivated.

The Water Signs

The first Water sign is Cancer, ruled by the Moon. Cancer expresses the maternal and nurturing instincts, growth, and fertility. Cancer is concerned with the home, family, domestics, heritage, country, and homeland. The Moon rules large crowds, the public, women and their interests, and popular subjects of the moment. It rules silver and governs water, the tides, and liquids in general. The Moon is sensitive and its energy is fluctuating and variable, thus it corresponds to changeable public sentiments. Those dealing in domestic products or services of interest to women will find that eclipses in the sign Cancer precede a transitional period.

The second Water sign is Scorpio, ruled by the planet Pluto. Scorpio is passionate, magnetic, and concerned with reproduction. It is associated with healing and regenerative processes. Pluto rules miners, the masses, healers, gangsters, morticians and mortuaries, sewage workers and refuse, toxins, venereal epidemics, pornography, nuclear energy, and atomic science. Sex, death, and taxes are in Pluto's domain, as are legacies, wills, and insurance. Its energy is coercive, purging, and uprooting. Franchise owners, debt collectors, insurance companies, loan officers, and others engaged in Pluto-governed activities will find that eclipses in Scorpio announce the need for changes. Mars was considered to rule Scorpio before Pluto was discovered.

The last Water sign is Pisces, ruled by Neptune. Pisces expresses the principles of bondage, captivity, the struggle of the soul in the body, and concern with life after death. It is associated with spirituality, charities, hospitals, and institutions of recovery or confinement. Neptune rules the sea, sailors, prophets, mystics, dancers, actors, medicine, alcohol, drugs, oil, gases, chemicals, and fluids. The energy of Neptune is to occlude, dissolve, cloud, or fog. Pharmaceutical and drug companies and those pursuing activities linked to

Neptune will find that eclipses in Pisces are particularly relevant for them, as they bring an accent to their industry. Jupiter co-rules Pisces.

A Water-sign eclipse may signify increased mortality among common people, widespread unrest, treasonous acts, drug-related problems, excessive rain, tidal waves, accidents by sea, or the destruction of fowl and fish and things living near the water. The Water signs are emotionally motivated.

Table 2: Eclipse Elements in the appendix provides examples of the people, events, and effects signified by an eclipse in any of the twelve zodiac signs according to their element.

Obviously there are a number of things and people represented by each sign and its ruling planet. In fact, each eclipse produces more than one manifestation, as we saw with the eclipse that announced the holy wars. For any scenario or event one could think of, one sign and Lord should symbolize it better than another.

Now, what about very unusual events, such as the arrival of aliens? We don't have a lot of experience with alien encounters, so how would we know to be prepared? Which sign and Lord might such an occurrence be placed under?

Actually, an eclipse in the Fire sign Sagittarius could be the precursor to the arrival of extraterrestrials here on earth.

It was an eclipse in Sagittarius in 1946 that was the forerunner of the controversial alien encounters in Roswell, New Mexico, in 1947.[1] Because the sign Sagittarius is related to distant travelers, Jupiter, as eclipse Lord, should be most descriptive of aliens. However, it is not so easy to pinpoint one specific ruler to these far-out visitors because of the many complications they entail. They arrive on a UFO, ruled by Neptune (the unknown) and by Uranus (flying object). Because they may be hostile invaders, Mars comes into the picture, and this planet reflects the rush of military activity whenever there are UFO sightings. Mercury would signify our ability, or lack thereof, to communicate with the visitors, and the Moon is a factor as it relates to the reactions of the public to their arrival.

In any case, we may have a chance to study this further, as significant eclipses and planetary alignments may encourage such encounters. In 2011 and 2012, there are two eclipses that energize Roswell's birth chart in the same way that one did prior to the 1947 alleged encounter. We'll talk more about this in chapter 10.

Special Conditions for Assigning a New Lord to an Eclipse

Usually the planetary ruler of the sign where an eclipse takes place becomes the Lord of the eclipse. That planet reveals much about how an eclipse is apt to manifest, the affairs it will spotlight, and the people whose interests will be brought into the limelight.

We know that during an eclipse, our luminaries, the Sun and Moon, are involved in a unique relationship, either together in one zodiac sign during a Solar eclipse or in opposing signs during a Lunar eclipse. If another planet happens to be close by when the eclipse occurs, within 3 degrees of the Sun or Moon, it becomes the new Lord of the eclipse. In this scenario, that extra planet dominates the eclipse message. The strongest influences can be seen in that accompanying planet, as if the eclipse, or in truth, the Lunar portal, opens a doorway for this planet's dominion. When the extra planet holds the very same degree as the Sun or Moon, the nature of that planet may override the planetary ruler of the sign of the eclipse, and it is given the power to reign over affairs. This is more serious if the planet is a malefic.

A good example of this was notable in the Eclipse of July 1, 2000, when Mars accompanied the Sun and Moon during a Solar eclipse that fell in the sign Cancer. Mars, associated with heat and fire, modified the meaning of the eclipse in a Water sign. It dried up the water, bringing drought and raging wildfires, more than in the previous fifty years, especially troublesome for the western United States for four years. We will take a closer look at this eclipse in chapter 8, but taking the root meaning, it translated to many "water-related dangers," so while some parts of the country suffered floods, other parts suffered wildfires and forty-nine states came under drought conditions.

Some eclipses reveal major pinnacles on earth, and these are not confined to the places where the eclipse is visible or the area of the globe over which the eclipse shadow sweeps. An eclipse carries a message to the whole world, so each eclipse is followed by multiple manifestations with varying effects by region.[2]

In the next chapter you'll find out about the epoch of an eclipse, the length of its duration, and what happens during its secret life.

---

1. See Roswell's horoscope in the Annotated Catalog of National Figures in the appendix for more about this eclipse.

2. Chart the event of the eclipse for the time it occurs locally or the time it occurs in the location in question.

CHAPTER THREE

The Secret Life of an Eclipse

An eclipse has a definite life span based upon the length of time that the Sun, Moon, and earth are aligned in the skies, with the sunlight temporarily blocked during a Solar eclipse or with a shadow cast upon the Moon during a Lunar eclipse. This shadow period varies from one eclipse to another, with an average shadow period of three to four hours.

Several formulas exist for determining the life span of an eclipse, with conflicting formulas purportedly coming from the same highly reputable source, none other than Ptolemy, so this has been a somewhat murky area. As already mentioned in the introduction, the most often heard rule is that a Solar eclipse has an effect that lasts as long in years as the eclipse lasts in hours, which gives the average Solar eclipse a life span of about three and a half years. This means that at certain times within that period, events signified in the eclipse chart will occur and that conditions symbolized by the eclipse will continue.

The formula for figuring the duration of a Lunar eclipse is more obscure, and the Lunar eclipse has been treated as inferior to the Solar eclipse by most modern astrologers if not by the older mathematicians themselves. The most often heard rule applied to the Lunar eclipse is that it has an effect duration, or life span, of one month for every hour of the eclipse shadow, equaling up to about six months at most.

These formulas were the ones that I personally tried to apply. However, in many years of research, I was never able to get the Lunar eclipse to fit this formula. Lunar eclipses and their effects consistently gave results indicating that they were sensitive much longer than a few months. There were numerous cases in my client files that indicated they were connected to personal processes requiring quite some time to complete. In one extreme case involving a young woman, a Lunar eclipse remained sensitive for nearly six years, during which time her domestic and home life underwent many extreme changes and transitions.

As a dedicated astrologer, I really wanted to apply the proper rules, but with evidence stacking up to suggest that a Lunar eclipse was of longer duration than any formula I'd heard of, this became quite a point of thoughtfulness.

Wondering how my results could be so at variance with what sounded on the surface to be a reasonable equation, I began to question what these formulas were based on. To be sure, whenever one of the old rules as to the duration of effect of eclipses is stated, the reasoning behind the equation is never explained.[1] Although the Moon's cycle is monthly while the Sun's cycle is yearly, and although the light of the Moon is a reflection from the Sun, a Lunar eclipse is a rare occasion, just as a Solar eclipse and both types of eclipses involve a unique alignment of the Sun, Moon, and earth. The Moon is actually at maximum power when Full, which is the only time a Lunar eclipse can occur. After a great deal more study to compare the effects of Solar and Lunar eclipses in the lives of individuals as well as in worldly matters, it finally dawned on me that there were actually two possibilities as to why Lunar eclipses were significantly underrated outside of the fact that they were probably less scrutinized than Solar eclipses.

From the earliest of times, the Moon was considered as most influential for all of earth's inhabitants due to its close proximity to the earth. The phases of the Moon were found to be consequential in all changes from conception to birth and were linked to all beginnings of actions. However, due to the fact that the regular cycle of the Moon is synchronized with the menstrual cycle of fertile women, it has likewise been associated with fertility, nurturance, and feminine principles since the dawn of time. Because the Sun reflects the masculine principle, an eclipse of the Moon might well have been treated as less important than a Solar eclipse. Could this be an interesting case of repression of the feminine principle? Come to think of it, the great mathematicians and astrologers of old were nearly all of the masculine gender. However, in their defense, there may be yet another reason for paying so little attention to the Lunar eclipse.

The Lunar principle centers on soulful stirrings and experiences that affect us on a deeper level. We are less conscious of these processes than we are of the identity and ego processes attributed to the Solar eclipse, so whether or not it's been intentional, it may be easier to dispose of these eclipses as quickly as possible rather than to query them. Even I kept trying to give them reduced significance in spite of conflicting evidence. By now I'm convinced that the rule Ptolemy and others might have passed along and couldn't bring themselves to utter, for whatever reason, was that the Lunar eclipse, like the Solar eclipse, be given a life span of one year for every hour of the eclipse shadow.

A Lunar eclipse can actually have a life span that lasts longer than a Solar eclipse. Considering that the Lunar eclipse shows conditions shared by the common people, general trends and conditions usually do last for an extended period of time.

This means that the overall *average* eclipse life span is 3.5 years during which the degree of the zodiac where the eclipse formed remains sensitive. It is sometimes longer or shorter than that. For instance, the Solar eclipse on Christmas Day of 2000 was officially alive and sensitive until 2005, while the Solar eclipse in November of 2003 lasted only a year. You can see a sampling of the first twenty eclipses of the twenty-first century with conversions in Table 3: Eclipse Life-Span Conversions in the appendix.

Now that we have some general guidelines in place from which to gauge the duration of an eclipse, we can take a look at what happens during the life of an eclipse.

Sometimes there's a surge of events and new information within days of an eclipse, either just before or right after. This happens due to the sheer dynamics of the eclipse itself, when both "lights" of the Sun and Moon form a relationship and stress a theme according to their zodiac placement(s). The events taking place near the time of an eclipse often serve as an announcement of the issues that need to be addressed and those that will come under review in the months or years ahead.

Weeks, months, or even years following an eclipse, other planets provide fuel and energy as they travel across the degree of the zodiac where the eclipse formed. As we discussed in chapter 1, the Lunar portals that were opened at the time of the eclipse remain open for the life span of the eclipse, which we understand now is about three and a half years. These times of planetary stimulation, or *transits*, often coincide with dynamic earthly events that were indicated by the eclipse. All of the planets in the sky will sooner or later pass by these portals, either by moving directly through the zodiac degree of the earlier eclipse, by conjunction, or by passing through the opposite degree in the zodiac, in opposition. If the previous eclipse is still "alive" and sensitive, certain planets provide new energy or allow for a release of pressure, so the dates of these planetary passes often coincide closely with events that are necessary to bring eventual resolution to a specific area of imbalance.

Part of the hidden power of an eclipse is that it is only the beginning of a lengthy process and has delayed manifestations. An eclipse reveals a descriptive era and can be used to find the timing of major significant events.

Perhaps the ancient astrologers came close to perfecting these celestial rhythms. Their only technology and the first science was the observation of the stars and planets from an earth-centered perspective, where they had lots of time to search for answers to the causes of conditions around them. It's even possible that a simple set of principles was lost with other astrological material in the seventh century or that it came to be disregarded later with the discovery that the earth was not the center of the universe. Still, most of us do feel that the universe revolves around us, and most astrologers continue to use the earth-centered horoscope because it works.

Although the ancients believed that the warrior planet Mars was responsible for activating an eclipse and that the taskmaster Saturn was responsible for consummating an eclipse, it is also true that when an eclipse receives the energy from *both* those planets while the eclipse is still sensitive, the force of the incoming or releasing pressure is greater, seeming to come all at once. Great changes take place; time may seem to speed up as we seek to acclimate to new and constantly changing conditions. Due to the very slow movement of the massive ringed planet Saturn, it is fairly rare for an eclipse to get this pass by Saturn while it is still active and sensitive. However, such were the times at the opening of the new millennium, and another of these periods approaches in 2007 through 2009 and again in 2011 through 2015.

Eclipses falling in this select group may coincide with exceptional periods of rapid progress if they fall on an important place in the individual nativity. In world affairs or personal quests, there is a special window of opportunity available with these eclipses—from the time of the eclipse to the closing pass of Saturn—to make changes and attend to important matters signified by the eclipse.

According to these principles, there are two ways for an eclipse to "end." One way is by the expiration of the eclipse itself, and the other way is through Saturn's pass—by conjunction or opposition—to the eclipse degree. Up until one of these two things happens, that eclipse degree is still sensitive, and each pass of Mars, which comes about once a year, can stir the eclipse potential, often coinciding with a conflict relevant to the original eclipse message.

For example, in the case of the lengthy Lunar eclipse mentioned earlier in this chapter, that Lunar eclipse had fallen on the planet Pluto in the chart of this newly married young lady. Having the Moon in such a close relationship with Pluto usually denotes some fairly major domestic transitions. Disruptions transpired at each planetary pass of Mars for five years following the eclipse, when domestic moves were made and her home and family underwent many upheavals and transformations. Finally, Saturn's transit over the eclipse coincided with a smoothing-out process, bringing stable conditions. This had been a lengthy Lunar eclipse with a life span of nearly six years when converted from hours to years.

In some instances a transit of a planet over a natal planet can produce a noteworthy event even without an eclipse having taken place there. Yet a simple transit, even from Mars, to a natal planet doesn't always bring a significant event. If the natal planet or point has been eclipsed, however, events tend to be more outstanding, sometimes spectacular and sometimes lasting for years. The eclipsed planet remains supercharged and sensitive. Then every transit of a planet such as Mars is more likely to produce an event of consequence.

You'll see many examples ahead that show the Lunar eclipse to be as important as the Solar eclipse, and having a lengthy life span.

The dates that the Sun, Mars, or an outer planet stimulates any eclipse from 2000 to 2015 are shown in table 1 in the appendix. Eventful happenings are likely to take place near the transit dates shown, with the nature of the event described by the nature of the stimulating planet, as discussed in the next chapter.[2]

---

1. One possible explanation that a Solar eclipse was regarded more highly than a Lunar eclipse is because a conjunction of planets is considered a stronger aspect than an opposition; the Sun and Moon are conjunct during a Solar eclipse, and opposed during a Lunar eclipse.

2. A planet within 3 degrees +/- of an eclipse, by conjunction or opposition, is in the zone of stimulation. For the Sun, this is three days either side of the exact transit date, and for Mars, up to seven days, al-

though usually less. Jupiter begins to stimulate an eclipse degree about two weeks before the transit date and lasts for two weeks after the precise date if Jupiter is moving at his speediest. Due to retrograde motion—the apparent backward motion of planets from our earth-centered perspective at certain times of the year—an eclipse may be stimulated multiple times by a planet. Due to exceptionally slow movement combined with retrograde motion, Jupiter, Saturn, or an outer planet could remain in range of an eclipse for several weeks.

CHAPTER FOUR

Planetary Stimulation to an Eclipse

In this chapter we'll take a brief look at each of the planets in terms of the kind of energy it brings when crossing over an active eclipse degree by conjunction or opposition. A few examples from the opening years of the new century will help make these points clear.

The Moon is actually a luminary, although astrologers refer to it as a planet. It has proven to have an effect on all our earthly cycles due to its close proximity, and is influential upon all, whether animate or inanimate. Without the Moon, life as we know it would not exist. It exerts a helpful pull upon the earth that keeps it stable in its rotation. Without the Moon, there would be no regular seasons. The Moon actually appeared larger to the ancients than it does to us. It is slowly inching away from the earth, about an inch and a half each year. That's practically nothing in the vast ocean of space, but eventually, a Solar eclipse will never appear as total because the rim of sunlight around the Moon during the eclipse will get larger as the Moon recedes from the earth.

The Moon is a most delicate sensor, and our moods are influenced daily by it as it travels speedily through the zodiac, forming first one and then another relationship to the other transiting planets and to our natal planets. In world affairs it reflects the fluctuations in the mood of the public. Because it is so transitory, the Moon is not sufficient on its own to produce spectacular events when it travels over an eclipse, although it may join in with a heavier planet at times of important events.

The Sun provides vitality, spirit, and animation. It is partly due to the great strength of the Sun that notable events sometimes transpire within days of an eclipse. Taking one year in its apparent revolution through the zodiac, the Sun reactivates an eclipse three months following the eclipse and then again three months later, when it arrives at the opposite degree in the zodiac from where the eclipse occurred. Since the place of the earlier eclipse is still sensitive, this passage of the Sun often coincides with a specific event that was suggested by the eclipse, or a central issue is brought to focus.

You can easily observe some of these dynamics of the Sun simply by noting your experiences precisely six months following your birthday, when you must confront a barrier and spend a few days working through a challenge, usually a challenge to your ego. This happens even if things have previously been going smoothly, or should I say, especially if things have been going smoothly. This personal Solar stimulation allows you to improve your methods, do some tweaking, and make necessary adjustments to your long-term plans. Each birthday you experience the fresh refortifying energy of the Sun, modified each year according to other planetary influences in force. Similarly, an eclipse gets rejuvenated each anniversary of its life by the return of the Sun to the eclipse degree.

The fast-traveling social planets Mercury and Venus are quite congenial and less dynamic in regard to worldly events as they travel over an eclipse. They are never far from the Sun, often traveling the same zodiac sign at about the same time and merely bringing an accent to daily affairs. Like the Moon, they may join in with other planets stimulating an eclipse at eventful periods; however, they are less likely to produce worldly events of outstanding note on their own.

We'll concern ourselves mainly with Mars and Saturn here because evidence points to their unquestionable link to previous eclipses at the times of major eventful happenings. Often there is also one or more other outer planet that gets into the picture, and it is when multiple planets stimulate multiple active eclipses that the most notable events transpire. Mars and Saturn may be most able to show future trends and to help us arrive at the most precise time at which specific types of event potential is greatest.

Mars is action-oriented, a real fighter; therefore this planet will often initiate the most dynamic events related to an eclipse. Mars travels pretty rapidly, making a complete circle through the entire zodiac in about two years, so it will frequently get to an eclipse degree very quickly to present a *conflict* and get things started. Later on we'll talk more about several dynamic events coinciding with Mars at its crossing to a significant eclipse, including the attacks on the Pentagon and the World Trade Center. Mars may represent a bully or an antagonist, and its transit to an eclipse may bring one forth. Mars energy is best utilized when fighting for causes on behalf of others. That's why it's appropriately associated with the armed forces and the military.

Planets farther out than Mars travel much more slowly and may not make it to the eclipse degree until much later. By that time, an eclipse may no longer be so sensitive, as it loses potency over time with the closing of the Lunar portals.

The planet Jupiter brings expansion when it stimulates the zodiac degree of an eclipse. Although it is called the Greater Fortune and is symbolic of abundance, gain, and acquisition, Jupiter's expansion can be a good or a bad thing, depending upon what it has to expand on.

In chapter 8 you'll get a picture of what can happen when Mars, the planet of fire, war, and conflict, teams up with Jupiter, the planet of expansion. What you often get is excessive waste and destruction. This was seen as fires raged through the West in the summer of 2002, coincident with the passing of Mars and Jupiter together over the Eclipse of July 1, 2000. That Solar eclipse occurred at noontime in the West, already the hottest time of the day in the desert, so this eclipse was high in the sky over the Western states, and fiery Mars accompanied the Sun and Moon at the time of the eclipse. This eclipse forewarned of drought and various dangers relating to water because the eclipse fell in the water sign of Cancer and Mars represented the dangers. Mars heat significantly dried up the available water, affecting especially the desert regions.

Just one final note about Mars and then we'll talk more about Jupiter. The kind of heat symbolized by that same Eclipse of July 1, 2000, courtesy of the influence of the planet Mars, also has another form. The verb "to mar" comes from Mars. To illustrate, it was ten days prior to that eclipse in 2000, as the Los Angeles chart reflected stress from the approaching eclipse, that a number of L.A. Lakers fans staged a riot, resulting in damage in their city. This was following a game they won against the Indiana Pacers. This type of mass hysteria is prone to develop there from time to time and was reflected in the L.A. horoscope during previous riots. This illustrates, too, how notable activity sometimes arrives just ahead of an important eclipse.

Now, let me give you an example of Jupiter's role as it crossed an eclipse during an unfolding in the case of missing intern Chandra Levy. The Lunar Eclipse of July 5, 2001, also notable for George W. Bush and the USA, fell on a point called the Vertex in Chandra Levy's horoscope. The Vertex is symbolic of fate and destined encounters. When this eclipse spotlighted her Vertex, the question of her fate was brought squarely into public view, even though she had already been missing for two months. A Lunar eclipse brings revelations, and her case came into view with Congressman Gary Condit's admission of their affair. Later, on May 22, 2002, as Jupiter transited her eclipsed Vertex, some of her remains were found. The acquisition symbolized by Jupiter provided clues regarding her fate.

Unless showing its excessive nature, Jupiter usually adheres to its reputation as the Greater Fortune, often bringing no less than a needed reprieve or perhaps a bit of kindliness or good fortune, whether conjunct or opposing an eclipse. Taking twelve years to complete a revolution through the zodiac, it may or may not travel over an eclipsed degree while the eclipse is still sensitive.

Crossing an eclipsed degree, the planet bringing closure is Saturn. The presence of Saturn symbolizes the matured development in the state of affairs indicated by the eclipse. Saturn is symbolic of changes shaped by the passage of time and has long been associated with karmic happenings as it is most intimately connected to the dense material manifestations of the earth world. In fact, there's a special condition shown in the progressed horoscope in which an individual comes into a period where he or she undergoes a long series of tests and trials that could be compared to the repayment of karmic debts. There are also times, reflected in the personal horoscope, when an individual can draw upon reserves of karmic credits.[1]

Saturn tests for weaknesses in structures in order that they be remedied, and you'll see many examples of this input. Saturn is crystallizing and often shows contraction as it moves through the degree of an active eclipse, either by conjunction or by opposition. Such shrinkage or constraint can be traced to the original symbolism of the eclipse, outlined in chapter 2. Even the rings around Saturn suggest limitations and boundaries. Due to its restrictive vibration, Saturn frequently points to something that is taken away. However, Saturn also brings hard-earned rewards. Remember, an eclipse frequently shows a place of imbalance, so Saturn's demands for karmic balance may bring major shifts, with power taken from one place and placed in another.

Because it is a rare eclipse that gets a passage of Saturn while it is still active, there is present a special window of opportunity to take command of a situation, and often this comes about very naturally as a result of the motivation provided by Mars. Stress, and even conflict, is frequently mobilizing and motivating. This window of opportunity is open until Saturn's closing pass, when it arrives upon or opposite the eclipse degree. At that time, Saturn lets us know via earthly and material events how our efforts can stand up under final pressure. From this final review, we adjust our long-range goals with more wisdom.

Saturn is slow and deliberate, and its influence is associated with conditions that seem to drag on forever. Efforts appear stalled and frustrating barriers slow progress as Saturn seeks perfection. If Saturn does come into range of an active eclipse, it may remain within range for weeks on end, drawing out the interval of time during which we're learning what we've accomplished and tending to any remaining flaws.[2]

Uranus, Neptune, and Pluto travel the zodiac so slowly that it is totally dependent upon their zodiac position as to whether they'll have the chance to bring their special energy to an eclipse while it's still active. Certainly it's fairly rare for an eclipse to receive stimulation from one of these outer planets, although each of them has a definite type of energy, and you'll have the opportunity to note specific examples of their input in this and coming chapters. The actions of these planets are frequently of a challenging nature, as with Mars and Saturn.

Uranus is associated with originality, uniqueness, and eccentricity. The energy of Uranus is best described as that bringing the unusual or unexpected. It is an irresponsible and nonconforming agent and therefore the most difficult to predict of any of the planets. These forces linked to Uranus match the unusual tilt of that planet on its axis, unlike any other planet in the solar system, cocked at an almost 90-degree angle. Uranus demands absolute independence, and its influence is observable in those who suddenly adhere to the old cliché of throwing out the baby with the bath water—doing whatever it takes to break free of restraints and then some. Uranus represents the rebel and genius as well as the technician and humanitarian. Uranus will play a crucial role from 2007 through 2010, as it has opportunities to stimulate several active eclipses.

Neptune introduces an element of mystery. This planet often clouds the picture, leaving a hazy fog, so it is hard to distinguish between what is real and what is imagined. Just like the deceptive nature attributed to Neptune, it was only because of the wavering influence it exerted upon Uranus in its orbit that Neptune was first discovered. Only later was it actually sighted. Due to its illusive nature, even in an astrological chart, an astrologer more often overlooks Neptune than any other planet. Neptune represents the mystic, and while Neptune can be a beautiful influence, inspiring creativity and selfless service among those of elevated consciousness who live according to the belief that "all is one," in mundane affairs it is more often descriptive of deceptions, and is linked to secret enemies, to treachery and ambush.

Neptune's influence was apparent during 2001, when it stimulated the Solar Eclipse of July 30, 2000, at 8 degrees Leo, an eclipse that fell on the Dragon's Head of the United States. During Neptune's influence to that eclipse (as Mars also stimulated the Solar Eclipse of June 21, 2001), Osama bin Laden secretly coordinated terrorist attacks upon the U.S., striking like a covert and cowardly thief in the night, and afterward eluding all efforts to trace his whereabouts. As you'll see in chapter 8, Osama bin Laden has been a major player in U.S. affairs, as noted by the connections from his horoscope to the nativities of both the United States and George W. Bush.

Pluto is somewhat like Mars in influence, although more transforming and often more destructive. For its small size, Pluto really packs a punch, and this planet suggests the need for complete renovation starting from scratch. Our dealing with terrorism and the upstart of it was partially reflected in the positions of Pluto and Saturn, which held in a struggle of opposition to one another in the zodiac for a lengthy time. Saturn is representative of the authority figure, and Pluto is the one that seeks to tear down and destroy the structures built by the authority. We'll be looking at Pluto more closely later on, because those energetic influences will play a role in cosmic processes here on earth in the not-so-distant future as Pluto comes calling upon active eclipses. Pluto is concerned with the process of renewal, and its power is slow, subtle, intense, and very deliberate, but it can also be explosive.

Using table 1 in the appendix, you can track the major planetary movements over eclipses through 2015, and in the next chapter you'll find out why these planetary transits will produce more spectacular events over or opposite some eclipses than others.

---

1. Saturn denotes particularly karmic happenings when involved with the Lunar Nodes or the Moon; thus the distinctive importance to an eclipse, which requires both of those. A prolonged contact of transiting Saturn to the progressing Moon (Saturn chasing the Moon) denotes karmic processes, discussed in my book *Predicting Events with Astrology* (St. Paul, MN: Llewellyn Publications, 1999) pp. 17, 259–261, and in the Glossary.

2. Using a +/- 3-degree orb, Saturn enters the range of influence to previous eclipses in May 2002, continuing in its transit to cross the degrees of multiple eclipses. It spends most of 2002, 2003, 2004, and into 2005 completing passage over several active eclipses, bringing results to efforts begun early in the new millennium. A similar scenario occurs in 2008–2010, as Saturn brings tests, trials, and results to multiple efforts originating in the years 2006–2008.

CHAPTER FIVE

Rating an Eclipse for Power

In table 1 in the appendix, you'll observe a number ranging from one to seven next to each eclipse listed. This is the raw power rating assigned to the eclipse, with one being the least powerful and seven the greatest to date following the formula given here.

A few simple steps can be taken to determine the power potential of any eclipse. The variables surrounding an eclipse have each been discussed in the preceding chapters, and an easy formula is provided here that eliminates a great many technicalities and mathematical equations for those who wish to apply an easy, workable system.

An eclipse automatically starts with a point value of one for the simple reason of being an eclipse. It is already many times more powerful than an ordinary New Moon or Full Moon due to the accompaniment of the Dragon's Head or Tail, opening a special portal that invites zest and energy for an extended time and thus lengthening the duration of the things signified.

Add one point if the Dragon's Head's or Tail is within 10 degrees of a Solar eclipse, or within 5 degrees of a Lunar eclipse. A "T" indicates these eclipses in table 1 in the appendix.

Add one point if the eclipse receives a transit by Saturn, by conjunction or opposition, within four years. This indicates that the critical matters signified are going to mature rapidly and offers a special window of opportunity to deal constructively with challenges.

Add one point for any additional planet that falls within 3 degrees of the Sun or Moon during the eclipse. If there are two or more planets meeting this criterion, give one point for each. This adds complexity to the eclipse message, as discussed in chapter 2.

Add three points if the eclipse falls in the critical opening degree of the sign Aries, Cancer, Libra, or Capricorn. These zero degrees, sometimes called Aries Point degrees, are always indicative of important world matters at hand, where one event has a domino effect that leads to ramifications in many areas and around the globe.

Add one point if the eclipse falls in the 13th degree of Aries, Cancer, Libra, or Capricorn. These are also critical degrees, crucial in matters of balance and equilibrium. Events stemming from these eclipses can shift the balance of power in the world.

Add two points for an eclipse that falls within 3 degrees of a conjunction or opposition to one of the luminaries (Sun or Moon) of the dominant world power. Presently, this is the USA.[1]

Add one additional point for an eclipse that falls within 3 degrees, by conjunction or opposition, of any other planet or angle[2] in the horoscope of the ruling world power.

The preceding calculations result in the raw power rating of an eclipse. This number appears next to the eclipse listings in table 1, and those with a rating of three or above are italicized.

Once you know the raw power potential of an eclipse, note whether the eclipse has the influence of the Dragon's Head or Dragon's Tail, as discussed in chapter 1. Then note the zodiac sign to determine the general theme of the eclipse, and note the Lord of the eclipse for more information, as outlined in chapter 2. In general, a Solar eclipse is more visible and manifests in an outer way, indicative of events affecting nations and global leaders. Lunar eclipses show conditions affecting the common people. Note the arriving transits to the eclipse, as discussed in chapter 4.

From here, the eclipse can then be compared to an individual chart or any other chart. For example, if any eclipse taking place in the years to come shall happen to fall on one of the luminaries (Sun or Moon) of the person holding presidential office in the United States at the time, it will make the eclipse worthy of two more points. If the eclipse falls on another planet in that president's chart, it would be worth one more point. Because he or she holds the most powerful seat in the world, and his or her actions and interests are key in world matters, this adds to the potential range of influence of that eclipse. This occurred in 2001 when the Lunar Eclipse of July 5 fell prominently in the chart of George W. Bush, adding two more points to an already powerful eclipse, bringing it to a rating of seven, and matching the preceding Solar eclipse that fell in the critical opening degree of Cancer, an Aries Point degree.

If an eclipse of a power rating of three or above should happen to fall on a luminary of another country, that eclipse will be quite profound for that country and its citizens, even more so if the eclipse also falls conspicuously in the chart of the leader of that country. Even an eclipse of a low power rating is of extra significance for those countries to which it makes important connections in that nativity. For example, the Lunar Eclipse of November 19, 2002, had a power rating of only one. However, this eclipse rated an additional two points in China, falling close to both Venus (harmony and tranquility of the people) and Mercury (communications and transport issues) in the People's Republic of China chart; and subsequently, the SARS virus emerged there, having an impact on the things symbolized by Venus and Mercury for the country. Quarantines and special masks were in order to prevent the spread of the virus.

There may be a special condition in which a judgment call must be made regarding the power rating of an eclipse. An example of this can be found in the Eclipse of July 1, 2011, which is marked with an asterisk in table 1. This eclipse falls *almost* within range of both the Sun and the benefic Jupiter in the USA chart, spotlighting the chief executive, wealth of the country, and productivity. It actually falls midway between the two, and although it was not given a higher ranking, it is likely to operate at a power potential of at least four, especially since transforming Pluto will transit the eclipse point soon after.

In the Catalog of Annotated Eclipse Charts in the appendix, you'll see some brief observations of the general planetary influences in play at the time of each eclipse up to 2012. These are not specific predictions but give the more prominent characteristics of each eclipse. The suggestions given are based on the concept that the eclipse points to a place of crisis, emphasis, or change, where attention is focused in regard to mundane affairs. An eclipse has multiple manifestations, and these vary by region. While an eclipse chart can be calculated for the time it occurs in any particular location in question, all but one of the eclipse charts in the appendix have been calculated for the time they occur in Washington, D.C., the capital of the USA. This provides a basis from which to judge the impact of the eclipse not only for the U.S. but also for other areas of the world.

As we saw in chapter 2, the sign of an eclipse announces the general area of change and points to the people upon whom it will have an impact. Eclipses in Taurus will affect bankers, for example, and wages will be a source of attention. Similar themes are brought into focus by an eclipse falling in the Second House of an eclipse chart. That is because Taurus naturally corresponds with the Second House. Similarly, appropriate associations can be used to predict the general impact of an eclipse in any of the twelve houses of an eclipse chart.

If an eclipse is listed as emphasized for your country or city in the Catalog of Annotated Eclipse Charts, you can then trace the planet it falls on in the Annotated Catalog of National Figures in the appendix. Then check Table 4: Planetary Keys in the appendix to see what that planet rules to find the people and things brought to prominence in your area.

To determine the importance of an eclipse for an individual, the first step would be to compare the eclipse chart to the chart of the person to see if ties are made from the degree of the eclipse to a planet in that person's nativity. If a natal planet should receive the rays of an eclipse, the nature of that planet will suggest the various things and people to which the eclipse is bringing an emphasis. These personal eclipse effects will be discussed in part 3.

If an eclipse of a high power rating falls on a luminary in the chart of an individual, it will be exceptional for that person, and events taking place in that person's life may be directly related to the impact of the eclipse in larger world matters. Say an eclipse in Capricorn, suggesting that business matters are due for some changes, should fall on the Sun of a corporate administrator. This person may be one who experiences the result of transitions in a direct way; his or her job duties may change. Several high-power eclipses in Capricorn preceded the corporate scandals that began in 2001.

Astrologers have their own favorite techniques they employ to find out more about how an eclipse might function for their clients.

For instance, in the sixteenth century, it was suggested by Jerom Cardan, an astrologer of some genius, that should any planet fall in the 29th degree of a sign at the time of an eclipse, it signified a temporary period of difficulties for those whose First House in the horoscope is ruled by that planet. This ruling planet is most influential, referred to by Cardan as the Significator of Life. This astrologer's research indicates that there is merit in his observation; however, this need not be any great or catastrophic event and may be more easily managed by having this knowledge prior to the occurrence. Eclipses with this feature are few and can be tracked in the Catalog of Annotated Eclipse Charts. If the rest of the personal chart concurs, one may expect some disappointment or worry and perhaps plan for a period of low-key activities.

In another of his choicest aphorisms, Jerom Cardan revealed that he may have applied rules similar to those given herein when he made the statement that "no eclipse whatsoever can threaten a scarcity or plague to the whole Earth, nor can the pestilence continue above four years in one place."[3]

In his statement pertaining to the specific incidence of scarcity, plague, or pestilence, Cardan suggests that he also included Lunar eclipses under his four-year rule due to the impact on the common people that such problematic conditions would obviously have.

In part 2, we will explore eclipses past, present, and future in regard to their influences on worldly affairs. In part 3, you'll learn about their meaning in your personal life.

In the coming chapter, you'll find out what Benjamin Franklin had to say about eclipses, himself an expert astrologer.

---

1. The USA horoscope appears in the Annotated Catalog of National Figures in the appendix.

2. The angles are the cusps, or dividing lines, of the First, Fourth, Seventh, and Tenth Houses.

3. Guido Bonatus and Jerom Cardan, *The Astrologer's Guide: Anima Astrologie* (Montana, USA: Kessinger Publishing Co.), p. 100.

PART TWO

Eclipses & World Events: Past, Present & Future

CHAPTER SIX

The Impact of Eclipses upon National Figures

In terms of world trends, the destinies of nations and large groups of individuals, a form of astrology called mundane astrology, is applied. While mundane astrology is said to be the most difficult branch of any, interpreting a chart of any type involves an inspection of the same four fundamentals: the signs, houses, planets, and relationships of the planets, or aspects.

Just as an individual has a personal horoscope, which maps out major crossroads in life, each country and city also has a horoscope. When comparing an eclipse chart to that of a country, one can find the times of magnified importance: a time when it comes into the limelight, sometimes dominating the global scenario. Even though the kinds of events that stem from crucial eclipses in the charts of national figures are sometimes anything but mundane, that is what it is called.

Whereas a house sector in an individual's birth chart represents a specific area of life for that person, when one looks at this house for what it rules in terms of world concerns, it takes on a broader meaning since it must accommodate a larger group of people. Instead of looking at individual choice, we're looking at collective choice.

Similar to the way an eclipse can amplify or distort an individual trait when falling on a natal planet, an eclipse can also magnify or warp a facet of the national character when it falls closely in alignment with an important planet in the birth chart of a nation or city.

Generally, the eclipse with the Dragon's Head attending is more indicative of outward ambition and materialism. If the nature of the planet that receives the eclipse becomes distorted by the influence of the eclipse, it can lead to compulsive actions as the lustful tendencies are aroused. This may then manifest as greed or grasping, and actions may be based on inaccurate perceptions. A more positive scenario would demonstrate a degree of enlightenment and the ability to direct the drives and motivations constructively to realize achievements.

Let's take the example of an eclipse falling on the Sun in the chart of a country. This automatically brings a spotlight to the interests and actions of the leader of that country. The same eclipse might distort the traits and characteristics of one world leader while bringing out the best features in another, leading to a fight between good and evil, where one becomes a world antagonist while the other plays the role of world savior or global policeman. If the same eclipse touches upon two countries, it may indicate a timely connection between the two, when they are brought together to accomplish some higher cosmic purpose necessary for world evolution

When it is the South Node or Dragon's Tail eclipse that falls on a planet, a lack of self-confidence and feeling of inferiority may at times lead to inappropriate outbursts or a complete loss of control. The more constructive side of these eclipses is found in humanitarian services, compassionate deeds, and selfless service.

The Annotated Catalog of National Figures in the appendix contains the horoscopes of many countries as well as a sampling of USA cities and enterprises. This catalog gives a listing of all the eclipses through 2011 that fall conspicuously in each of the national horoscopes, and identifies the particular planet that is stimulated by each eclipse. The planetary keys in table 4 in the appendix offer a condensed list of the things and people ruled by the planets so that you can track the effects of eclipses around the world.

The most important national figure to compare an eclipse chart to is the USA. That's because it is presently the leading world power. It is good to have a starting point to compare an eclipse chart, so this is the logical point of reference used by mundane astrologers.

The United States of America Horoscope

There are several variations of the USA horoscope. Without official documentation as to when our forefathers who drew up the Declaration of Independence initially signed it, this topic has always been debatable. It is agreed that it was on July 4, 1776, but beyond that there is wide-range speculation. In fact, all of the charts for the birth of the nation have been rectified based on whatever shreds of evidence have been found.[1]

Up until the attacks on America in 2001, my favorite chart for the USA was the Scorpio Rising chart, also called the Penfield chart for the astrologer who constructed it based on documentation in a biography on John Hancock. Astrologer Michael O'Reilly makes a good case for it.[2]

The Scorpio Rising chart makes interesting parallels to the White House chart, the data for which I recently came across, and in my studies I'd been utilizing both to watch for patterns involving eclipses over a long period. In late 2000 I noticed a particularly "heavy duty" eclipse coming, and as I worked on the June 2001 U.S. forecast I made note of urgent factors surrounding that total Solar eclipse:

> The Solar Eclipse of June 21 [2001] is a total eclipse and falls on the first day of summer in the first degree of Cancer, an Aries Point degree. The Aries Point degrees portend major and far-reaching events, so this eclipse suggests an escalation of notable global events in the coming weeks. History is in the making.
>
> Charting the eclipse for Washington, D.C., which gives indications for the U.S., the eclipse falls in the Twelfth House, governing secret enemies. The Solar eclipse falls on Venus in the United States chart, indicating the potential for turbulence affecting the public.
>
> The Full Moon of July 5 is a Lunar eclipse that also happens to fall conspicuously in the charts of President Bush and the USA. Not only are relations stressed with foreign nations and our interactions with them, but there could be actual conflicts that arise and call for military action by the USA in the coming months. President Bush himself may come under threat, and this is a particularly troublesome time for him in fulfilling his presidential duties. The total impact of these eclipses will not be realized until 2004, although events will begin to transpire when the Solar eclipse is fueled by Mars in September 2001.

I was talking about the transit of Mars as it opposed that eclipse at 0 degrees Cancer. Mars is known to greatly excite eclipse conditions, often operating to bring about a conflict, and the dates of its stimulation to this cataclysmic eclipse were September 8–13, 2001.

By this time I had verified from my studies that the conjunction or opposition to a previous eclipse point by Mars and Saturn can be profound, as it coincides with eventful affairs for the U.S.; however, an eclipse in one of the Aries Point degrees is extremely rare and immeasurably magnifies the potential severity and range of effects.

Following the 9/11 attacks, astrologers scrambled to track down the indicators of such an event. Truly, you'd think the astrological "chatter" would have been buzzing quite loudly with an event of such magnitude on the horizon. Perhaps it was the beautiful trine configurations forming from transiting planets to the U.S. planets and Jupiter approaching a conjunction to the U.S. Sun that relaxed everyone. As a matter of fact, it was those configurations that contributed to the generally relaxed mood of the whole country.

The Gemini Rising chart is the longtime favorite for the USA, and another popular chart is called the Sibley chart, which has Sagittarius rising. At this point I decided to take a look at both of them in light of the events of 9/11. I found key results in the Gemini chart.

The Gemini Rising chart is also rectified, with a few variations, and based partly on an old story that Ben Franklin arranged an early-morning signing of the Declaration of Independence. Now, if a time was arranged for signing the document using astrological expertise, this chart reflects such a selection. Benjamin Franklin was admittedly an astrologer and a pretty good one at that. From his own account, he could predict the weather based on astrological laws, although he surmised that people probably believed he consorted with the devil to make such accurate predictions. Going by a pen name and under the guise of Richard Saunders, Benjamin Franklin authored his *Poor Richard's Almanac* from 1733 to 1758.[3] In fact, Franklin himself had experience with eclipses, and in the 1736 edition of his almanac he had this to say:[4]

> Suffer me to observe that whoever studies the eclipses of former Ages and compares them with the great events that happened (as every true astrologer ought to do) shall find that the fall of the Assyrian, Persian, Grecian, and Roman monarchies, each of them, was remarkably preceded by great and total eclipses of the heavenly bodies. Observations of this kind, joined with the ancient and long-tryed rules of our art . . . make me tremble for the Empire now in being.

He made that statement in 1736, obviously concerned about the future of the Empire. By the time of the signing of the Declaration of Independence years later, he'd have been even more astrologically adept and, as an astrologer, unable to resist electing the best time for signing such an important document as the Declaration of Independence. Astrology was in vogue at the time, used to choose times for the best hunts and many less important matters than the birthing of a country. It is quite relevant that he'd have chosen the courageous Mars rising in the First House as a statement of the country's independence. As one of the most important planets in any enterprise chart, an angular Mars gives initiative, makes an entity competitive, and leads to accomplishment, especially if supported by other planets. Also, where better for Franklin to arrange the fortune planets—the Sun, Venus, and Jupiter—than in the Second House of national wealth, where they would fairly ensure prosperity for the country?

The Gemini Rising chart was also used by Evangeline Adams to predict World War II, and of the most popular U.S. charts, it is the only one in which the Moon is not void of course. This is a critical impairment of the Moon, signifying that "nothing more will come of the matter." It would not have been possible for the U.S. to become a world power had it been born with such impairment. Certainly Franklin would have avoided it under any circumstances. It would explain why he'd have kept his colleagues up to the wee hours in order to sign the great document before the Moon went void, and to capitalize on its applying trine to Mars in the First House. The Moon on the MC also describes a government "for the people."

I can now safely say that I favor the Gemini Rising chart over any others. The decision is based largely on some perfect aspects of the Moon that were forming among the natal, progressed, and transiting planets in this chart on September 11, 2001, which underscored the unexpected events and the anguish for the American people.

To be brief, transiting Uranus (21 degrees Aquarius) was within a conjunction to the USA Moon at 18 Aquarius while square the progressed Moon at 21 degrees Taurus. These suggested unexpected upset for U.S. citizens. Transiting Venus (18 degrees Leo) opposed the natal Moon, while also approaching a square to the progressed Moon, signifying a very saddening occasion. Nothing as profound and convincing involving this sensitive luminary was found in the other USA charts. The Moon reveals the conditions affecting the masses.

Utilizing the eclipse formula is perhaps the only technique that would have shown trouble ahead, and the time of the trouble, no matter which USA chart was used. However, more proof of the validity of the USA Gemini Rising chart comes from the Cancer Eclipse itself, which fell precisely on the Second House cusp of banking, national wealth, and financial structures, indicating potential for grand transformations in those areas. From there, trouble could have been traced directly to the World Trade Center towers, where the powerful eclipse fell prominently on the Ascendant.

Of course the World Trade Center Towers chart would make an important tie to the U.S. chart. As an emblem of financial power, the Twin Towers Ascendant is linked to the U.S. house cusp of finances and financial structures. Both were tragically marked by that Total Solar Eclipse at 0 degrees Cancer in the summer of 2001. Both were greatly affected following the eclipse. In fact, a similar eclipse pattern was in play in 1993 when an attack on the World Trade Center took place, although that eclipse was much less powerful. We'll talk more about this in chapter 9.

The White House Nativity

Having the White House horoscope as the backdrop to trace eclipses adds a whole new dimension and offers a more personal look into the life of the president and First Family.

The White House itself has become a place to go lavish, as it is a representation of our nation and the values for which it stands. It's also a place to show allegiance. In many ways, the affairs at the White House show the pulse of the nation.

Although the cornerstone for the White House was set on October 13, 1792, it was November of 1800 before President Adams and his wife, Abigail, took up first residence. They moved in on a Saturday, the first of the month. For the White House to function as intended, this date marked its true birth.

Over the years the White House has played an increasingly large role in our statement as a nation, becoming an icon for our country. Honor and nobility, faith and pride, have been attached. And, undoubtedly, the first president and man who did so much for his country deserved all the best of what the White House finally came to be. Unfortunately, George Washington never even lived there. At the time the cornerstone was set, Washington was acting president and shortly after was reelected to his second term in office.

By the time Mrs. Lincoln arrived at the White House in the 1860s, many of the rooms were rat-infested and unlivable. She, "the First Lady of the land," for whom the term was coined, redecorated lavishly and went several thousand dollars over budget. She managed to keep this a secret for a while, but her husband became quite upset when he finally found out. He himself gave little thought to any of the frills that came with his job and spent every ounce of his energy working through the war.

Well educated and from the South, Mary Todd Lincoln was snubbed by the Southern women in D.C. for supporting Mr. Lincoln in the Civil War. Then, she lost a child while in the White House, which took a great toll on her.[5] Unable to deal with her grief, she is said to have held eight or so séances in the White House, with her husband in attendance for at least one of them, mostly in an effort to find out who was interfering with her mind. After that, she dealt with her emotional loss by splurging uncontrollably on clothes.

It was a tragic story and in the end, when the Civil War ended, it was on one of their first evenings out together, taking in a night at the theater, that President Lincoln was shot by an assassin, dying hours later.[6]

So, the nativity of the White House allows us to see how the First Family is faring, even down to reconstruction and facelifts of the Presidential Palace, as it was once called. Fires, like the one in the West Wing on Christmas Eve 1929, have visited the White House, and it has also been visited by death and disarray.[7] Confusion was especially notable when phones and lights came on the scene so close together. Wiring was intertwined and looped from the ceiling of the main offices. It has also surely had its days with heavy smoke odor with the men puffing away on their cigars during political meetings.

The White House birth chart is calculated for noon on November 1, 1800. Features show a Full Moon across the signs Taurus and Scorpio, and connections between this chart and the nativity for the setting of the cornerstone show that the Sun of the White House chart occupies the prior Venus position precisely and is just 2 degrees away from the prior Jupiter. These planetary connections suggest that the ideals held when the first cornerstone was laid have finally become a reality. The White House should provide a safe and comfortable haven for the president and a place for strategic planning. This home would undergo many deaths and rebirths as it served a new family every few years. The Scorpio Sun, ruled by the regenerating Pluto, is a perfect illustration of all these requirements.

On the day of the terrorist attacks on America in 2001, the White House chart reflected imminent danger, with many clear indicators that it was under threat. However, there was one incredible saving grace that was shown to be coming compliments of the brave planet Mars. That saving grace shown in the White House chart came in reality from the heroic actions of the passengers on United Airlines Flight 93, who died in the crash in Pennsylvania as they courageously rushed the cockpit to take on the terrorists of the hijacked plane to prevent it from destroying its target.

The Annotated Catalog of National Figures in the appendix shows the White House horoscope and lists coming eclipses of special note for the White House through 2011.

That catalog also shows the horoscopes, coming eclipses, and anecdotal information for major U.S. cities, such as Los Angeles, Manhattan, New York City, Phoenix, and Roswell. The Twin Towers horoscope is included in the catalog, although we now call the area Ground Zero. Eclipses falling in that chart may continue to show activity around Ground Zero until there is a new structure and memorial in place.

Other enterprises and horoscopes in the catalog include the New York Stock Exchange, NASA, and United Nations. Other countries and entities shown are Afghanistan, Australia, Canada, China, Cuba, Egypt, France, Iran, Iraq, Israel, Japan, Mexico, North Korea, Palestine, Russia, United Kingdom, and Vatican City. If your country or city is listed, you can follow the important eclipses taking place through 2011.

---

1. Rectification is a process of correcting a horoscope to precision based on astrological laws and a study of events that match up experiences with planetary prominence at the time of the event.

2. Michael O'Reilly quotes Marc Penfield's *Horoscopes of the Western Hemisphere*, in which Penfield refers to the biography by Herbert S. Allan, *John Hancock: Patriot in Purple* (New York: Macmillan Co., 1940), p. 228: "At last, about 2 o'clock in the afternoon of the 4th, the great white paper was reported . . . and immediately ratified." From this, Penfield rectified the time to 2:20 p.m., giving 8 degrees Scorpio rising. O'Reilly, who used it for his "Tomorrow's News" column in *American Astrology*, from 1992 to 2000, rectified it to a minute later.

3. H. W. Brands, *The First American: The Life and Times of Benjamin Franklin* (New York: Doubleday, 2000), p. 131.

4. Thanks to Lina Accurso for sharing these quotes from her own copy of *Poor Richard's Almanac* in her July 1998 article, "Ben Franklin: America's Astrologer-General," in *Horoscope Magazine*, p. 35.

5. Willie Lincoln's death on February 20, 1862, coincided with a transit of Mars over a prior Lunar eclipse falling in the Twelfth House of the White House chart that occurred in June of 1861.

6. Lincoln's death followed an eclipse to his Mars when transited by Saturn.

7. On the night of the fire in the West Wing of the White House, the area utilized by the president's staff, Mars was stimulating a prior Solar eclipse that had fallen on the cusp of the Sixth House in the White House chart.

CHAPTER SEVEN

Rare Predictions & JFK

Utilizing eclipses and other favorite tools of the trade, astrologers often take it upon themselves to get a glimpse into the future. An astrologer basically arrives at a forecast from a combination of planetary configurations. Based on mathematical calculations and hundreds of years of combined observations, astrologers decipher the most probable effects of a combination of planetary stimuli, one upon the other. Sometimes their endeavors are chillingly accurate and other times not, depending upon the experience of the astrologer and the technique employed.

There are both positive and negative manifestations associated with each planet, so there is always a choice of response to incoming stimuli available for each of us, which all combined give the resulting bigger picture. Although one's star karma may be set at birth, it is a human matter as to what we make of it and how we choose to express it. Our efforts and activities can influence the outcome of an eclipse, whether personally in regard to our private lives or in consort with the actions of others, where we are contributing to outcomes in a much larger sense. The planetary forces can be called into play and used constructively as long as one is aware of what there is to work with. As the admirable astrologer

Evangeline Adams advised, "The wise man cooperates with his stars. The fool thinks he rules them."[1]

Here's a perfect illustration of this. In May of 2003, with planetary configurations and both recent and upcoming eclipses suggesting the potential for viruses, epidemics, and sundry other troubles such as terrorist attacks, and with SARS affecting China quite severely at the time, in Seattle and Chicago, mock drills were carried out to prepare for a possible crisis caused by an epidemic or biological attack. The drills were an extremely positive use of the available energies, and they helped offset the more destructive potential. They provided a constructive channel for the available energy.

Some planetary forces in combination can be especially difficult to curb, a struggle for anyone; therefore an astrologer is able to identify problematic times with a heightened tendency for things to go badly. Even the warrior planet Mars plays a necessary role in the overall process of things. We would not survive for long without the energy and aggression of Mars that's necessary to defend ourselves when we come into danger. But, the ancients noted Mars as a "malefic" force, some going so far as to call it evil, due to its reputation for being conspicuously involved in various types of conflicts, illness, and accidents.

In 1648, for instance, astrologer William Lilly predicted both the outbreak of the bubonic plague and the great fire that befell London in 1665 and 1666, respectively. His is among the more spectacular prophecies, and with his prediction, citing a grand catastrophe as never before, with fires and a consummating plague, he submitted an illustration of the Gemini twins plunging into a great fire, symbolic for London by Gemini's prominence in the London horoscope. Lilly was so accurate with his warnings that he was called in and questioned when his predictions came true fifteen years later. After a lengthy inquiry he was exonerated, and as an astrologer his reputation was made forever.

In 1899, the popular American astrologer Evangeline Adams predicted the fire that ravished the famous Windsor Hotel on Saint Patrick's Day in New York City. According to her own story, when persuaded to give the hotel proprietor a personal reading upon her arrival to the hotel the night before the fire, she revealed to him that he was under the worst possible configurations.[2] Asked what had happened on two previous occasions during his life when conditions were similar, he replied that there had been fires in the hotel. That very night, his hotel burned and he lost several family members. As for Adams, her correct assessment of the situation began her lucrative career and her fame as an astrologer, with an office at Carnegie Hall, where she charged fifty dollars for a thirty-minute session. It also proved her accurate assessment of her own chart and her prediction for herself, where she saw that the middle of March 1899 was a good time to relocate to New York to pursue a successful career in astrology.

So when it comes to Mars, events signified by this planet are fairly predictable because Mars reflects elements of risk and carelessness. Mars is associated with war because it also shows times when men will fight for what they believe belongs to them. In your own nativity, Mars shows where you become engaged in conflict whenever Mars receives sufficient stimulation from passing planets.

As the new millennium approached, most of us couldn't help but recall the many prophecies we'd heard over the years. Numerous prophets and seers left us hanging shortly after the year 2000. According to many, we were approaching our Armageddon, when all kinds of horrors would befall us, including earth changes, viruses, and the war to end all wars. Astrologers also issued warnings in view of the Solar Eclipse of August 1999.

Sir Isaac Newton departed from this view, however. From a lifetime of bible study and a thorough understanding of the cosmos, this great mathematician and physicist felt the end time will not be until 2060. I did not know of this until recently, but it has sparked a sudden interest to reread the bible and I plan to take a good look at the planetary alignments of 2060 more closely as soon as I'm finished here. I notice an emphasis of planets in the sign Taurus, which is all about "earthly" matters.

Of course, there have been predictions for the end of the world in the past. There were two in the sixteenth century, and the most recent of these predictions was for 1962, when an eclipse and planetary lineup took place in the sign Aquarius. American and European astrologers accurately predicted great sociological turmoil, but a handful of overzealous Indian astrologers, using a different zodiac and based on ancient Hindu predictions, placed the eclipse in the sign of Capricorn rather than Aquarius, apparently leading to their misinterpretation. Unfortunately they got a lot of press attention in their preparation for the end of the world and ceremonies to ward it off.

Many historical events did take place following that much-discussed eclipse of 1962, but we made it through intact and an improved social structure was the eventual result from many of those crises. Change is inevitable, and though uncomfortable at times, without it we would stagnate.

The Solar Eclipse of 1999, like that in 1962, made unmistakable contacts to the United States chart. We'll talk more about the eclipse of 1999 in the next chapter, but first a bit of reflection on that famous earlier eclipse and the events that took place as Mars and Saturn transited it.

There were actually three Solar eclipses that were of special note preceding the assassination of President Kennedy and the many critical events in our American history at that time. The Total Solar Eclipse of February 4, 1962, fell at 16 degrees Aquarius. In Kennedy's horoscope, this eclipse fell in stressful contact to his Mars, with Mars located at the point in his horoscope that is associated with death. This eclipse forewarned of a potentially violent death. It also fell on the Moon in the USA chart, signifying an event that would have a profound impact on the American people.

Another eclipse occurred on July 31, 1962, at 8 degrees Leo. This was a Solar Eclipse in a Fire sign that fell upon the United States' Dragon's Head at 7 degrees Leo, which is a potentially turbulent point and much connected to military moves by the U.S.

A third Solar eclipse took place on July 20, 1963, at 27 degrees Cancer, just four months before the assassination. This one fell directly upon Kennedy's natal Saturn while it also opposed the United States' Pluto.

Many astrologers warned of trouble for Kennedy, and although her accuracy is disputed because she apparently contradicted her own prediction with a later one, Jeane Dixon became famous for her call that the Democratic president elected in 1960 would die in office. Another most remarkable prediction about the danger to JFK and the "perils" of November 1963 was made months in advance by mundane astrologer Donald Bradley, who wrote a monthly forecast column in *American Astrology* magazine using the pseudonym Leslie McIntyre. His prediction gained notice in the press and the attention of newspaper columnist Walter Winchell for its degree of accuracy.[3]

Within a short time, Mars activated the first eclipse in the Air sign Aquarius, and numerous social conflicts developed. Issues became heated over racial segregation in Southern states. Riots erupting on college campuses led Kennedy to send in the National Guard to prevent further rioting in Mississippi and federal marshals to enforce desegregation in Alabama. The murder of civil rights worker Medgar Evers was followed by legislation to prevent discrimination in education, voting, etc., but these types of conflicts continued to escalate. The year 1962 also saw the Supreme Court rulings against prayer and devotional readings in public schools. Deteriorating relations with Cuba were of primary concern for U.S. foreign policy.

As already discussed, the Dragon's Head is always a sensitive point, especially to Mars transits. Following the Solar eclipse on this point in the U.S. nativity on July 31, 1962, the Cuban missile crisis began on October 22, 1962, just as Mars began to stimulate the zodiac degree of that eclipse. With Saturn also entering range of this eclipse, there was fear of the outbreak of World War III, developments were escalating for U.S. involvement in the Vietnamese conflict, and decisions made by Kennedy were creating fierce enemies for him.

On the day of Kennedy's assassination, Saturn was just completing passage across that eclipsed degree of 16 Aquarius, more than a year and a half after the eclipse formed! Neptune was throwing mystery into the mix, and Saturn brought what most considered a great loss. Neptune reflects deception and illusions; hence forty years following, facts surrounding the assassination are still shrouded in secrecy and uncertainties remain.

Kennedy's Saturn opposing the United States' Pluto was certainly a rather dangerous connection for him from the very beginning, for Pluto is the planet signifying death and Saturn shows his greatest efforts. Kennedy was not the first, nor will he be the last, to die for a cause.

To give you a little more illustration of the kind of power and sensitivity of the U.S. Dragon's Head, during the WWII era, in August of 1943, a Solar Eclipse took place at 8 degrees Leo, within 1 degree of the U.S. Dragon's Head. D-Day followed on June 6, 1944, coincident with Mars' passage across the eclipsed degree. From these examples, it's apparent that the U.S. Dragon's Head is a point of offensive action, especially following an eclipse that sensitizes it.

In the next chapter you'll see how a more recent eclipse upon the United States Dragon's Head also fell on the Sun of Osama bin Laden while spotlighting George W. Bush as well, creating a cosmic connection between the three, which began to manifest soon after the eclipse.

1. Evangeline Adams, *Evangeline Adams' Book of Astrology* (New York: Tower Books Inc., 1931), p. 24.

2. Evangeline Adams, *The Bowl of Heaven* (1926; reprint, Santa Fe, NM: Sun Books, 1995), pp. 31–37.

3. Leslie McIntyre, "Tomorrow's News," *American Astrology* (November 1963). The author relied on, and described, aspects involving the progressed Moon in the USA Gemini Rising chart to arrive at his correct assessment.

CHAPTER EIGHT

The New Millennium Eclipse Timeline

You may recall that there was much sensationalism surrounding the eclipses of 1999, in particular the Solar eclipse in August of that year. As far back as Nostradamus (an astrologer himself) in the sixteenth century, psychics, seers, and astrologers everywhere were issuing warnings as they pointed to the dire heavenly configurations.

At the time of that Solar Eclipse in August of 1999, the heavenly bodies were gripped in a cross configuration, called a Grand Cross in astrological circles, quite a formidable combination. It signifies multiple tensions, conflicts, and anxieties not easily put to rest. In fact, just prior to this Solar eclipse, there was also a Lunar eclipse featuring a Grand Cross. A much earlier eclipse with the feature of a Grand Cross preceded the outbreak of the bubonic plague in the fourteenth century. Originating in China, the Black Death killed millions in Europe. Perhaps the seer Nostradamus was recalling this when he gave his frightening prediction for 1999:

> In the year 1999 and seven months,
> From the skys shall come an alarmingly

> powerful king,
> To raise again the great King of the Jacquerie,
> Before and after, Mars shall reign at will.

Michel Nostradamus, born in France in 1503, was a healer and psychic as well as an astrologer. Some historians say he gazed into a bowl of water to get many of his accurate visions of the future. There is little doubt that he was speaking of that August 1999 eclipse when he wrote his famous Century X, quatrain #72, from *Les Propheties*, eluding to an alarmingly powerful king and a reign of Mars, associated with images of wars, fires, conflicts, illness, and epidemics. Although in this quatrain he spoke of the year 1999 and seven months, the calendar used in his day was changed slightly following his prediction, adding ten days, so that the Solar eclipse he saw occurring in the seventh month now corresponds to our eighth month of August.

The Great Divide Eclipses & the Years 1999–2006

That powerful Leo eclipse in 1999 heralded the approaching times and began a new era, suggesting many changes in store over the coming several years, a phase of instability, and struggles among leaders and nations. It and other eclipses of 1999 and 2000 fell in the signs Leo and Aquarius, signifying the need for a greater unity among mankind that would first require a great divide. There were indications of a fight for supremacy and a world power threatened. Terrorism was suggested and tensions spilled over into the economic picture. Leo is the sign of the individual ego, while Aquarius is the sign of the larger brotherhood.

As we know now, though, an eclipse is only the beginning of an extended process, and other than the Kosovo crisis and worries about Y2K, the major happenings in 1999 surrounded President Clinton's woes and impeachment hearings. These followed an eclipse in August of 1998 that fell on his natal Sun. Within days of that personally significant eclipse, he was forced to make his historical confession to the world about his affair with intern Monica Lewinsky.

As we recall from chapter 2, an eclipse in Leo, with the Sun as Lord of the eclipse, brings an accent and spotlight to the activities and interests of world leaders. True to form, this Leo eclipse had already started producing just that.

Uppermost on the minds of many in 1999 was how the millennium date change would affect computer network systems. Preparations and fixes took up the biggest part of the year, beginning shortly after the very first Solar eclipse of 1999, in February, at 27 degrees Aquarius, ruled by the technologically savvy Uranus. Mars' later pass to that Aquarius eclipse coincided with our very entry to the new millennium, when on the evening of December 31, 1999, there was much excitement in the air as the whole world watched together to see if the dreaded Y2K bug would bite. Thanks to all the technical preparations, patches, and fixes recommended by Uranus as Lord of the eclipse, it did not.

Another quite significant eclipse from the Aquarius and Leo group was the Solar Eclipse at 8 degrees Leo on July 30, 2000. This eclipse fell in close alignment with the ferocious Dragon's Head in the United States horoscope. As a point of offensive action, following eclipses on the Dragon's Head on previous occasions, Mars stimulation had coincided with the Cuban missile crisis and D-Day.

It was late in 2000 that my attention was drawn to some startling features in the horoscope of newly elected President George W. Bush, who had also just been touched by that Leo eclipse. Born on July 6, his natal Sun lies in very nearly the same degree of the zodiac as the Sun in the United States horoscope, for which the birth date is our Independence Day of July 4, 1776. With 360 degrees in the zodiac, this common tie might have been enough to give him an edge in the election. Soon, however, I saw that a Lunar eclipse would spotlight this very degree of the zodiac, and just prior to that significant Lunar eclipse was a Solar eclipse in the opening degree of the sign Cancer, a critical degree.[1] From years of observation and study, I knew this was no mediocre eclipse, but rather just the opposite, heralding global events of a spectacular magnitude.

I recalled that many celestial similarities had been in place during the early '60s prior to Kennedy's assassination and the great troubles our country faced at that time, including an eclipse that had set off the fierce Dragon's Head of the United States. It appeared that major changes were on the horizon and that President Bush would lead the U.S. though some difficult times, possibly at the risk of his own personal safety. He and the USA were evidently participating in a great cosmic process.

Following this discovery and armed with as many books and references on U.S. history as I could find, I spent the next several months amid stacks of horoscope charts, graphs, and event and planetary timelines as I attempted to find a common denominator at the time of historically significant events. I was aware from my study of individuals' charts that it was when a personal eclipse later received specific planetary stimulation that important life-changing events took place. I wondered if the same rules could be applied to world events. As evidence revealed that they could, by the first week of September 2001, I was aware that we had arrived at a crucial period, going by the number of eclipses that were due to receive special planetary stimulation.

According to my researched timeline, a significant historical event was coming due; actually the dates I'd noted as a dangerous period for the U.S. were September 8–13, 2001. Still absorbed in my research of the early twentieth century, however, I overlooked the forest for the trees, and when the attacks on America came on September 11, I was overwhelmed with shock. Even with all my research pointing to a global event with wide ramifications, what happened was incomprehensible—by far the worst of any event I had studied. Though temporarily immobilized at the full meaning of those danger days, I began to wonder if this unimaginable event might be a prelude to further incredible events, as several significant eclipses were to continue to receive energetic forces of testing in the years to come. Truly the era we'd entered was unique to any to which I could previously compare.

As a matter of fact, many astrologers warned of the danger that President Bush might be prevented from completing his full term in office based on the simple fact that he was elected in a year ending in 0, which has historically coincided with the assassination or death of a president while in office, all except Reagan since 1840. Bush's horoscope even showed similar features to those of Kennedy and Lincoln, and these eclipses falling so soon after he took office were quite powerful.

It appeared there were many issues that we'd be forced to deal with, including this recent national tragedy, wars, fires, floods, drought, and a host of other problems. Remaining strong during difficult economic times would be part of what was required. However, I noted that there was a window of opportunity to learn about terrorism lasting until 2006.

This recent eclipse falling on the Dragon's Head of the United States and on Bush's Ascendant had also made a tie to the chart of none other than Osama bin Laden.

Osama bin Laden's natal Sun and Uranus are within a degree of the U.S. Dragon's Head; thus the friction between his interests and those of the U.S. The U.S. became engaged and initiated the fight against the whole of the terrorist network within a little more than a year of this most recent eclipse.[2]

To top this off, President Bush had a remarkable connection to bin Laden, whose aggravation would be experienced quite personally regardless of other factors. Overall, the connection between them signifies a competitive contest, even physical in nature if such an opportunity would present itself.

It gives much food for thought that both Bush and bin Laden have such remarkable planetary ties to the U.S. horoscope and that there are such striking planetary links between their personal horoscopes, especially in light of the timely appearance of bin Laden's coordinated attack on the U.S. coming so soon after Bush took office. Talk about cosmic connections.

Because all factors were not yet in place and Bush not yet in office, Mars' very first pass over this most recent eclipse on the U.S. Dragon's Head did not produce the major event signified but did coincide with the peak in the political season to elect a new president. The Leo eclipse promised this focus on leadership and was still operating true to word. Much later, as Neptune stimulated this Leo eclipse (while Mars stimulated the critical Cancer eclipse), there came the covert attacks upon the U.S., so that by the next pass of Mars to this Leo eclipse, in 2001, U.S. troops were in Afghanistan carrying out mission Enduring Freedom and trying to track down the illusive bin Laden, who was believed to have been the mastermind behind the deadly attacks.

Then around the Full Moon of July 24, 2002, just as Mars came to stimulate the eclipsed U.S. Dragon's Head again, the story was leaked through the media about the Bush Administration's plan to attack Iraq, in its continued quest to eradicate terrorism. With stimulation from Jupiter to the eclipsed Dragon's Head in early 2003, the U.S. bombed Iraq, using strategic maneuvers to remove Saddam Hussein from power without causing mass casualties (as is Jupiter's benevolent nature). Saturn does not come into range of this eclipse until late in 2005, where it remains in close touch until mid-2006, finally bringing closure.

Although this eclipse may be relatively spent by then, if bin Laden manages to remain at large that long, the Saturn transit could coincide with his capture or demise. The result of the U.S. efforts to overcome terrorism should be obvious at this point, victories as well as losses. Some things could look a little bleak. We saw in the previous chapter that Saturn's transit to a more active eclipse on the U.S. Dragon's Head coincided with fear of the outbreak of world war as the U.S. was drawn into the Vietnam conflict.

It appears the U.S. could be involved in conflicts for a prolonged period of time. By 2008 and 2009, new eclipses will fall in close alignment with the U.S. Dragon's Head and Dragon's Tail, so there are yet more causes to fight for ahead.

The Homeland Security and Big Business Eclipses
& the Years 2000–2007

The eclipse in the first degree of Cancer in June 2001 was particularly significant for all the nations of the world and all the people of the world. This eclipse in a critical degree pointed to critical worldwide events and an accent on homeland security. For the U.S., this eclipse warned of secret enemies, and nearly three months following the eclipse, when Mars stimulated this eclipse, nineteen suicide hijackers, apparently followers of Osama bin Laden, carried out a covert and orchestrated attack on the U.S.

Out of all the eclipses in the opening years of the new century, this one was most powerful, with ramifications far and wide.

While the Cancer eclipses of 2000 through 2002 also spotlighted the family structure, all the way down to issues such as stem cell research and women's issues, the related eclipses during those years in the opposite sign of Capricorn emphasized themes surrounding big business, free enterprise, and capitalism. Those Capricorn eclipses were ruled by the business-savvy Saturn, as Lord of the eclipses.

We definitely saw evidence of shifting and adjustment as corporate scandals underscored the message of these Capricorn eclipses, indicating that some things in the business world were in need of an overhaul. It is in this area that we could experience some of the greatest tests and trials in 2004 and 2005, when Saturn consummates the several eclipses that fell in the signs Cancer and Capricorn, important ones for the U.S. by the fact that they fell on crucial places in the U.S. nativity as well as in the nativity of the U.S. leader, President Bush. The last time Saturn transited the sign Cancer, where the U.S. Sun resides, President Nixon resigned from office following the Watergate scandal, and the Vietnam War came to an end, a war that the U.S. lost. Certainly, with the added impact of crossing several important eclipses, including the powerful Lunar eclipse in the critical 13th degree of Capricorn, 2004 should prove to be a historical year in matters of national business as well as homeland concerns. As a result of lessons learned, many changes affecting the way big business is conducted will continue to be implemented until 2007.

The Summers of Fire Eclipse & the Years 2000–2004

Quite by chance, I had the opportunity to monitor one of the Cancer eclipses up close and personal from the very beginning. This dynamic eclipse occurred on July 1, 2000, at 10 degrees Cancer. I ended up calling it the Summers of Fire Eclipse.

The Solar eclipse that day was high in the sky over the Western states, and what made this eclipse unique was that fiery Mars accompanied the Sun and Moon by falling in the same degree of the zodiac as the eclipse. As Lord of the eclipse, Mars was given the power to reign over affairs. Although Cancer is a water sign, the heat from Mars quickly evaporated it, an especially dangerous combination for desert communities. Commencing near the time of the eclipse, the number of wildfires increased, and there were numerous cases of arson in Phoenix. Living in Phoenix, I was able to observe each of these surges of increased fires over the next few years as they coincided with planetary stimulation to the eclipse.

In this particular scenario for hot and dry conditions, expansive Jupiter increased the heat and inflammation of Mars, and as Jupiter teamed up with Mars for a pass to the eclipse in 2002, fires raged throughout the West, with the worst fires ever in Arizona and Colorado. Two Arizona fires were set within days of one another as Mars approached the eclipse degree, merging soon after. That it was a firefighter who set one of these fires in order to have summer work displays some of the characteristics of the eclipse as well, with a type of self-inflicting nature. It was a similar story in the Colorado fire, except it was a woman firefighter in that case.[3] A lost hiker set another of the blazes to attract attention.

By the time of Mars' precise inflammation to the eclipse on June 12, 2002, the Colorado fire was being compared to a war, and by Jupiter's final passage,[4] the media carried the news that America was in drought.

Paying close attention to how long the effects of a planet's stimulation lasted, I was amazed at the lasting power of Mars when combined with Jupiter. The fires seemed to burn forever. Speculating on what might happen upon the arrival of the Sun to the eclipse that followed close behind Jupiter and Mars, I felt it would bring some degree of command or control over the fire. Keep in mind that this was the second pass of the Sun over the eclipse point since the eclipse originated, or the second anniversary of the eclipse. Besides gaining some control over the fires, first reported as the Sun approached the eclipse within a degree, this transit also brought the arrest of the responsible party in the largest of all the fires.

This illustrates the dynamic effects of an eclipse and the extended period in which the degree remains sensitive. Even as the Sun brought some mastery over the fires, it also helped to revitalize the initial eclipse, and fires continued to burn intensely throughout the West until well after all the planets cleared the sign of Cancer.

On the third anniversary of the eclipse in 2003, fires once again escalated to their peak in the West; however, without Mars or Jupiter in the picture, the number of fires was only one-third as many as the year before.

The most destructive side of the eclipse, we hope, was seen two years afterward and only because Mars and Jupiter teamed up at their most excessive to ignite the flames shown by that eclipse.

One wonders if the pass of Saturn will bring an end to the drought and all the related problems or if it will show the face of the worst conditions first. Although Saturn makes three passes to this eclipse due to retrograde motion, its final pass in May of 2004 coincides with a final pass from Mars, which could bring severe conditions. By the eclipse's fourth birthday in July of 2004, we should see the final outcome of damages and new incentives resulting from the eclipse.

We could even surmise about what steps might have been taken as a preventive measure, had this message of the stars been heeded. Maybe some carefully controlled burning would have been a good solution, a win-win solution in fact, since it would have given the firefighters work, possibly saved much of the forest areas from destruction, and prevented the losses and disruption suffered by the evacuees.

While shark attacks also escalated under this eclipse,[5] some areas of the United States suffered from floods. Other countries also suffered floods and fires, all manifestations reflected by this eclipse in which we have the message of "water-related dangers."

Foreign Affairs, Religion, Travel, and Communications & the Years 2001–2006

Eclipses falling in the signs of Gemini and Sagittarius in 2001 and 2002 emphasized education and religion, travel and communication, as well as foreign affairs and international economics. If we take a look at the focus from the airline industry, to the fates of journalists in foreign lands, to attention on a holy war and scandals involving priests, to how the international economy was affected by various factors, it's easy to see that the themes indicated by the eclipses in these signs were reflective of the very issues that were of concern between 2001 and 2003.

Two of these eclipses were critical for the U.S. as they fell closely in alignment with the United States Mars, the warrior planet. While the eclipses were still in their infancy and quite sensitive, they received Saturn's testing-phase pass. Things were brought to a head very quickly in terms of wars in two foreign countries, Afghanistan and Iraq. Gemini is a dual sign and Sagittarius is linked to foreign affairs. The foreign mission also focused on the removal of two suppressive enemies to the USA, Osama bin Laden and Saddam Hussein, but the latter mission was attempted without the backing of the larger foreign alliances as imposed by the restrictive Saturn as it crossed the Solar Eclipse at 23 degrees Sagittarius (of December 2001) in early 2003, during UN talks.

By 2003, we still have eclipses falling in the signs Gemini and Sagittarius, still bringing transformations in the communications and travel industries and in religious and foreign affairs. Gemini has special significance over relations with bordering countries, while Sagittarius relates more to countries overseas.

Publishing is also spotlighted with the Gemini and Sagittarius eclipses, as well as the interests of people connected to these activities. A couple of these eclipses are quite stimulating to journalists and the media, appearing to mark a period in which there is much debate, analysis, and theorizing about the past and future, with each commentator putting his or her particular spin on what has been and what will be happening.[6] Several controversial books and publications followed close on the heels of one of the Gemini eclipses, including the tell-all book by Hillary Rodham Clinton. It was also announced that a book about rescued POW Private Jessica Lynch was in the works, criticized by many. Also shortly following, Bush was harshly criticized for relying on bad intelligence (Gemini/Mercury) to make a case for war in Iraq.

There are also changes occurring that affect our experiences and outlook in regard to travel and communication. These changes may materialize in our daily or long-distance communication, in our mode of transport, and in how we move about our neighborhood and relating to long-distance travel. Interestingly, at this time, there was controversy about the SUV and whether driving one supports terrorism due to its gas-guzzling tendency. Whether or not it supports terrorism, fuel prices have been on the rise, with gasoline shortages also making our usual daily transport a matter of concern.

With the May 2003 Gemini eclipse falling on the USA Uranus, ruling electricity, the condition of the electrical power grid became a concern following a major blackout in August, which happened coincident with the Sun's first stimulation to that eclipse. This event greatly hindered transport for a time. In the same week, a computer virus cost Microsoft and the public millions and interfered with Internet traffic.

At about the same time, complications arose in Iraq, with rebels from various factions undermining progress, also reflected in the eclipse to the USA Uranus, signifying rebels and unexpected elements causing problems for the government. So you can see that there can be numerous manifestations of an eclipse, all of which can be traced back to the affairs symbolized by the sign and ruler of the eclipse as well as the nature of the planet receiving the eclipse in the chart of a national figure.[7]

As you'll see in the Catalog of Annotated Eclipse Charts in the appendix, the eclipses occurring in 2004 show some unfinished war business, apprehension, and high-society disturbances. Prominent eclipses begin falling in Aries and Libra, promising an era of major social change and matters of justice coming to the forefront. In spite of outer turbulence affecting public tranquility, for some this is a pleasure-seeking time; however, that could include an increase in prostitution, illegal moneymaking activities, or abuse of alcohol or drugs. There is a highly dramatic eclipse in regard to fashion and design, and there are some spiritually inspiring vibrations. There are changes in living conditions with regard to housing and in the interests of daily family living. Money matters tend to be grave.

In the next chapter you'll learn of the major impact on financial affairs that an eclipse can have and what the years ahead may bring.

---

1. Matters indicated are grave, serious, and climactic. Also known as an Aries Point degree. See the glossary.

2. Several possible birth dates exist for Osama bin Laden. Because the chart describes his charisma and terror tendencies and due to this connection to the U.S. horoscope, I believe his correct birth date is July 30, 1957, based on government data submitted by Robert Blaschke to Lois Rodden's online *AstroData-Bank*, www.astrodatabank.com.

3. On June 8, 2002, a wildfire was started by a forestry worker, which developed into the largest in Colorado history. The origin of that fire really exemplifies the nature of Mars, as it rules firefighters as well as fire itself. Having worked for the forestry service for eighteen summers to prevent such catastrophes, a firefighter was supposedly burning a letter from her estranged husband while on duty to enforce a fire ban when her own small blaze got out of control. Numerous fires across the Southwestern states, from California to New Mexico, peaked during this same week.

4. From our viewpoint on earth, the planets appear to stop and back up at regular intervals, called retrograde motion, before resuming direct motion. It's because of this that Jupiter made three passes to the eclipse.

5 I was unable to keep precise dates and records of the escalation of shark attacks that began under this eclipse.

6. Controversial talk show host Howard Stern was taken off the air coincident with Mars' transit to the Gemini eclipse, following fines for indecency.

7. A pass from Mars in April of 2004 to the Gemini eclipse that fell on the USA Uranus coincided with another intense resurgence of violence in Iraq.

CHAPTER NINE

Eclipses, the Stock Market & World Trade

Research on the financial end of things gives a clear picture that for each of the major market crashes in the U.S., certain criteria were met in planetary configurations involving a previous eclipse on an important place in the United States nativity. The hotspots for these eclipses are on or opposite the USA Mars or Mercury. The USA Mars is in the sign of Gemini, ruled by Mercury, which governs the marketplace, so both these planets are significant of trade activity in the U.S. Eclipses denote a potential upset, and Saturn's later transits to eclipses spotlighting the USA Mars or Mercury have coincided with significant crashes. The crashes I've studied include Black Monday of 1987, Black Friday of 1873, and the big crash of 1929. A similar eclipse was a presage of the severe depression of 1920.

Black Monday of 1987
On June 10, 1983, a total Solar eclipse fell at 20 degrees Gemini, within 2 degrees of the USA Mars. As Saturn later moved within 3 degrees of an opposition to that eclipse, Black

Monday resulted on October 19, 1987, when the erratic Uranus, the changeable Moon, and the dissolving Neptune added their influences.

Black Friday of 1873

A Lunar eclipse in 1870 fell upon the USA Mercury within 3 degrees. Black Friday resulted when transiting Saturn opposed this eclipse on September 19, 1873, again with the accompanying influence of the dissolving Neptune.

Black Tuesday of 1929

On June 15, 1927, a Lunar eclipse fell opposite the USA Mars within a couple degrees. Later on, in October of 1929, Saturn transited across this eclipse as it also linked to a Solar eclipse of 1928 in the sign of Gemini. The other closest planet adding its influence was Jupiter, thus producing the "great" crash.

Marketplace Activity & National Finance for 2000–2007

Because of the many criteria, it is only very infrequently that all factors are in place at the same time to bring about a crash. Research indicated that by 2000 many of the conditions of previous crashes were coming into place once more, suggesting the potential for extreme conditions in the markets and in economic affairs.

In 2000 there was an eclipse opposite the USA Mercury, and then in 2001 and 2002 there were two eclipses that touched the USA Mars. However, the eclipse on Mercury was not to get Saturn's closing transits until 2004 and 2005, still within the eclipse life span. And, the eclipses spotlighting the USA Mars would be unusual because they would get Saturn's transit fairly soon after the eclipses, one of them within ten days.

In a similar theme, nearly one hundred years ago, Saturn's closure to Lunar eclipses of 1916 coincided with a stock-selling panic and the entry of the U.S. into World War I. The first of these eclipses fell at 28 degrees Cancer, opposite the U.S. Pluto, and the latter at 22 degrees Capricorn, opposite the U.S. Mercury, ruling the marketplace. In this case, Saturn made its pass to the eclipsed Mercury ahead of Mars when the panic took place due to fears of entering the war.

As in the earlier case, by 2001 there were already signs of imbalance in our economic affairs, with a great amount of conflict impinging from many directions.

Noting that the Solar Eclipse of June 10, 2002, was within close range of the U.S. Mars and in the sign of Gemini, naturally governing the marketplace, and with Saturn dominating the eclipse by being Lord, I made a brief forecast in the early spring of 2002 to test my theory that Saturn's transit to the eclipse would bring constricting elements to trade activity, as follows:

> At the time of the eclipse, Saturn is near the Sun and Moon, becoming Lord of the eclipse and passing over the eclipsed degree ten days later, on June 20. The presence of Saturn in the eclipse configurations suggests that by the time of the eclipse, conditions are bleak and somewhat depressing as far as the U.S. economy. Some specific event or simply a combination of factors could impinge upon the activities of investors and a dwindling spiral as a result might be seen in the marketplace. Because Mars travels just ahead of where the eclipse forms, Saturn actually makes a pass prior to Mars. Earlier, in 1916, a similar set of conditions coincided with a stock selling panic.

Shortly after making that summary, I was able to gather statistical evidence of Saturn's pass over that eclipse. On a statistical graph of the Dow Jones Industrial Average for a three-month period, the point of Saturn's arrival to the degree of the eclipse coincided with a more extreme dip in a downward trend, falling well below 10,000. The main factor affecting the trading at this point was the MCI WorldCom scandal, this on top of earlier accounting scandals and the rising evidence of the need for accounting probes into the books of big companies. Uncertainties prevailed.

With Saturn's transit to that degree just days following the eclipse, we saw the stock market fall steadily as economic worries rose and the value of the dollar declined, equaling that of the European euro in mid-July of 2002. It is as if Saturn's transit clamped down on the existing slump and prolonged it. One might have expected it to delay any chance of growth until at least the spring of 2003 or even perhaps a bit later when well clear of the eclipse.

Normally, Saturn's transit to that Gemini eclipse might have shown the worst conditions, economywise, and then ended the hardest times as it has done previously in U.S. history. However, not only are Saturn's transits to the USA's eclipsed Mercury still to come in

2004 and 2005, in the meantime there are some unusual celestial phenomena that could bring complications to economic matters.

In a rare event, commencing in 2003, Pluto will cross the Gemini eclipse degree (20) by opposition, and due to extremely slow movement combined with retrograde motion, it will make a total of five passes to this degree. Even though Saturn should have ended the eclipse, Pluto hovers in a small portion of the zodiac and holds in an opposition to the U.S. Mars until 2005, after which its pressure will gradually subside. Even without any eclipse conditions present, this is a profound transit. What Pluto will contribute in the wake of Saturn should eventually bear out to real corporate restructuring and many financial reforms.

We might surmise about some of the likeliest events to transpire through a brief look at previous times in U.S. history when Pluto made stressful contacts to the U.S. Mars, as it does through 2005. At a fundamental level, Pluto is concerned with taxation, and Mars with war, equaling a special war tax, which is just one of the themes observed at earlier times when these two planets have been linked. Both are also concerned with new enterprise, and you'll see this connection too in several of the seven occasions since 1776 that they've come into contact.

The following summaries with an asterisk indicate the most stressful of the previous contacts from Pluto to the USA Mars. However, the contact in 2003 to 2005 is more stressful than any since the USA gained independence. We shall move backward in time:

1986: Several separate terrorist attacks brought repercussions upon foreign trade. The space shuttle Challenger exploded. A captured agent divulged CIA connections to the Nicaraguan Contra mission. A Lebanese magazine disclosed secret U.S. sales of arms to Iran.

*1968: Strategic Air Command carrying four hydrogen bombs crashed near Thule, Greenland, spreading radioactive material over a wide area. A U.S. Navy vessel was seized by North Korea in the Sea of Japan. The release of eighty-three crewmen came a year later with a formal apology by the U.S. for being in territorial waters. Communist strikes in Saigon. Martin Luther King Jr. killed. Robert F. Kennedy assassinated.

1943: World War II was costing $8 billion per month. Twenty percent was deducted from the pay of wage earners, with a pay-as-you-go income tax that was signed into law. The FBI captured and held eight Nazi spies, all of whom were found guilty and died later by lethal injection. Race riots developed in New York and Detroit. War Bond rally auction held in New York. Coal miners strike continued. The United Nations Relief and Rehabilitation Administration was formed to supply food and essentials to newly liberated people of the world. The Pentagon was completed, the largest office building to date, covering thirty-four acres. Frank Sinatra was all the rage; fans were so violent at his New York appearance that riot teams were called out and 441 police personnel responded.

1904–1906: Construction of the Panama Canal began. The New York subway opened. Fire destroyed 2,500 office buildings in Baltimore. The steamer General Slocum caught fire and collapsed in midstream on a trek up the East River, taking the lives of 1,021. The rich man's depression of 1904, the nineteenth financial setback since 1790, lasted one year. The U.S. established its third mint in Denver, Colorado. The Staten Island Ferry opened in New York. A San Francisco earthquake and fire ravished the city.

1857–1859: After twelve years of prosperity, America entered its twelfth depression since 1790, hitting the industrial north especially hard. The Supreme Court came through with the Dred Scott decision 5–3, which stated that Negroes were not citizens even when they moved into free states and could not exercise any constitutional rights. The 120 emigrants of a wagon train were massacred in Utah by a band of Indians alleged to have been supported by Mormons. Fire destroyed the Crystal Palace in New York. The cornerstone of St. Patrick's Cathedral was laid in New York. The first oil well opened in Pennsylvania. Gold was discovered in Colorado and Oregon.

*1814–1816: The War of 1812 entered its final stages, and a peace treaty between the U.S. and Great Britain was signed December 24, 1814. Unaware that the war had ended, Major General Andrew Jackson defeated powerful British naval forces in a needless battle outside New Orleans, killing 2,000 British. The government raised funds by taxing watches, hats, boots, and other consumer goods. The nation's currency was in chaos, with 245 state corporations individually issuing their own money.

1781–1782: The Revolutionary War concluded with the surrender of 8,000 army men under the command of General Charles Cornwallis as they were surrounded in Yorktown, Virginia; however, the British did not leave New York until November of 1783. Spanish settlers established Los Angeles, calling it El Pueblo de Nuestra Señora la Reina de los Angeles de Porciúncula. General George Washington established the Purple Heart, an award for military merit.

If the previous events are any indication, between 2003 and 2005 we might expect natural disasters or accidents, terrorist activities, and war efforts that have a major impact on the economy. Given a worst-case scenario we could be dealing with extreme threats, even nuclear threats, during this period. We can also anticipate firsts, new establishments, and new enterprises as a result of the powerful desire to renew and regenerate. New York continues to take center stage, as it has done since the country's beginning.

Overall, economically, we get the image of the phoenix rising from the ashes although with floundering spurts as events continue to impinge and produce setbacks, especially during the period from August of 2004 through mid-2005 as Saturn crosses the USA's eclipsed Mercury.

Financial Collapse & Structural Growth: The World Trade Center

As far as new enterprises and seeing the phoenix rising from the ashes, this is certain to be seen at Ground Zero as well, when a new structure will eventually stand in the place where the Twin Towers stood.

A study of the eclipses pertinent to the collapse of the towers allows a look from a different perspective at U.S. trade activity and economic affairs, since the World Trade Center is an emblem of our nation's prosperity, also paramount in world trade.

In 2001, in the midst of the other eclipses that were affecting the USA's Mercury and Mars, relevant to trade activity, another important eclipse fell on the Second House cusp of the USA chart, governing not just national wealth but also important financial buildings and infrastructure. That same eclipse fell prominently in the horoscope of the Twin Towers, a warning that something critical and potentially dangerous was about to take place.

The ribbon-cutting ceremony and dedication of the Twin Towers took place on April 4, 1973, at 9:40 a.m. This established a birth time and date from which to draw up the nativity, which can be found in the Annotated Catalog of National Figures in the appendix. The 2001 eclipse at 0 degrees Cancer fell in alignment with the rising degree (the Ascendant) of the Twin Towers. In the chart of an individual, the Ascendant represents the physical body, and it is likewise symbolic of the physical structure of an entity such as this. This critical degree rising in the chart of the Twin Towers was a signature of the importance of this trade building in world affairs, and it very much reflects the name of the building itself since these degrees, when prominent in a horoscope, symbolize worldly connections.

Having such a powerful eclipse in such a conspicuous degree and prominent placement in the Twin Towers chart was truly significant of a huge event.

Although the eclipse occurred on June 21, 2001, it was not until September 11, while transiting Mars was activating the eclipse, that the terrorist acts unfolded, bringing the collapse of the towers, an event that greatly impinged on the image of pride and prosperity in the country.

A similar set of eclipse phenomena was at work on February 26, 1993, when the World Trade Center was bombed; however, in that case the eclipse that later received the activation from Mars was much less critically placed. The eclipse pertinent for the World Trade Center that preceded the 1993 bombing fell on June 30, 1992, at 9 degrees Cancer. That Solar eclipse fell upon the First House Dragon's Tail of the Twin Towers, indicating vulnerability. The bombing itself occurred as Mars was making an extended pass to that eclipse. Following a retrograde period, Mars made a station at this eclipsed degree. This long, involved back-and-forth stimulation by Mars to the eclipse point aptly described the months of preparation by the terrorists preceding the bombing.

Now, to note the difference between an eclipse of great meaning from one of less significance, there was a prior Solar Eclipse on June 21, 1982, that fell near the Twin Towers Ascendant. However, this eclipse occurred before the Sun had entered the critical first degree of Cancer. That eclipse occurred in the last degree of Gemini, shy of falling on the conspicuous rising degree of the Twin Towers chart and therefore much less indicative of problems.

You can be sure that when a new structure is dedicated at what we now call Ground Zero, the birth map of the building will also make important connections to the U.S. nativity.

The Financial Outlook for the USA

As you can see in the Annotated Catalog of National Figures in the appendix, an eclipse in 2010 falls on the USA Mercury and in 2011 on the USA Mars. Once again there are likely to be fluctuations in trade activity. As you track the planetary passes to those eclipses in table 1 in the appendix, you'll see that neither of them receives a transit by Saturn during the time the eclipses are active, although one gets a pass by Jupiter in 2013, so there's less potential for a crash and more potential for growth.

Of course the eclipse of June 21, 2020, is extremely meaningful in terms of finance and monetary concerns for the U.S., and we shall look at it more closely in chapter 11.

In the next chapter we'll take a look at some prominent eclipses to come, and you'll see how Uranus plays an outstanding role for some time as the planet of experimentation, innovation, and surprise.

CHAPTER TEN

Surprises & Twists
from 2007–2015

Up until this point we've discussed many past events for the U.S. that have been connected to eclipse patterns. We've covered the ups and downs in the struggling U.S. economy and we've gotten glimpses of the future on several fronts.

In this chapter we will set out to decipher the messages from the eclipses of 2007, and the nature of the impact they may have since they are the recipients of much planetary stimulation soon after they occur.

There are some limitations to jumping so far into the future. Since we are constantly creating our tomorrows through choices we make today, collectively we make a huge impact on the conditions we'll have created by 2007. We can speculate from what we see today about certain conditions we are creating. And, as is the nature of astrology's laws, high-profile themes repeat themselves in many ways through the planets that will help pinpoint the areas due for attention.

The eclipses occurring in 2007 have the added impact of a Saturn transit while the eclipses are still active. As you've discovered, it was several eclipses of this influence that helped bring about many major changes early in our entry to this new century. Eclipses with this Saturn influence show situations that mature fairly rapidly once we're aware of them. If the eclipse shows an out-of-balance situation, it will require solutions and resolve pretty quickly. Conflicts that arise that are associated with the eclipse are frequently timed to Mars stimulation to the eclipse. And, it is not just Mars' first transit that can produce this friction but any of this planet's visits to the degree of the eclipse during its life span.[1] Saturn's transit generally coincides with the most restrictive periods in regard to the themes shown by an eclipse, and this transit often concludes the difficulties. It appears preferable to have Mars transit prior to Saturn.

The eclipses in 2007, however, get not just the transit of Saturn along with the usual Mars transits, but they also receive stimulation from Jupiter and Uranus, a really outstanding group of heavies. While Jupiter brings increase and expansion, depending upon what it has to expand upon, Uranus can be counted on to bring the unexpected. Uranus is actually the very first planet to reach one of the eclipses. Usually Mars would have at least brought a conflict to make sure we were aware of a critical situation. The energy of Uranus is more like having the rug pulled out from under you, suddenly and without warning. Yet, we must not forget that Uranus is also responsible for sudden strokes of luck, flashes of genius, discoveries, and new inventions. In any case, Uranus' effects tend to be rather shocking, and at times no less than electrifying.

Knowing that the eclipses of 2007 are outstanding, first of all by receiving the effects of Saturn within the life span of the eclipses, we next note that they are falling in the zodiac signs of Virgo and Pisces. The signs will provide a general theme about how these eclipses might affect the whole globe and the general population. Going by those signs and their rulers, we will first place these eclipse messages into one of two categories.

Virgo is an Earth sign, related to harvests, crops, the food supply, nutrition, and public health. Mercury, concerned with details, critical analysis, and the ability to make wise use of natural resources, rules Virgo. Virgo is motivated by practicality and concerned with health, work, and service. At best, an eclipse in Virgo could suggest an era of feasting and robust good health for the multitudes. At worst, it could indicate just the opposite—problems with crops or resources that lead to illness, malnutrition, etc.

Pisces is a Water sign, related to the sea and marine life. Neptune rules Pisces and is associated with charities, nursing-care facilities, and social movements. Neptune rules medicine, drugs, chemicals, and oil. Uncertainties often prevail with Neptune, and it has a dissolving effect. Pisces is also a spiritual sign, sensitive and idealistic. At best, an eclipse in Pisces might relate to a whole new social movement that is spiritual and seeking enlightenment. At worst, there could be widespread unrest, criminality, drug abuse, or serious dangers affecting our oceans or marine workers.

Together, the sets of eclipses in these two signs in 2007 bring a focus to our most basic needs as supplied by the earth: our food and water resources. When the very oceans are part of the equation, it is impossible to overlook the huge implications for all the lands and people should this involve shifting coastlines, melting icecaps, or some kind of contamination.

As a matter of fact, it is in 2006 that eclipses begin falling in Virgo and Pisces, signs naturally associated with public health services, and they suggest a worldwide focus on environmental concerns. In 2003, we heard that the hole in the ozone sheath over Antarctica was the largest ever, and during these years there is likely to be greater focus on environmental hazards, with increased efforts to clean them up.

Since an eclipse brings varying effects by region, we will next look at these eclipses in a chart cast for Washington, D.C., which will show an overall theme for the USA. Although these eclipses with their themes relating to health and environmental factors are more pronounced in other countries than in the U.S., the West Coast and California in particular may take a high profile during this period, with attention or special efforts to deal constructively with a potential threat.

Even though there are apparent challenges attached to these eclipses, we shall most assuredly handle them, for these are not the end times. Venus promises a measure of protection.

The first of the series of eclipses is a Lunar eclipse occurring on March 3, 2007, at 13 degrees Virgo. In the chart set for Washington, D.C., which you can see in the Catalog of Annotated Eclipse Charts in the appendix, this eclipse falls in the Twelfth House, the house in a mundane chart that pertains to charities, hospitals, welfare, convalescent centers, and similar rehab facilities. This same house also governs prisons, crime, and criminals. The Moon, which occupies the Twelfth House, reflects crowds, women, and the working classes, so this position suggests that many people are connected with places of rehab, possibly as recipients of welfare or as charitable workers helping others. Concerns with crime or prison conditions could also escalate. We know that eclipses occurring in the sign of Libra in 2004 were to bring a shift in morality, and on top of hard economic times, an increase of criminal activities was possible. That may be part of what this chart is reflecting.

On the opposite side of the chart, there is a great deal of activity in the Sixth House, the house that is naturally associated with Virgo, emphasizing concerns involving civil servants, medical employees, the Red Cross, and health services. The Sixth House reflects the well-being of the people, and here we see Neptune on the cusp, showing possible health hazards or vulnerability. Neptune is opposite Saturn, indicating disorder in these areas, and there could be delays, confusion, or setbacks. Saturn on the cusp of the Twelfth House necessitates responsibilities, adding to the burdens in places like hospitals, rehab centers, charitable institutions, and welfare programs. Seniors may be facing difficulties.

The Sixth House also contains retrograde Mercury, indicating a review of issues as they concern public health, welfare, and conditions affecting the working classes and civil servants. There could be peculiar disorders and drug experimentation. With an easy aspect from Pluto, research could result in a scientific discovery leading to a cure for a contagious ailment. The Sun in the Sixth House shows the area of activity and concern of the country's leaders and government, so there is a lot of attention on directing and overseeing civil servants, medical needs, and the health of the public. In the Sixth House, we also find Uranus, suggesting some unforeseen elements or an emergency that upsets the public and necessitates the action of civil servants.

Jupiter is on the cusp of the Fourth House and forms a trine to Saturn on one side and a trine to Venus on the other, producing a Grand Trine in Fire signs, a spiritual tone. This suggests a demonstration of patriotism and loyalty and an increase of charitable movements. This is also good for producing vision and foresight in solving practical problems.

When a benevolent planet like Jupiter is found on one of the chart angles and stressed by another planet, however, it often shows a disruption to the ease and benefits associated with it. Here, Jupiter receives an unfriendly aspect from Uranus, suggesting an interruption to the benefits promised by Jupiter. Because of the mutual reception of Uranus and Neptune, Neptune must also be regarded as unfriendly to Jupiter, so this likely disturbs peace and order. It indicates trouble for the government in some way. We should also keep in mind that Jupiter's expansion factor is not always of a positive result, nor is a Grand Trine without its potential to make things seem so cozy that we fall off guard when precisely the opposite is needed. However, Jupiter's promising planetary relationships help greatly to offset the difficulties seen otherwise.

The Dragon's Tail rises in this chart, denoting potential vulnerability on the part of the public. The Dragon's Head near the cusp of the Seventh House with Uranus close by denotes the possibility for unexpected complications in foreign or national affairs. Also, when a planet falls this close to an eclipse, it becomes Lord of the eclipse, so again we're reminded of unpredictable possibilities. With Uranus as Lord, anything is possible.

When a particular theme comes up time after time, it points to some of the most observable effects. I think we are starting to get the idea that Uranus will introduce volatility, but it is unfortunate that this is the target planet to decipher. Many astrologers will not attempt to judge Uranus for the simple fact that this planet is nonconforming and therefore almost impossible to pin down. With Uranus, astrologers say that if you can name what it is, then that isn't it. Nevertheless, we shall make an attempt here. At least we'll test theory.

Uranus suggests unusual or unforeseen conditions affecting our health, jobs, or military. It verifies trouble for the government. People are discontented, and there is apt to be confusion in national life.

We cannot rule out the possibility that at least some of the problems we encounter during this period will be the result of threats or actions taken by an enemy. The Twelfth House, where two of the eclipses fall in 2007, also rules secret enemies, and it appears our military is actively dealing with conflicts throughout this period. Because of the military themes as well as Uranus' placement in Pisces, trouble could fall to the Navy. The military may be responding to threats, and it may be the conditions they face in other lands that are of concern to the American people.

The emergency may be related to health or the environment, and while it may be new or more forms of pesky viruses requiring vaccines and making high demands on health care workers, there is potential for these concerns to be connected to the oceans, seas, water, or energy supplies.

Moving on to the next eclipse, which is a Solar eclipse on March 18, 2007, there is much agreement from this chart that these are some challenging times with serious difficulties in national life and sudden, unexpected trouble. There is potential for discomforting circumstances, whether arising through violent storms or a natural disaster. Oil, fuel, and electrical energy issues are in high focus throughout this period, so blackouts or outages could lead to other complications.

Keep in mind that everything does not happen immediately after an eclipse occurs. Having said that, the spring of 2007 does appear to be an active time.

The next eclipse of 2007 is a Lunar eclipse falling on August 28. There is a Grand Cross involving Jupiter, Mars, Mercury, and Uranus. This Grand Cross, which is representative of conflict, falls in the angular houses of the chart, emphasizing the personal effect it has on the country. It falls in changeable signs, indicating fluctuating conditions and an atmosphere of inconvenience or unrest. On the positive side, there is also potential to negotiate solutions for whatever problems exist.

The planets Mercury and Uranus in their opposition fall in Virgo and Pisces, respectively, suggesting from their First House and Seventh House positions that there is much public excitement and debate, possibly due to complications or unexpected troubles arising in foreign quarters. Mars is elevated in the chart, showing movement of the military and potential problems for the Army. It applies to a square with the First House Mercury, ruling the people, suggesting possible health risks as well as debate, argument, and warlike tones.

Mars and Jupiter in their opposition show potential suffering in hospitals, charitable institutions, or rehab centers. Venus in the Twelfth House of rehabilitation opposes Neptune in the Sixth House, repetitious of health-related themes as well as indicating discontent among the working classes or difficulties for the Navy.

The first planet to reach this eclipse is Saturn, which does so less than two months following the eclipse. In times past, we've seen that it is best for Mars to make contact to an eclipse degree ahead of Saturn. When this doesn't happen, Saturn sometimes presses down on existing conditions and drags them out.

The final eclipse in 2007 is a Solar eclipse that takes place on September 11. Again, the eclipse falls in the environmentally and health-conscious sign of Virgo, and Uranus closely opposes the eclipse from the Sixth House.

Since Uranus is quite prominent in two of the eclipses this year, we must not forget that in 1999 Uranus played a very positive role when everyone was so worried about the Y2K bug. Thanks to all the patches and fixes recommended by the technologically savvy Uranus as Lord, we weathered that storm. Uranus was strong in its own sign, Aquarius, at that time. Now in Pisces, there remains that element of mystery, illusion, and uncertainty. Its mutual reception with Neptune appears to bring more complications than advantages, compounding difficult aspects. This suggests disorder, confusion, and unexpected trouble.

If there were to be preventive measures that could be taken ahead of time, they might lie in the area of upgrading and improving our water filtration systems and facilities to avoid contaminants, including security measures to prevent the event of sabotage. Uranus rules rebels, and Pisces' ruler, Neptune (where Uranus falls), rules deceptions and poison. Being aware of the need for flexibility and of surprise elements of inconvenience will help to deal with them when they come. On an individual level, we could each do what we can to conserve energy and to reduce strains on the environment and the pollutants we contribute. Driving less and walking more might produce a win-win solution to some problems regarding both health and the environment. Improve your nutrition, guard your health in practical ways, and become innovative about bringing a more healthful quality of living to your area. Donate your time, effort, or money to good causes.

In table 1 you will find the times of planetary transits to the 2007 eclipses, and you'll notice that the Solar eclipse of March 2007 gets planetary stimulation from several celestial bodies around the same time in early 2010. Included in the listings are all the transits to these eclipses by the outer planets, even those occurring after the "closing" transits of Saturn, just for the purpose of observation.

The Catalog of Annotated Eclipse Charts in the appendix gives a condensed description of the prominent features for each eclipse up to 2012, and there you'll find a list of countries brought to emphasis by each eclipse. For example, two of the eclipses in 2007 bring a spotlight to North Korea and its leader. Iran is affected by three of the 2007 eclipses.

It seems we'll always be handling one challenge or another—that's the way life is. It really makes one appreciate the daily blessings. However, things begin looking better a little later on, and in fact there is an era that looks like it could be quite exciting, at least in one respect.

From 2010 to 2012, you'll notice that several eclipses spotlight the chart of Roswell, New Mexico. Two of them emphasize Roswell's Moon and Mars, the same kind of eclipse pattern the occurred prior to the controversial alien sightings there in 1947. The eclipse itself occurred in 1946, and it was when Mars transited the eclipse in early July 1947 that all of the excitement took place. At first, the news of an alien spacecraft crash appeared in newspapers and was discussed openly, but soon the whole matter became hush-hush and the government insisted that the entire incident could be explained by tests of weather balloons.

In the mid-1990s, a couple eclipses fell similarly in Roswell's chart, and these were followed by a great deal of new speculation about that first encounter, including an aired interview with the children of military personnel who were present and had knowledge of the facts in 1947. Now grown, they spoke about how they were forced to keep this secret and how it had affected their lives. Another documentary that aired showed an alien autopsy, very authentic looking, said to have taken place shortly after the alien spacecraft supposedly crashed during an accident in a lightning storm.

Now, as if two new eclipses within a few months weren't enough to make one sit up and take notice, a third eclipse also falls across Roswell's Uranus and Pluto, a pair of planets suggesting unusual (Uranus) encounters (Pluto). A similar Lunar eclipse spotlighted those same planets in late 1946, just a few months before all the excitement took place in Roswell. Could these coming eclipses portend another alien encounter or at least the opportunity to learn the truth about the first one? To me, this sounds captivating (pun intended). Surely aliens couldn't be any less friendly or more threatening than some of the characters we share the planet with. In any case, it may be wise to have a contingency plan in place. My curiosity is definitely peaked because whatever is going on in Roswell, the same eclipses are of interest to NASA and to the White House. With much stimulation to these eclipses over the couple of years following the eclipses, Saturn does not bring closure until 2015, as indicated in table 1 in the appendix. Do watch especially the dates of the transits of Mars over these eclipses, as they are likely to coincide closely with some of the more outstanding activities.

In the next chapter we will look at the potential for the year 2020, based on the powerful eclipse that year, so extremely rare and so important for the USA.

---

1. Note all conjunctions or oppositions +/- 3 degrees that occur within 3.5 years following the eclipse. See table 1 in the appendix for dates of major stimulation to eclipses through 2015.

CHAPTER ELEVEN

The Powerful Eclipse of 2020

While all eclipses carry an important message of change and transition, in this chapter we will take a look at some of the most powerful eclipses of all.

Just after the turn of this new century, we experienced an eclipse that fell in the opening degree of Cancer. These critical degrees are the 0 degree of Aries, Cancer, Libra, or Capricorn, the days that correspond with the start of our four seasons, as the Sun passes into one of these signs called "cardinal," associated with action and initiative. Whenever a planet occupies a position in one of these degrees, that planetary energy can manifest quite easily, so to have an eclipse in one of these points is an event of some spectacular notice. These eclipses are exceptionally rare, and they signify events of wide-range effect, setting a historical marker.

The next time we'll have one of these will be in 2020, on June 21 of that year, as the Sun moves into Cancer, the same sign and degree as the eclipse of 2001 that preceded the attacks on America. Fortunately, the eclipse of 2020 has a raw power rating of only six, as compared to seven for the one that fell in 2001. Still, it is quite a powerful eclipse.

To illustrate just how rare they are, there were no eclipses falling in one of these degrees during the entire twentieth century. The last time a Solar eclipse fell in one of these degrees prior to 2001 was December 22, 1889. That eclipse fell in the opening degree of Capricorn, the sign concerned with business affairs. Saturn, as ruler of Capricorn, is associated with scarcities and is especially representative of industry, organizational affairs, statesmen, public buildings, and national calamities.

One thing that these Cancer and Capricorn eclipses have in common is that either would fall on one or the other of the two most important financial house cusps in the USA chart. And, either would fall on or opposite the USA Venus, also symbolizing money and creature comforts. These connections are indications that either type will precipitate changes in national wealth and in economic and financial affairs. Other than that, the eclipse of 2001 in Cancer was more concerned with homeland security, and by sign, suggested an era of great concerns for many countries around the world. In the chart set for Washington, D.C., it additionally indicated secret enemies, so the overall message of this eclipse was quite different than the previous eclipse in 1889 in the opening degree of Capricorn. Even though the planetary configurations at the time of that earlier eclipse were actually somewhat beneficial, helping people to weather the difficulties of the times, it was still a time of certain crisis that followed.

Following that historical eclipse in late 1889, it was not until the spring of 1893, coincident with Mars' fourth pass to the eclipse, that the direst of financial circumstances for the U.S. occurred, when a panic of stock selling plunged the nation into a deep depression. It was called the Silver Panic and was the result of the U.S. being out of step with the rest of the world on the values set for gold and silver. Even though there were Wall Street failures totaling $10 million in 1890, there had still been an image of prosperity on the surface; but in the second week of May 1893, the greatest losses were suffered, totaling $169 million. Cordage Trust, a stock-market favorite, went into receivership, with shares falling from $70 to $12. Banks closed their doors, unemployment soared to 9.6 percent, and mercantile failures totaled almost 3,500. Specific events that signaled the end of the boom and the start of contraction were price declines across the boards, including wheat and iron, which had previously been on the rise. The Philadelphia and Reading Railroad collapsed and went into bankruptcy. The Treasury's gold reserves fell to a record low, finally falling below the minimum necessary to protect greenbacks.

This was an eclipse with the influence of the Dragon's Tail.

By 1894, the U.S. was forced to borrow $50 million in gold on two occasions, indicative of unrest on the labor and political scenes, with 16.7 percent of industrial wage earners now idle.

The following is a time capsule of just some of the events noted around the world and in the U.S. after that powerful eclipse of 1889 to show how these critically placed eclipses bring grand historical markers.

- Russia began the Trans-Siberian railway system, marking the project by a ceremonial service in mid-1891.

- Great Britain declared all territories in South Africa up to the Congo to be within its sphere of influence on July 1, 1891.

- Germany renounced claims to Uganda, Zanzibar, and Pemba.

- Chile broke out in a civil war in 1891 as a result of what started out as a political fight between the president of the republic and the national congress. The president committed suicide after his forces were defeated.

- The idea for the world Olympic games was born on November 25, 1892, and the first games were held in Greece in April 1896.

- In the USA, Ellis Island opened on January 1, 1892, the first federal immigration station.

- Carnegie Hall opened on May 5, 1891.

- Francis Bellamy wrote the Pledge of Allegiance in August of 1892.

- The United Mine Workers of America came together in Columbus, Ohio, in 1890.

- Polygamy was prohibited in the U.S.

- Lizzy Borden was acquitted of the crime of killing her father and stepmother with an ax.

- The Sherman Anti-Trust Act was passed, making it illegal to restrict interstate trade. This paved the way later on for a federal suit against Standard Oil for its monopoly, eventually dissolving all thirty-three of its corporations.

Unrelated to the financial themes but nonetheless a historical marker for America, another set of events developed in the U.S. coincident with Mars' very first pass to this eclipse.

The autumn of 1890 marked a historical crossroads for Sioux Indians, now living on reservations in the Dakotas. The result of the incident is known as the Massacre at Wounded Knee, when Chief Sitting Bull and Chief Big Foot were both killed by U.S. troops, along with 300 Sioux Indians.

With their buffalo gone and themselves dependent on Indian agents, the proud Sioux Indians missed their previous way of life and freedom to roam, now confined to reservations. In a final effort to return to the old days of their glory, the Sioux began to follow a new mysticism preached by a shaman in Nevada named Wovoka. They traveled from the Dakotas to hear him speak. Wovoka, who called himself the messiah, prophesied that the dead would soon join the living in a world in which the Indians would live as in the old days. According to his prophecy, a tidal wave of new soil would cover the earth, burying the white man and restoring the prairie. To hasten the event, the Indians were encouraged to dance the Ghost Dance. This they did, dressing up in colorful shirts with images of eagles and buffalo, believing that the emblazoned shirts would protect them from the white man's bullets.

The practice of the Ghost Dance spread through the Sioux villages of the Dakota reservations, bringing fear to the whites as it revitalized Indian resistance. Finally, an Indian agent at Pine Ridge wired his Washington, D.C., superiors, calling for military intervention. The order went out to arrest Chief Sitting Bull. He was killed in the first attempt, and Chief Big Foot moved into command, himself sick from pneumonia and dying. Then, during a sunrise powwow of negotiations with his warriors and the U.S. Army officers, a shot outside the tent pierced the early morning quiet, leading to a chaotic defense from both sides. As women and children ran for cover, they were cut down in the rapid crossfire. When the gunshots ended and the smoke cleared, a total of 300 Sioux Indians and 25 Army troops were dead. This incident ended the Indian wars.

Overall, that Capricorn eclipse certainly has a ring of governmental authority and national business about it. The difference between this and the Cancer eclipses of 2001 and 2020 is that while the Capricorn eclipse emphasizes corporate and business affairs, the Cancer eclipse emphasizes our home, land, and living conditions, and the security of those.

In looking back on the events following the 2001 Cancer eclipse, we can see that on a group level, the way we felt about our basic security was shaken and transformed.

The events of September 11, 2001, corresponded with Mars' first pass to the Cancer eclipse of the previous June. A Mars transit to an eclipse point often coincides with a crisis of conflict.

The Cancer eclipse of 2001 had the influence of the Dragon's Head, associated with new incoming energy that is sometimes sudden and catches us unaware. The eclipse of 2020 is also of the influence of the Dragon's Head.

The major passes of Mars to the eclipse of 2020 come in the spring of 2021, in January of 2022, in March of 2023, again late in December 1923 through January 1924, and finally in late August to September of 1924. The eclipse also receives the rejuvenating rays of the Sun each year during June and December, with a particularly sensitive period indicated in December of 2023.

We know from the past that our financial interests as well as our values face transformation. For the USA, the eclipse of 2020 will likely bring many challenges for the country. Other nations that this eclipse will particularly affect are those with planets in the critical Aries Point degrees.

This powerful eclipse of 2020 also falls on Prince William's Sun, occurring on his thirty-eighth birthday, so this will likely be an important period for him, for his father, Prince Charles, and for the royal family.

It seems as if all of the most momentous worldly events may be traceable to an eclipse. There are obviously many discoveries to make. And, while eclipses may be most important in terms of world events, in the next chapter we will take a look at how eclipses denote your personally important periods and how they signal vital cosmic connections.

PART THREE

Eclipses: Your Personal Cosmic Telegrams

CHAPTER TWELVE

An Eclipse & You

Signs and symbols appear daily in our lives that reflect our personal exchange with the universe if we choose to pay careful attention. These are so subtle sometimes that they may hardly be noticed, although many individuals are becoming more aware of the odd synchronicities or unusual "coincidences" that happen from time to time, an apparent signal of being in sync with universal forces and in the right place at the right time on the destined path.

There is nothing we are more synchronized with than the heavenly bodies, however, and special cosmic messages come to us at regular intervals to keep us informed of our personal exchanges and earthly duties. These important cosmic telegrams come via eclipses.

Eclipses prove that we are connected to a greater force and that there's a definite purpose for each of us. The specific message an eclipse holds for you depends on where in your personal horoscope the eclipse falls. In the coming chapters you'll discover what each eclipse through 2011 means for you.

No one has the same chart, or blueprint for life, as you do, and no one will for at least another 25,000 years. From the moment of your first breath and for the rest of your life, your personal horoscope mirrors every major crossroad you come to. If you don't have one yet, refer to the list of resources in the back of the book to acquire a free copy of your horoscope, and you'll be able to learn the area of your life where eclipse energy is due to raise your consciousness in the years to come. This will give you a heads up about areas that will require your attention.

When it is time for you to serve in a cosmic task, an eclipse signifies it by plugging in to one of your birth planets, which thereafter becomes a conductor for various universal energies that are each available for a certain period of time, providing the opportunity for you to complete your work. An eclipse sometimes points to where you've been investing your energy for an extended time, and indicates the need to bring this out into the external world. In this way, an eclipse often brings a dream into reality because you'll work very hard to make it so. Other times it can seem especially difficult to get a project off the ground, and you feel tested at every turn even though you know you're on the right track. Believe it or not, there's a purpose for this too, and you can become better equipped to work with the forces at your disposal.

When it is time for you to take a new, important step on your life path, an eclipse also signifies this, sometimes bringing the feeling that it's time to prepare by wrapping up an old matter or ending an old association in order to create a vacuum. Eclipses reveal the escalating steppingstones in our lives, when we complete one of our prearranged tasks or are summoned to the next. They offer the opportunity to break free of old habit patterns, enabling us to move beyond our self-appointed limitations. If we allow them, they can even show us how to gracefully accept times of melancholy, to actually become fortified by getting to know the nature of our soul.

Even though eclipses respect the multitudes and appear to be most influential over worldly matters, providing for cosmic balance upon earth, they also touch each of us and sometimes in a most intimate way.

Eclipses of great global importance have an effect upon your life, even if somewhat indirectly at times. The cost of living, the price of gas, the loss of jobs through mergers, or other situations beyond your control that come unexpectedly also have an impact on those around you, and some people are more personally affected than others. When things begin to shift and change in a big way, you can be sure there's a great cosmic process at work. Life and times are changing, and at times the only wise choice is to adapt and make the best of it with the knowledge that smoother times lie ahead and that there's a purpose for what is happening, even if you don't quite understand what it is at the time.

The best example I can give you of one of these major eclipses is the one that occurred on the first day of summer in 2001 and in the first degree of the zodiac sign of Cancer. As we've already discussed, the first degree of the cardinal signs—Aries, Cancer, Libra, and Capricorn—are called critical degrees. These represent the beginning of each of the four seasons. Because one season follows the other, these specific degrees, if occupied by a planet, or especially if an eclipse occurs there, are symbolic of a kind of domino effect, when a single event eventually touches upon many personal facets of life. These degrees symbolize worldly events and have wide ramifications. Because an eclipse mirrors conditions affecting the multitudes, this eclipse symbolized a sensitive spot that would be felt around the world by falling in the opening degree of the nurturing sign Cancer, representative of fundamental securities within the homeland.

Basically, the degree of this eclipse announced that major events were in the making that would bring many countries to their feet, that events would have a ripple effect felt by everyone all over the world. On the opposite end of the eclipse spectrum in 2001 were the Capricorn eclipses, bringing industry and big-business themes to light, also certain to have wide ramifications. Of course, within less than three months of that all-important eclipse in the first degree of Cancer, we realized that the world as we knew it had changed dramatically as we began to feel the ripple effects immediately following the events of September 11, 2001.

In your personal horoscope, a planet in one of those critical degrees shows that in some way, a cause you work for does, can, or will receive the notice of the world at large. Fame is sometimes signified by a planet in one of these degrees, but then so is infamy. Such renown may come about swiftly. If not reflecting you, this feature of your chart could be symbolizing that it's your partner who has a direct link to worldly affairs, possibly a function for the government or a capacity that affects large numbers of individuals. Just to give you one example, Walt Disney had the planet Neptune in one of these degrees. Neptune rules fantasy and imagination; thus his name became associated with fantastic, fun escapes from the everyday world. In fact, Neptune is also the planet ruling dreams, and Mickey Mouse first appeared to Disney in a dream. His dream has had a tremendously positive impact on children and adults around the world for several generations.

The eclipses of 2001, some of which have effects lasting until 2006, were falling in two specific areas of your horoscope, representing two specific areas of your life, raising your awareness about certain relationships and bringing with them the exposure of certain elements in your life that required your special attention. If that critical Cancer eclipse happened to take place near one of your personal planets, you'd have felt the impact of that worldly eclipse in a very personal way. It would have had an even more pronounced effect in your life than it did for some people. Although an eclipse is not necessarily a precursor to a loss or to troublesome times, it sometimes is. Perhaps you lost a loved one as a result of the events of 9/11, or the company you worked for was directly affected in the aftermath. In either of these examples, your life would have been affected on many personal levels that would take time to work through.

Eclipses call individuals to their personal destinies, so whether it's time for you to serve in a cosmic task or time for you to make a cosmic connection with someone, an eclipse will signify it ahead of time. Sometimes this feels as if you're riding an ocean wave, that you've been picked up by a powerful, positive force and carried along. It can be quite an invigorating experience. Other times an eclipse may call you to wrap up a previous phase of experience because it must be done in order to meet your destiny. There's a promise to keep and a gift to leave behind. Though we are aware that something larger is at work, these eclipses are sometimes experienced initially as more difficult, almost as if we are leaking energy until we come to understand the process.

Our personal mission, complete with all the details about our prearranged plans, commitments, and meetings with others, is shown in our horoscope. When our prearranged plan requires us to meet up with someone with whom we have a contract, we may experience the meeting in an unusual way that we call fate. The definition of fate is a "predetermined and inevitable necessity." So, if we must say goodbye when one of our contracts comes to an end, we also refer to the experience as fate. Usually anything that happens, whether good or bad, that is unexplainable by the apparent use of free will, we tend to call destiny or fate.

Eclipses are often associated with the destinies and fates of individuals as well as the larger world karma. However, they are never meant to be omens of doom. An eclipse offers a *window of opportunity* to address a situation or condition. And, the nice thing is that as residents here on earth, each of us is also plugged in to these cosmic-energy flows, and they can be harnessed constructively to achieve our personal aims. Even when an occasional eclipse initializes changes that you'd prefer to have nothing to do with, there is an important learning experience at hand and an opportunity for growth. By examining it, you can come to better understand and work with the flow.

The fact that we are so in sync with the happenings in the heavens is a fascinating concept, especially when you consider that the planets were well established in their movements before any of us were born. If one reflects the other, are we an extension of them or they of us? As the saying goes, "As above, so below." It's really as if we choose to make our entrance when our vibration is synchronized perfectly with cosmic forces. And so it is. The same kind of magic portals through which cosmic energy flows at an eclipse are also symbolized somewhere in your personal horoscope, revealing a story about your evolving soul and the spiritual vibration you were in tune with when you arrived to take up life on planet earth.

CHAPTER THIRTEEN

Your Evolving Soul
& Your Prenatal Eclipses

In your horoscope, it is the Dragon's Head and Dragon's Tail that tell of the spiritual vibration under which you made your entry. These points, also called the North and South Nodes, reveal the continuous threads running from lifetime to lifetime. In space, the Lunar Nodes are invisible points of intersection of two orbits that pierce the celestial sphere.[1] In your horoscope, they tell the story of your evolving soul. The Dragon's Head shows where you're going, and the Dragon's Tail shows from where you've come. Always directly opposite one another in the horoscope, they work together, with the endowments from your previous experience furnishing a foundation, offering a gift, in exchange for the new experiential realms you've chosen to conquer.

Because we're more comfortable doing things we're familiar with, it's easy to become entrapped at the South Node, or Dragon's Tail. These are the talents and things we could just about do with our eyes closed because our accumulated experience in past lifetimes has made us experts in the things represented by the zodiac sign containing the South Node. The South Node reveals our most ingrained patterns of behavior; this is what we've learned through lifetimes of experience up to this point, and so it often signifies the path of least resistance. However, in the scheme of life, it's crucial to move on to our destiny that is reflected at the North Node and the attributes of its zodiac sign. This is where we feel somewhat uncomfortable, a bit nervous, or as if what we feel called to do is too risky to proceed. While we feel very comfortable at the Dragon's Tail, we are sometimes frightened to tread into the new territory symbolized by the Dragon's Head; yet we must gradually relinquish the old comforts and move on, for that was our plan. Even though it is all new territory, with experiences yet untried, the Dragon's Head shows the kinds of experiences we were excitedly anticipating when we made our entry this lifetime. You may feel this sense of calling as follows.[2]

- If your Dragon's Head is in the sign Aries, then your Dragon's Tail is in the sign Libra. This position suggests that in the past you estimated your own happiness according to the happiness of those around you. Now you must find your own identity rather than one that is an extension of others, learn to take a stand on your own, and give up the need to please all the people all the time.

- If your Dragon's Head is in Taurus, then your Dragon's Tail is in Scorpio. These positions suggest that having been through many emergencies and crises, you must let go of old anxieties about picking up the pieces or the need to scavenge, to learn moderation, and to have faith that the material abundance of the world will meet your needs.

- If your Dragon's Head is in Gemini, then your Dragon's Tail is in Sagittarius. This position suggests that in the past you were a free spirit, perhaps a wanderer, used to going it alone and unaccustomed to social responsibilities. Now, you must get intimately involved and connected with society, even though you feel clumsy in such unfamiliar territory.

- If your Dragon's Head is in Cancer, then your Dragon's Tail is in Capricorn. This position suggests that in the past you were of a business mind, cool, calculating, and proud of the public status you held. Now, the challenge is to open up and experience the feeling of nurturance, both from the receiving end and through the giving end, even though it is difficult to let down your guard about your privacy.

- If your Dragon's Head is in Leo, then your Dragon's Tail is in Aquarius. These positions suggest that in the past you worked with many friends to achieve goals that were common to a larger group. Now, you must learn to stand on your own, overcome self-doubt, and build strength within yourself, for you are ready to be a strong leader. Your longing for friendship only dissipates your energy and undermines your ability to build self-confidence.

- If your Dragon's Head is in Virgo and your Dragon's Tail in Pisces, emotional sensitivity impedes your good judgment, leaving you lackadaisical about managing your life. You've known the sorrows of others and have become used to putting others ahead of yourself, creating co-dependencies and relying upon favorite fantasies and superstitions to get you through life. Now, you must learn discrimination about those you choose to help, and learn practical planning skills and how to clearly define goals for yourself.

- If your Dragon's Head is in Libra and your Dragon's Tail in Aries, you have achieved a great deal of self-confidence from past experience. With a competitive drive, you've learned to make swift and critical decisions, concerned mainly with self-interests and self-love in the past. Now, you must take all that self-esteem and spirit of competition and put it to work on behalf of others. Sharing and cooperation are keynotes as you learn to be sensitive to the needs of others.

- If your North Node is in Scorpio and your South Node in Taurus, you've come to expect a great deal of stability and settled conditions in life, secured through accumulated possessions and hard work. Now, unable to let go of anything or anybody, you trap yourself with excess baggage that hinders you from seeing new possibilities or experiencing change of any kind. Eventually, you'll find yourself by learning to let go of those things that are now only decayed remnants of the past.

- If your North Node is in Sagittarius and your South Node in Gemini, you have learned the gift of the chameleon, ever flexible and able to maneuver splendidly without ever having to take a decisive stand about your personal beliefs. Now, you must move beyond your wealth of superficial knowledge and follow the target marked for higher knowledge as you seek wisdom, truth, and allegiance to one committed belief.

- If your North Node is in Capricorn and your South Node in Cancer, you have such attachments to the past that you constantly look there to analyze today, immersed in the child side of your nature and tending to become absorbed in the emotional ordeals of others. Now, you must look outside yourself to find a larger ideal with which you can identify, enabling you to grow up and eventually becoming a model of maturity.

• If your North Node is in Aquarius and your South Node in Leo, you've developed pride and dignity and have enjoyed admiration, as in the past you were used to being in the spotlight. While forming relationships with those who made you look good, you tended to look down on others. Now, you will learn to be more dedicated to the greater humanity as you work with others to further the goals of a group instead of working toward your own individual aims.

• If your North Node is in Pisces and your South Node in Virgo, in the past you've regimented everything according to material and finite principles, yet you fear contamination and seek perfect order through detail. A perfectionist? Yes. An analyst? Yes. Now, you realize there's more to life than meets the eye or can be measured; yet it's difficult to let go and dive into the uncharted seas of faith, where you'll learn that all is one, that you cannot separate yourself from others forever, and that it isn't up to you to make judgment calls on anyone.[3]

Throughout your life, opportunities and circumstances allow for you to make this transition from the old, familiar ways of the Dragon's Tail toward the new realms and adventures of the Dragon's Head. Events happen that pull you to toward your destiny. As you draw on your prior gifts and utilize them in their highest capacity, the past is eventually resolved and this releases you to explore more of the new territory and the new direction you're meant to move toward. Your previous gifts contribute to your onward journey.

If you have a planet near the Dragon's Head, it will help propel you more easily in the new direction as it urges you to leave the past behind. With a planet near the Dragon's Tail, you have a particular tie to the past that requires culmination in this lifetime.[4] In this scenario, you've brought with you special knowledge or talents that you wanted just one more lifetime to perfect or to utilize more fully.

As we'll see shortly, important eclipses falling in the personal chart are special announcements about these lifelong processes at work. You may recall from chapter 1 that the Dragon's Head and Dragon's Tail are the key players at an eclipse, the opening through which cosmic energy flows.

The placements of the Dragon's Head and Tail in your horoscope also reveal where eclipses were falling just prior to your birth. Often, these eclipses fell in the same signs as your Dragon's Head and Tail. These prenatal eclipses activated the essence of your spirit and soul. Astrologers are exploring the idea that the prenatal Solar eclipse indicates the actual time of entry of the spirit into the child's body yet in the womb. There is much consensus on this theory.

These findings are quite interesting for a number of reasons. Not only does this suggest that groups of spirits enter the earthly plane at the same time, but also that the spirit enters the unborn child's body during the last six months of a pregnancy—after the first trimester. This is due to the regular pattern of eclipses, occurring about every six months. Could such a possibility help solve the moral issues surrounding abortion? Maybe eclipses will eventually become times of celebration for expectant parents.

While my studies have centered primarily on post-birth eclipses, which act as guideposts throughout life to help us fulfill our life purpose, I have learned of subtle differences between Solar and Lunar eclipses that provide clues to the possible nature of the prenatal Lunar eclipse.

I don't know about you but I've always felt there's a difference between spirit and soul. Even though they are intricately connected, they are not one and the same. In his book *Care of the Soul*, Thomas Moore defines this difference, suggesting that the spirit seeks to rise and to transcend the personal, while the soul gets down in the personal emotions. He says that the soul tends toward melancholy.[5] His insights about this complex issue of spirit and soul match the differences between the Solar and Lunar eclipses, where one is felt at an identity level and the other is experienced at an emotional level.

So, before we go further, I'll offer the suggestion that the prenatal Solar eclipse is the activation of spirit, while the prenatal Lunar eclipse is connected to the roots of your soul, as it also bonds you with other souls.

For a number of reasons, I also believe that the prenatal Lunar eclipse is the mechanism that seals off our prior memories. The Moon is considered to be the planet of accumulated lifetimes. This is a theory, yet if it is true, according to the principles of an eclipse it may take up to four years or even longer for all of the prior memories to be completely blanketed. This may be the reason that young children sometimes have a gift of unusual awareness that eventually fades.

In any case, the degree of each of the prenatal eclipses should be plotted in your horoscope, using table 5 in the appendix to find the dates of the Solar and Lunar eclipses that occurred most recently prior to your birth. Mark them in your birth chart with a star, an asterisk, or another symbol of your choosing. They may be good places to start discovering the differences between your soulful stirrings as opposed to the thrust of your spirit.

Special karmic relationships in your life may be shown with those people whose Sun sign matches the sign of one of your prenatal eclipses, and especially so when another person's Sun falls on one of these prenatal eclipses.[6] Your experience of and feeling toward these people may be intensified in some way, as they are connected with your growth and evolutionary progress during this lifetime. You may feel a sense of a spiritual union or a soul bond with them.[7]

Following birth, another eclipse forms in that same degree of the zodiac as the prenatal eclipse every nineteen years or thereabouts, suggesting personal periods of some remarkable importance in one's evolution. This happens around the ages of 19, 38, 57, and 76.

---

1. The intersection of the Moon's orbit with that of the ecliptic (the apparent yearly path of the Sun through the celestial sphere as the earth orbits the Sun), as the Moon circles the earth. Occurring twice a month, we have a pair of Nodes opposite one another.

2. With a copy of your horoscope acquired from one of the resources listed in the back of the book, you can identify the zodiac sign of your Dragon's Head and Dragon's Tail.

3. These are general themes associated with the nodal positions. An excellent discussion of this subject is found in Martin Schulman's book *Karmic Astrology: The Moon's Nodes & Reincarnation* (New York: Samuel Weiser, 1975).

4. A planet within +/- 3 degrees of the Dragon's Head or Dragon's Tail would make its influence felt.

5. Thomas Moore, *Care of the Soul* (New York: HarperCollins, 1992).

6. Within +/- 3 degrees of a conjunction or opposition.

7. Soul connections in life are also found through one person's planet conjunct the Dragon's Head or Dragon's Tail of another person. Previous relationships are marked by the South Node, and future relationships are marked by the North Node. The particular planet making the connection would add definition to the nature of the relationship.

CHAPTER FOURTEEN

Eclipses as Guideposts on Your Life Journey

With the prenatal eclipses defining a basic part of you, the eclipses following birth help move you along your chosen path. They act as guideposts to help you fulfill your life purpose, sometimes by nudging you out of a comfortable rut, and sometimes by surprising you with a once-in-a-lifetime opportunity.

Even when eclipses are not precisely spotlight one of your personal planets, they are constantly providing the vigor, stamina, and attention to keep life interesting. A full set of eclipses sweeps slowly through all the various horoscope sectors approximately every nineteen years. The horoscope houses each correspond with a specialized area of life experience. So, regardless of other factors, eclipses allow us to take routine stock of each of these life areas on a regular basis, and this is the first place we'll look to check for imbalances or needed changes. Often, we are aware of the need for change, but understanding a little about the people and affairs of a house can help focus our attention and bring this out into the light more fully.

The House of an Eclipse

With your horoscope in hand, use table 1 in the appendix to find the house in your chart where the next eclipse is due to occur.

From the following brief house descriptions, you can begin to assess these areas for stagnant energy, need for change, something you've been putting off, etc.

- The First House governs your personality, temperament, appearance, and physical health. Attributes of the First House show the color lens through which you view the world and the experiences you attract based upon the first impression you make on others. The key phrase is "I am," and this house naturally corresponds to Mars. Your attitude is changing, and you are apt to take everything more seriously when an eclipse falls in this house. You become more health-conscious and may make changes in your appearance.

- The Second House governs your income earning power, portable possessions and property, and general finances and resources. It indicates how you earn and spend your money. It also reveals your value system and how you set your priorities. The key phrase is "I have," and this house corresponds to Venus. You may make or spend big money with an eclipse falling in this house.

- The Third House governs your mentality, communications, short trips, vehicles, immediate environment, neighbors, and siblings. It's the house of basic concepts, ideas, and written and spoken agreements. The key phrase is "I think," and this house naturally corresponds with Mercury. Life is busy with errands, contracts, and paperwork with an eclipse falling here. Communication and transportation are key issues.

- The Fourth House governs your home, family, parents, heritage, and real estate. It reveals the way you feel about yourself on the inside based upon the degree of security and the foundation provided to you from your heritage and background. The key phrase is "I feel," and this house corresponds with the Moon. Home and domestic and family matters are all important with an eclipse falling here.

- The Fifth House governs children, romance, artistic expression, entertainment, sports, and speculation. This house governs the urge to create something that will live on as an extension of the ego. This may be a child of the body or the mind, or another individual contribution. The key phrase is "I will," and this house corresponds naturally with the Sun. Children, the pursuit of pleasure, friendships, and hobbies are highlighted with an eclipse falling here.

- The Sixth House governs routine responsibilities, schedules, duties, service, occupation, co-workers, employees, health maintenance, and pets. The key phrase is "I analyze," and this house corresponds to Mercury. Job, schedules, pets, or new diet and exercise regimens are some of the things that often come into focus with an eclipse falling here.

- The Seventh House governs "others" who attract your attention. This house rules marriage partners, business partners, adversaries, open enemies, counselors, and advisers. The key phrase is "I balance," and this house corresponds naturally with Venus. This is an important relationship house, and multiple relationships are apt to be transformed with an eclipse falling here.

- The Eighth House governs taxes, insurance, inheritance, shared property, and resources as opposed to the personal resources and earnings of the Second House. It rules regenerative processes, sex, and death. The key phrase is "I desire," and this house corresponds to Pluto. You may take out a loan or have concerns about debts when an eclipse falls here.

- The Ninth House governs higher learning and the abstract mind, long-range vision, philosophy, professors, religion, publishing, propaganda, and long journeys. It is an outer extension of the Third House. It also rules in-laws and travelers. The key phrase is "I see," and this house corresponds to Jupiter. Education or travel may come into focus with an eclipse falling here.

- The Tenth House governs your public reputation and status, profession, career, and authority figures. Whereas the Fourth House is the most private area, the Tenth is the most public area and where you gain notice. The key phrase is "I use," and this house corresponds to Saturn. You'll definitely get noticed with an eclipse falling here, so be prepared.

- The Eleventh House governs friends, social groups, long-term hopes, wishes, and ideals. It is an outer extension of the Fifth; here creative goals are shared with a whole group. The key phrase is "I know," and this house corresponds with Uranus. Changes in friendships, clubs, and affiliations are likely to follow an eclipse falling here.

- The Twelfth House stores past deeds. It governs the subconscious mind, dreams, secrets, behind-the-scenes activities, recovery, confinement, or retreat. The key phrase is "I believe," and this house corresponds with Neptune. Introspection or the desire for solitude may follow an eclipse falling here.

All together, the houses govern every single activity, association, interest, and so on.

Throughout your life, eclipses sweep through your horoscope wheel in a clockwise motion, cleansing and revitalizing the various areas of your life, two at a time, as pairs of eclipses fall in related, opposing houses. The house position of an eclipse shows where a more balanced state of affairs will evolve. For more insight into the potential changes brought by an eclipse to one of your houses, see the next chapter for the descriptions of eclipses on the planets, and read the description of the planet that naturally rules the house. Mars rules the First House, for example, and the Moon the Fourth House.

Now, let's see if we can define the characteristics of each of the four types of eclipses. Using table 1 in the appendix, you can identify the nature of the next one to arrive.

The Difference Between a Solar & a Lunar Eclipse

One thing that can be said of any eclipse is that it is the forerunner to change, but beyond that, is there a way to determine the kind of change symbolized by an eclipse? If an eclipse activates spiritual or soulful processes, can we define the way it might be experienced?

Since an eclipse can take place only at the time of the New Moon for a Solar eclipse or at the time of the Full Moon for a Lunar eclipse, we can rely on the nature of those general Moon phases to understand some of the specific dynamics behind an eclipse.

The New Moon, or "low ebb" of the Moon, signals preparation for a new cycle. From the time of the New Moon to the time of the Full Moon there follows an increase of energy. People in general are more receptive to new ideas, and it's a good time to lay the groundwork, or plant seeds, for new projects. The New Moon is very positive in nature, but it is dark at the time of the New Moon and astrologers of old warned to begin nothing at this time unless you wish it to remain secret and out of sight. From the New Moon to the Full Moon, the Moon is increasing in light. Our bodies tend to absorb and retain water as it nears and responds to the hot and dry influence of the First Quarter Moon. Wherever the New Moon falls in your horoscope, you'll experience a sense of rejuvenation and renewed spirit relating to the matters of that house. The various issues of this house absorb your attention; there are new beginnings and exciting new possibilities.

Things set in motion at the New Moon tend to come to culmination or maturation at the "high tide" of the Full Moon. Important decisions are made now as one sees a situation in full light. Conditions and circumstances are in full bloom at the time of the Full Moon, for good or ill. From the Full Moon to the New Moon, energy is decreasing as the Moon decreases in light. The body tends to lose a couple of pounds as it nears and responds to the cool, moist influence of the Third Quarter Moon. Sleep is sound, and it is time to reap the harvests. You may notice that something comes out in the open regarding the affairs of the house in which the Full Moon falls. You may sometimes notice a slight separating trend in regard to the people and things associated with that house and its opposite. There is finalization in these areas.

So, a Solar eclipse, akin to the New Moon, is about being refueled, planting new seeds, laying the foundation for new projects, reaching outward, and striving toward new experience. The personal Solar eclipse is about ego, identity, spirit, and vitality and suggests experiences at the ego/spirit/identity level.

The Lunar eclipse, akin to the Full Moon, represents sudden awareness of things previously out of sight, revelation, culmination, and completion. Relationship themes are stressed. A Lunar eclipse may call you to explore some raw emotional depths, and these eclipses bond us with others, who also relate to these deep, dark recesses of the soul that allow us to experience joy or to suffer pain. Whether for good or ill, a personal Lunar eclipse is likely to bring pinnacles or changes that other people would find easy to relate to.

The North Node Eclipse versus the South Node Eclipse

Solar and Lunar eclipses are also of different natures depending on whether the North or South Lunar Node is in close proximity at the time of the eclipse. The Nodes show connections in time and space, with the North Node, or Dragon's Head, offering an inflow of new energy, and the South Node, or Dragon's Tail, offering an outlet for the release of old energy. The South Node is a drawing-out force. The nature of the North Node is compared to the dynamics of Jupiter and considered luckier and more auspicious than the South Node, which is compared to Saturn, where there are restrictions or boundaries.

In a general way, in terms of a personally significant eclipse, the North Node eclipse appears outwardly in the material world to be of a more positive force than a South Node eclipse. This does not mean that the South Node eclipse is negative, only that it more often tends to be experienced as difficult initially. An old phase of experience may be ending in preparation for a new phase, and something is expected of you before you are free to move on. You are working through something or working something out.

There may be a feeling of newfound power and strength with the North Node Solar eclipse; one is finally able to push through a barrier or there's a sudden break. A Solar eclipse with the North Node attending is often quite positive in regard to the types of experiences and material manifestations that may come from it, although one must have the courage to grab on to an opportunity that suddenly arises, tap into the expanding influence, and accept it graciously. The wave of inrushing energy can take one by surprise so that it's experienced as upsetting because an old set of comfortable conditions may have to end in order to move into the new experience.

With the South Node Solar eclipse, there may be the feeling of an energy leak or drain unless we understand that something is required to wrap up the previous phase of experience. A valuable final product is required. There is perhaps a gift to contribute, even if it is only our own clarity and truthfulness to ourselves in regard to what we've learned to this point. Here, there is the demand to release the desires of the ego, although this process may be challenging because some part of the identifying self is suddenly under focus. One is forced to recognize what is valid and what is not. There may be an identity crisis, the sense of self may feel depreciated, and vitality may be lacking.

A Lunar eclipse with the attendance of the South Node may correspond with low points in life as far as the emotional vibrations coinciding with it due to the process of letting go of old emotional habit patterns, and letting go of persons we've come to depend on and things we've taken for granted. Remember that the Dragon's Tail shows a comfort zone, so not only are the processes here difficult to observe, operating as they do on a subconscious level, but the habits here are particularly hard to cast aside, however necessary it is to do so. There may be melancholy.

A Lunar eclipse with the attendance of the North Node represents an influx of new elements that will positively affect the most personal side of life. Lunar eclipses generally link to elements of our closest environment, usually rooted to home, security, and the people most intimately connected to these. And, even though this particular eclipse has very positive potential, one still must be able to appreciate change.

In all, we have four types of eclipses for which we might sketch some key attributes:

- North Node Solar eclipse—Beginnings, courage to allow new energy in; spirit and ego.
- South Node Solar eclipse—Beginnings depend on release; spirit and ego; filtering.
- North Node Lunar eclipse—Culmination creates opening; soul and emotion; joy.
- South Node Lunar eclipse—Culmination and release; soul and emotion; filtering.

The processes attributed to eclipses are about moving from one level of growth to the next. Considering that there are overlapping eclipses falling rhythmically through your chart, and a special one here and there that singles you out to receive new flows of cosmic energy, it becomes easy to picture this process as a kaleidoscope of patterns until the perfected blossom eventually appears.

CHAPTER FIFTEEN

Preparing for Your Special Personal Eclipse

In the previous chapter, you learned of some general guidelines to help decipher the kind of energy coming due from each of the four types of eclipses. This will help you as we continue here to explore your most personal eclipses.

Falling on or opposite a personal planet, an eclipse represents a call to task. And, there are advantages to understanding the processes at work. It enables you to become more conscious of areas in your life that needs adjustment and where there are opportunities for new experiences. Most importantly, it allows you to extract the best of whatever lesson is at hand. Considering that you had a hand in ordering up the lessons you wanted to learn, each personally significant eclipse symbolizes a gift on the proverbial silver platter. Once called to task and this process is set into motion, you won't be able to stop it, but you can always choose your response to the changes occurring.

You may go for several years and not have an eclipse fall directly on or opposite one of your birth planets. Then, there may come times when you have several eclipses spotlighting personal planets and points in your horoscope within a short period. In this case, life becomes busy with changes, the shedding of old habits of behavior, or letting go of a relationship, as well as the adventure of new experiences and meeting new people. There are inner and outer processes at work at the same time. In between the two extremes is more the norm, when an eclipse highlights one particular realm of experience and specific people in your life every couple of years or so.

On some level you may be aware of where change is needed. An eclipse is the meeting of time and place, so on a personal planet, change is due, or perhaps overdue, as symbolized by the planet receiving the eclipse. If a situation or relationship has been neglected or allowed to deteriorate, an eclipse can trigger what seems at first to be an upheaval in the associated affairs.

It is also likely that you'll have one particular planet in your nativity receiving more eclipses over the course of your lifetime than any other, indicating many varied opportunities to perfect one key element in your nature that is required for you to achieve your most important spiritual aims. Other planets in your horoscope may rarely receive an eclipse, showing an element of the nature that is comfortable in this lifetime, with no need for testing or perfection, while another facet of the personality or character is under focus. One learns a great deal from an exploration of this interesting phenomenon.

The following are some general frames of reference for the types of events coming due, as represented by a personal planet or point as the receiver of an eclipse.[1]

In preparation for an eclipse, you should note any eclipse of importance coming up within six months and continue to monitor any in the last couple of years. Plot these in your horoscope, using an asterisk, star, or another symbol of your choosing. Table 1 in the appendix provides the date, degree, and other details of each eclipse through 2011.

An Eclipse to Your Horoscope Angles

A most dynamic place for an eclipse to fall is on one of the four angles of the horoscope; these are the dividing lines, or cusps, of the First, Fourth, Seventh, and Tenth Houses.

Earlier, we talked about the critical degrees as representative of the four seasons. Well, in your personal horoscope, the angles of these four houses form a cross, representing your personal seasons and most crucial concerns. The Ascendant, or First House cusp, represents you; the IC, or Fourth House cusp, represents your home, closest family, and domestic conditions at the end of the day. The Descendant, or Seventh House cusp, represents your partner, intimate or otherwise; and the Midheaven, or Tenth House cusp, represents your public status and career. The zodiac signs and degrees that align with these four angles in your horoscope are most personal for you and you alone, so an eclipse falling here promises a period of dynamic personal and relationship changes.

An eclipse sensitizes the area in the individual horoscope in which it falls, so when an eclipse falls on one of these four points, you might move and/or change occupations. Important decisions are at hand. Remember that these seasonal points indicate an event that automatically affects several personal areas. So, if an eclipse falls on your Seventh House cusp, pertaining to your partner, you may end a relationship or form a new one, which then requires a move. Or if the eclipse falls on the cusp of your Fourth House, reflecting your home, you may change residence, which may require a change of occupation. If the eclipse falls on your Tenth House cusp of career, you may make a professional change, which may require a move and may eventually lead to finding a new partner. If the eclipse falls on your First House cusp, indicating your persona, a new outlook may lead to other changes, and with this eclipse you might even alter your physical appearance as well. There are various scenarios, but these eclipses are most commonly the forerunners of domestic and job changes and important relationships undergoing transformations. They indicate a busy time with many personal changes.

For more insight about an eclipse on one of the four angles, check the following descriptions for the planet naturally associated with the angle: an eclipse to Mars would be similar to an eclipse on the Ascendant; an eclipse to the Moon would be similar to an eclipse on the IC; an eclipse to Venus would be similar to an eclipse on the Descendant; and an eclipse to Saturn would be similar to an eclipse on the Midheaven.

Now, in a general way you can track the transiting Dragon's Head through your chart to note areas of opportunity, rewards, good fortune, and happiness. The North Node attracts all of these. Similarly, you can track the Dragon's Tail to find potential areas of vulnerability, loss, or sacrifice, where you are working through issues. However, you can have a combination of influences. When it comes to an eclipse, it requires some special handling because it doesn't matter if it falls on or opposite an important planet or point. If within 3 degrees by conjunction or opposition to a planet or point, you will have the eclipse energy enter your life via the planet or point. A South Node eclipse on your Ascendant may call you to make sacrifices to others or for the sake of others. You have to give in to others and make concessions. That same eclipse is also sending its vibration (South Node) to your Descendant, so that there are occasions when you can't rely too much on others. Even so, the North Node transiting the Seventh House promises that some gain will come from others.   A North Node eclipse on the IC attracts good things at home as it also attracts career rewards. At the same time, the South Node moving through the Tenth House suggests a general time period in which some sacrifices are being made in the area of profession. The eclipse factor would take precedence over a simple transit, especially one that links to a planet or another important point.

Keeping this in mind, let's now explore the possibilities of an eclipse falling on each of the planets.

Your Eclipsed Planet

An eclipse falling on or opposite one of your personal planets is usually a prelude to an active period in your life according to the nature of the planet receiving the eclipse. Along with the Ascendant and Midheaven, an eclipse to a luminary (the Sun or Moon) or to your chart ruler is most important. As you'll discover in the real-life examples in the next chapter, there are enjoyable as well as challenging effects from these eclipses; however, because the energy of the Sun is so vital, an eclipse to this benefic star is apt to be experienced most profoundly.

Remember that when an eclipse stimulates a personal planet, it can temporarily magnify or distort a facet of your personality or character, so you can observe this tendency near the time of the eclipse. Be particularly mindful of initiating actions that would or could have dramatic consequences near the time of one of these personally important eclipses, especially in regard to the people and affairs ruled by the eclipsed planet.[2]

Your Eclipsed Sun

An eclipse to the Sun may very well get you noticed, and it often signifies important contacts and crucial decisions. A close association brought about by this eclipse is often the source of new experience. With a positive eclipse, your confidence gets a boost and obstacles that have previously slowed your efforts may suddenly clear. Doors open and there are positive changes in the degree of recognition you enjoy. Rewards are forthcoming. Your sense of personal power and importance may soar, but be very careful how you utilize this newfound strength because developments here can have a major impact in the long term.

With a difficult eclipse to the Sun, you may initially experience an identity crisis or wonder about your handling of life, feeling quite unequipped to handle all that's expected. Self-image may be at an all-time low, and there are feelings of inferiority. Problems crop up, and the ego/identity may feel trampled upon. Ego desires must take a back burner, and it is an effort just to maintain position by remaining inobtrusive, demanding little.

The Sun is associated with central figures, so this eclipse often brings to light issues or concerns involving the losses or gains of a benefactor, usually a masculine figure. Events in connection with a close father figure or another important supporter may arise, where their fortunes have a direct impact on you. There may be new connections or separations. Persons whose affairs come into focus include the father or husband.

The energy of the Sun is most likened to the affairs of the Fifth House of the horoscope. This is the spirit that animates us, and it is involved in those activities where we really come alive and experience joy. If you look back, you will probably notice that there were times in your life when you felt exceptionally fulfilled as opportunities allowed you to easily express your natural passion. Other times, it may have seemed that life just didn't allow for much fun and play. An eclipse to the Sun will bring an emphasis to the way you feel about these things.

The Sun is symbolic of the vital life force, and therefore any health irregularities should not go unattended. The Sun, sensitized by an eclipse, sometimes causes one to be vulnerable to accidents, similar to an eclipse on the Ascendant. In matters of health, the Sun is associated with the heart and circulation and with vital energy afforded through the chest area and lung capacity.

Your Eclipsed Moon

An eclipse to your Moon often announces new domestic conditions and changes involving family members.

For a time, relationships with women come into higher focus than usual. The Moon is associated with the mother, motherhood, and feminine issues, so events in keeping with these themes are all very normal at this time. There may be a birth in the family, or the health of the mother may be a concern. Some particular woman may play a significant role in the life, either as an asset or a drain. With a difficult eclipse, you may feel that she is trying to dominate you and make your life difficult.

The Moon is naturally delegated to the most private area of one's life—the Fourth House area: your subjective security, how you feel about yourself on the inside, how stable you feel about your place in the world, and how "connected" you feel. This may be an introspective time and a time when it is hard to express your feelings as you fight through some temporary clouds. Sensitivities may heighten, and the emotions fluctuate more than usual. You may be moody and particularly drawn to the past. With a difficult eclipse, there may be a feeling of apprehension or fearfulness. A bit of melancholy or a need for a period of solitude or separateness is not unusual.

The Moon denotes popular appeal and the reception of others, so this eclipse also suggests fluctuations or changes in this respect. One's popular appeal could plummet or soar as others let you know whether you've earned their respect or disapproval.

The parts of the body and bodily functions that are associated with the Moon are the stomach, abdominal cavity, digestion, and fluids.

Your Eclipsed Mercury

When Mercury is eclipsed, it may be time to carry through on an important idea or to let go of one. The mind becomes activated, and nervous energy needs a good outlet as the mental stamina is tested.

Mercury is naturally associated with Third House affairs, so correspondence, important paperwork, transport, and vehicles are all highlighted with an eclipse to this planet. Travel plans may be made. Legal agreements and contracts of various types come strongly into focus and will have to be dealt with most diligently. Problems relating to these agreements or the need to revise them often come up. Revisions at a more basic level also occur with this eclipse due to Mercury's governing of the mental processes. Your point of view on many matters comes under focus to be tested. You may need to revise basic ideas, and this could be accompanied by an intellectual crisis of sorts. Tension and stress are common, as ideas that have been taken for granted are now challenged.

Since Mercury governs your communications skills, one of the first things you should check is whether your communications are coming across as you intend, especially if this is an eclipse with the influence of the Dragon's Tail. Negotiations could be hindered and contacts unreliable, and your ability to represent yourself may become flawed under these eclipses. Chances are that there will be some misunderstandings, and things could begin to get garbled just before the eclipse.

Perceptions change with an eclipse to Mercury, and the outcome of an eclipse on Mercury may be an enhanced memory, greater capacity to store data, increased efficiency, a brighter outlook, and a lighter disposition. Writers could aspire to achieve lofty goals. And, in carrying out your idea, do not expect results overnight or even in six months. By the time this eclipse process is complete, you're whole outlook will be refreshed.

Mercury also naturally governs over Sixth House affairs, including your daily work routine, and since the sign Mercury was in at your birth shows the characteristics of your thought processes, it is often a good indicator of the kind of work you do. Therefore, a job change is sometimes made when an eclipse falls on Mercury. Making long-term business plans is recommended only if this is a positive eclipse; otherwise, the chances are that you will align yourself with the wrong individual.

Persons whose interests are highlighted by an eclipse to Mercury are siblings, relatives, youth, and neighbors. Mercury rules the brain and all the body's pairs, including the lungs, and it rules the intestinal functions.

Your Eclipsed Venus

As a planet providing us with certain benefits, Venus is most often associated with material comforts, money, decorative items, art, finery, festivities, and happy social occasions. This eclipse may increase your desire to entertain or to accumulate beautiful objects. Venus has natural rule over Second House matters, including all portable property, so this eclipse brings a focus to earnings, money matters, creature comforts, and material assets. You may experience the arrival of gifts or a sudden and ongoing drain to assets. Much thought and concern are given to these matters. An eclipse to Venus with the Dragon's Head attending is generally more favorable in this respect than an eclipse with the influence of the Dragon's Tail.

Known as the Lesser Fortune, Venus usually provides a measure of good fortune, benevolence, and protection somewhere in life. This place of special gifts is often found relating to the house of the natal horoscope where Venus is located. With an eclipse to Venus, there may be an increase or a decrease of such fortune, but there will likely be a change.

Venus also centers on the affectionate nature, those things and people that attract us. There may be karmic attractions or sudden separations. With a difficult eclipse, an attraction may be misdirected, or the feelings misunderstood, and this can be an especially tough period emotionally.

Venus rules young women, whose affairs may come into focus. For a man, this eclipse may be the forerunner of marriage since Venus symbolizes his significant other. Partnerships of the Seventh House, intimate and otherwise, come into play, as Venus is the ruler of Libra.

Venus also shows how we pamper ourselves and others, so this eclipse can make one feel more desirable, attractive, and charming. A tendency toward overindulgence must be kept in check.

Associated with Venus are the senses of taste, touch, and smell, as well as digestion requiring saliva, secretion of insulin, and assimilation of carbohydrates. Venus rules the pancreas and spleen through Libra, and the throat, jaw, and thyroid gland through Taurus.

Your Eclipsed Mars

Mars signifies the aggressive urges, the point where we feel instinctively opposed or the "front line" of battle in life where we meet and overcome opposition. Therefore, a conflict of some type usually comes to the fore with an eclipse to Mars. As the natural ruler of the First House, an exaggerated sense of self-importance is common with this eclipse. An individual becomes stimulated, energized, or aggravated under the rays of Mars. Astrologer Evangeline Adams says that Mars is the most "unbalanced of planets; the one most in need of restriction or direction."[3]

Frequently when an eclipse activates Mars, we feel a newly acquired confidence in our beliefs and actions, and a desire to start something new. We feel ready to fight for what we believe in or for what we believe is rightfully ours. Mars' motto is "I want to do what I want to do when I want to do it." With a difficult eclipse to Mars, serious conflicts could arise or you may be asked to make a compromise that seems unthinkable. Getting involved in a project where you can work independently and receive personal recognition is favored under this eclipse.

Because Mars is naturally associated with the physical body, and the way in which we literally maneuver it, a difficult eclipse to Mars could be the forerunner of a health issue or an accident unless its energy is directed constructively. Activities that require physical exertion, including exercise, sports, or just plain old hard work, are favored under this eclipse. Physical energy is at its peak, but beware of overdoing it by taking on a workload that is too heavy or attempting especially large projects that can sap the energy. Accidents are more likely if the assertive nature is repeatedly repressed, when one is more likely to become accident-prone.

Sexual issues may arise, and this is one of the most often eclipsed planets prior to the marriage of a woman because Mars is the chief ruler of a woman's partner. Associations linked to Mars are similar to those of the Sun, with masculine figures and their affairs emphasized.

Mars rules machinery, mechanics, athletes, heroes, those in the military, surgeons, those who work with sharp instruments, and men in general. Mars is associated with the head and rules the blood and adrenaline.

Your Eclipsed Jupiter

As the Greater Fortune, Jupiter is associated with expansion, abundance, increase, and acquisition. With an eclipse to Jupiter, we often feel motivated to expand our place in the world in some way. Feeling exuberant, you may believe you cannot fail, so one of the problems arising with this eclipse is taking on too much or promising more than can be delivered.

Business losses or legal disputes may follow a difficult eclipse to Jupiter, and this may be due to the bad judgment of a close associate. Whether bringing advantages or disadvantages, an eclipse to Jupiter often involves a close association. A positive eclipse suggests helpful associations, whereas a problematic eclipse warns not to rely on the judgment of another.

Jupiter naturally rules Ninth House matters, including higher education, publishing, religion, long-distance travel, and distant visions. Jupiter, as the recipient of an eclipse, may bring a time in which long-held spiritual beliefs are questioned, reviewed, or changed. There's a distinct drive to explore distant targets, often of the mind rather than in the physical world. An urge to theorize leads to an examination of many beliefs, and then to proposing them to others. This may be through publishing, marketing, preaching, etc.

Jupiter symbolizes material prosperity as well as spiritual prosperity. With an eclipse to Jupiter, a person often attracts that which is most important. So, with this eclipse you may attract material goods or money, a promotion, title, or badge of honor, or you may attract spiritual growth and blessings in the form of increased awareness and a greater degree of enlightenment.

The placement of Jupiter in the chart shows where there is some amount of protection, luck, or fortune. With an eclipse to Jupiter, something about our usual luck in these matters is about to change. With a difficult eclipse, the abundance we're used to may cease. Something we've always counted on to be there could be in jeopardy. Circumstances may force us to cut our losses, or we might squander benefits. Overindulgent tendencies should be checked. With a South Node eclipse, count on increased expenses.

Those people associated with Jupiter are professors and philosophers, lawyers and judges, philanthropists, clergymen, in-laws, and uncles. Jupiter rules the kidneys and liver functions, the sciatic nerve, and the thighs.

Your Eclipsed Saturn

Saturn is the natural ruler of the Tenth House, the house governing status, career, and the immediate supervisor or boss. An eclipse to Saturn brings professional and business concerns into focus and may promise more stable and permanent conditions in the long term. The way this eclipse is experienced is related to how we feel about accepting responsibility because we'll now be required to take on more of it. If we have a great plan but could use a bit of discipline, the eclipse to Saturn brings the potential to get organized and tackle tough jobs. The Saturn eclipse offers the ability to handle practical matters and brings with it a more sober attitude. Thus, this eclipse era may correspond with a time when life itself takes on a serious note. There are important learning experiences, but this is usually along very constructive lines, and there may be a feeling of contentment or even joy from working within boundaries or limitations.

Saturn rules older people. Old ideas or methods may come up for review or have some special significance now. Older people often begin to play an important role in life, perhaps an elderly relative or a parent. One may find an important mentor among these people. Saturn signifies authorities and those who've acquired some degree of wisdom, so new associations may be formed along such lines. Saturn indicates longevity, so associations begun at this point could be long-lasting ones, and conditions created now are apt to remain stable.

With a difficult eclipse, there may be a health issue surrounding an older person in the near family. Or, you may be more susceptible to colds, circulation problems, or physical weakness, and this may be a discouraging period. Obstructions encountered may be revealed through the natal house ruled by Saturn. If Saturn is in friendly relationship to the

Nodes in the natal chart, there are some benefits promised from this eclipse, even if it is of the South Node influence.

Saturn rules the bones, teeth, and skeletal structure as well as the assimilation of minerals.

Eclipses to the Outer Planets

Because they move so slowly, when the outer planets—Uranus, Neptune, and Pluto—receive an eclipse, people around your age are experiencing the same eclipse, so these eclipses do not always represent issues as personal in nature as those indicated by the previous planets. However, if one of these planets is prominent in your chart, perhaps by falling on one of the angles, it is very important. Such a planet reflects a basic component of what you're all about. Maybe the planet rules your Tenth House of profession, or, if the planet receives a lot of aspects from other natal planets, it is a chief element in the functioning of a whole range of areas. These eclipsed planets tend to operate on both a physical and a psychological level.

Your Eclipsed Uranus

Uranus is the natural ruler of the Eleventh House of hopes and wishes and circumstances over which we have no control. With an eclipse to Uranus, exciting times are ahead. Sudden turns of events are especially notable in the affairs ruled by the house where Uranus is located. Uranus is associated with originality, freedom, and independence, so life provides all manner of experiences that ensure we do not become overly dependent on a pat set of conditions. Learning to be flexible and handling change are requirements. You can be assured that falling into a rut is not a worry with these eclipses. Some disruption may follow these eclipses, which can be both exciting and unnerving at the same time.

An eclipse to Uranus often brings an exciting masculine figure into the life but may also bring one of the most important connections ever made, whether male or female. This relationship, whatever it may be, is likely to be erratic and short lived; however, it nonetheless will play an important function and have a profound and positive influence, resulting in changes in your life that could not otherwise have happened. Uranus rules astrologers, inventors, eccentrics, rebels, and humanitarians. It also rules new technology and gadgets. Uranus is associated with the lower legs and rules the nervous system. It is associated with oxygen intake, asthma, and allergies.

Your Eclipsed Neptune

Ah, the illusive Neptune. An eclipse to Neptune can bring inspiration, creativity, spirituality, and absolutely blissful times. There may be creature comforts and luxuries as never before, happy times of money, travel, cruises, and general contentment. Activities that fare well under an eclipse to Neptune are gardening, artistic pursuits, or interests that call for imagination and inspiration to be a guide. Dreams may become particularly vivid and informative. However, there are some pitfalls to be aware of.

Neptune naturally rules the Twelfth House of self-undoing, so it is important to be very clear and honest about things within yourself because self-deception could lead to problems. Neptune tends to bring some degree of confusion or uncertainty about the matters of the house where the planet resides. Some missing piece of information may make it impossible to resolve an issue, leaving it up in the air. Things hang in limbo. It may be difficult to get an agreement from someone, or, even worse, someone attempts to deceive. Understanding that you may be more vulnerable to scams, use caution in trusting anyone who comes into your life at this time. Be careful of trusting your own judgment, and if possible get advice from someone trustworthy before making important new commitments. Be as aboveboard as possible in all your dealings.

With an unfortunate eclipse, there could be involvement with drugs or alcohol, a minor phobia, or simply a vague feeling that something is wrong. Neptune is associated with mystics, actors, prophets, recluses, and seafaring. Neptune rules the lymphatic and immune systems and is associated through Pisces with the feet.

Your Eclipsed Pluto

An eclipse to Pluto generally brings some permanent changes in life; however, this may be a slow and lengthy process. Pluto governs the Eighth House of death and rebirth. It works from below the surface, although its subtlety should not lead you to think that it is not a powerful force at work. With a natural understanding that bringing improvement sometimes requires the destruction of the old, once the source of blockage is exposed, it is often eliminated for good. This process may be related to many things and brings an opportunity for self-improvement, such as kicking a bad habit. There may be contacts with healers or counselors, and a new association could mark a major turning point in life.

The kinds of activities that are favored by this eclipse are new undertakings or projects that require time and effort to produce dividends, those where persistent efforts will eventually revitalize a situation. Pluto is particularly related to financial matters, and investments may prove favorable. Pluto rules your joint resources, as well as taxes, insurance, and inheritances, any of which may be of concern with this eclipse.

Intense and complicated relationship themes may also come to the fore with this eclipse. Pluto sometimes points to power struggles or confrontations. Pluto shares many similarities with Mars. There may be manipulations, jealousies, or resentments that interfere with normally healthy relationships. It may also symbolize sexual frustrations or desires that are not being met, leading to experimentation in an extracurricular affair.

A Lunar eclipse upon Pluto brings the potential for many changes within the domestic sphere. In rare instances, an eclipse to Pluto may be followed by the death of someone dear. Pluto rules the reproductive organs and the reproductive system.

Once a personal planet has been the recipient of an eclipse, it is sensitive to coming transits. The energies of transiting planets as they cross over the eclipse tend to stir up the eclipse potential as they also produce events. Again, the planetary transits over the eclipse point can bring a brief period when the judgment may be a little distorted or overzealous. Consider the concerns and nature of the planet that has been eclipsed for clues as to where and how your judgment may be impaired. It is a time to practice caution if the transiting planet is Mars. If there's a problem, it may show itself when Mars energizes the previous eclipse. Uranus also is pretty quick on the draw but can be a very positive force. Benefits arising from the eclipse often come with the transit of the Sun or Jupiter, planets of good tidings, for the most part. The dates of major transits to current eclipses are found in table 1 in the appendix. The next chapter includes some examples of the kinds of energy brought to an eclipse by the passing planets in individuals' charts.

Eclipses usually come in pairs, and sometimes two eclipses spotlight two natal planets within a short interval. Checking the symbolism of each of the planets involved helps to clarify the process set in motion, and the two may assist one another. Table 4 in the appendix give keys for each planet, indicating the various people and things ruled by each.

If a Solar eclipse doesn't fall within 3 degrees of any of your planets, check the eclipse's house position and then look to the last planet in your natal chart that the Sun passed over.

This is the nearest planet, in a clockwise direction, from the place of the eclipse in your chart. That planet will give you a clue to the nature of experiences coming due.

A last pass over the Sun may call for a crucial decision and important contacts. A last contact to the Moon signifies issues with women or changing domestic conditions that could provoke an emotional response. With Mercury, correspondence or travel may be required, and with Venus, artistic or social pursuits come into focus.

If the last contact was to Mars, a conflict of some sort is likely, so be sure to properly vent these energies into physical activity rather than become accident-prone. With Jupiter, the possibilities are endless, but be careful not to go overboard in your current optimistic frame of mind. Of course, Saturn reminds you of the need to work hard and indicates a period of increased responsibility.

If the Sun's last pass was over Uranus, things are rather unpredictable, so prepare to be flexible in regard to matters symbolized by the house where the eclipse falls. With Neptune, confusing elements and uncertainties require waiting before putting plans into action. Pluto suggests ongoing and persistent efforts to revitalize or improve a situation.

---

1. In this discussion, we are concerned with an eclipse that falls on or opposite a planet or point within +/- 3 degrees.

2. Watch for an eclipse that falls on or opposite a personal planet within +/- 3 degrees. It is important to understand that an eclipse falling in conjunction with a planet is not necessarily more desirable than an eclipse by opposition. The influence of the eclipse is experienced according to the nature of the planet receiving it.

3. Evangeline Adams, *The Bowl of Heaven* (1926; reprint, Sante Fe, NM: Sun Books, 1995).

CHAPTER SIXTEEN

Real People
& Their Eclipse Stories

This chapter highlights eclipses in the lives of various people, with examples of different eclipsed planets. They show that an eclipse is not necessarily a bad thing, often preceding a fortunate era. As they say, a picture is worth a thousand words, and these true-life illustrations demonstrate the impact of various eclipses, sometimes reflecting more than one event. Even the problematic ones may help show how an eclipse could be utilized constructively.

Debra Quits Corporate World
with Eclipses to Her Dragon's Head & Tail

Debra experienced a pair of Lunar eclipses, one to her Dragon's Head, then to her Dragon's Tail about six months later. Midway between the two eclipses, just as Mars moved into range of stimulation to both eclipses, she quit the corporate world and began working independently. Earlier, we spoke about how the Dragon's Head and Tail represent where we're going and where we're coming from and how moving toward the destiny shown at the Dragon's Head feels like taking a risk. In this example, it's easy to see how this was a big step for Debra. Giving up the security of working in a big company in favor of long-term self-fulfillment took courage. By the end of this eclipse process, she had successfully established her new place in the world. An eclipse on the natal Nodes often brings a critical turning point in life.

At Age Fifteen, Jennifer's Life Turned Upside Down after Eclipses to Her Midheaven & IC

This next example is quite a showcase to illustrate the importance of eclipses to the angles of the horoscope, or the seasonal points discussed in the last chapter, which frequently announce a move. These angles, or the cusps of the First, Fourth, Seventh, and Tenth Houses, are termed the Ascendant, IC, Descendant, and Midheaven, respectively. They relate to your four most personal areas of self, home, partners, and profession. When your horoscope shows an eclipse to one of these personal angles, your life is about to change significantly.[1]

Jennifer was the recipient of two Lunar eclipses to these angular house cusps, first to the cusp of her Fourth House, representative of her home, and about six months later to her Midheaven, associated with career ambitions and also governing authority figures. With the Lunar eclipse suggesting potential separations, a little more than two years later as Saturn came to cross the place of the eclipses, her family moved across country, at her father's determination, forcing her to leave behind her friends, boyfriend, and grandparents. This was a very difficult change for her and yet before two years had gone by, she was happy and in love with her husband-to-be, and she realized that for what she wanted in her career, the move had actually been a blessing.

Carla Buys Home, Gets Promoted, Becomes Grandma with an Eclipse to Her Midheaven & IC

Carla, a hard worker who had been looking for the right home to meet her needs, got just the jump-start she needed when an eclipse spotlighted her Fourth House cusp of home and family. She moved into her new place a few weeks after the Solar eclipse and heard a little later that her application for reevaluation of her job had been approved. As a result she got a year's back pay for responsibilities she'd been handling and automatically moved up a step in seniority and status. This had been a Solar eclipse with the Dragon's Head attending. As the Sun came along later to spark this eclipse, she found out she was going to be a grandma, another manifestation of the family changes that were promised.

Jane Sees End and Beginning to Relationships with an Eclipse to Her Descendant

Around the time that Jane experienced a Solar eclipse on her Seventh House cusp, she broke off a long-term relationship and became involved in a new one.

Stewart and Donna Blessed with Grandchildren after an Eclipse to Her Moon

Stewart had a Solar eclipse spotlight his Seventh House cusp of partners, bringing a focus to his wife, Donna. This was an eclipse with the North Node attending, and in Donna's horoscope it fell on her Moon, denoting emphasis on family and motherhood. In the coming year, both of their children produced offspring. Then, following a couple of gall bladder attacks, incorrectly diagnosed as heartburn at first, Donna underwent gall bladder surgery without complications. This shows both the connection of the Moon to motherhood and family issues as well as its association with the digestive system.

Nikki's Mother-in-Law Finally Accepts Her after an Eclipse to Her Sun

Recently married and while her husband was away in the service, Nikki gave birth to their daughter. Up until a Lunar eclipse with the North Node attending fell on her Sun, her husband's family wanted nothing to do with her. Within four weeks of this eclipse, her new husband returned home and his family opened their arms to Nikki and the baby. As an eclipse to the Sun frequently brings a masculine figure into prominence, we can see this connection as well as the influence of the Lunar eclipse as a time of completion for her husband, also common when there are domestic and family changes.

Bill's Vitality Suffers Following an Eclipse to His Sun

A South Node Lunar eclipse fell on Bill's Sun. Several months later, a seemingly minor injury on the job led to gradually declining health and multiple mysterious symptoms. Over a year following the eclipse, as Mars moved over the degree of the eclipse, he underwent multiple tests, eventually learning that he had fibromyalgia. In this particular case, the eclipse also fell in close opposition to his Pluto, indicating more serious potential than if the eclipse had only touched upon his Sun. Fibromyalgia often follows an emotional trauma, suggested here by the melancholic South Node Lunar eclipse.

Jason Is Promoted to Major and Called to Duty
Following an Eclipse to His Sun

Jason had always had a special sense of mission and loved the military. He was in Special Operations in the Air Force as well as a navigator and chief of tactics. He was promoted to major some months following a North Node Solar eclipse to his Sun. At the time of the promotion, Uranus had just moved across to newly stimulate this eclipse. He was called to Afghanistan to help fight the war on terror, and as the eclipse remains active, he and his family will move in a few months to South Korea, where he's been asked to serve in Seoul.

Bob Experiences Accidents with an Eclipse to His Sun

A Lunar eclipse opposed Bob's natal Sun from his Third House cusp, the house ruling vehicles, transport, and close vicinity. He had two accidents, resulting in fairly minimal injuries, one while riding a motorcycle just prior to the eclipse and another in his car several months later—both accidents within a few blocks of his home. This had been a Lunar eclipse with the South Node influence.

Elsa Can't Move with Eclipses to Her Mercury

Elsa had two eclipses spotlighting her Mercury. The first was a Solar eclipse and then a Lunar eclipse some time later. Both of these eclipses were accompanied by the South Node, or Dragon's Tail, and though she wanted desperately to move across country, it was not possible because as a single parent, her home, work, and family responsibilities prevented her from doing so until more than three years later, when Saturn moved into range to cross over her eclipsed Mercury and end the eclipse process. By that time, she'd handled all the necessary details to make the move successfully, though not without making some sacrifices.

Larry Has Scrapes and Troubles with Vehicles
after an Eclipse to His Mercury

With a South Node Solar eclipse to his Mercury, Larry had virtually every kind of problem one could imagine involving vehicles. These included multiple citations, repossession of one car (as Mercury also symbolizes contracts), then buying a lemon, and two minor fender-benders with the other drivers at fault both times, both uninsured. The eclipse fell in his Eighth House.

Darlene Has Contract and Job Problems
after an Eclipse to Her Mercury

Darlene had a Lunar eclipse fall on her Mercury that had troublesome consequences for the next three and a half years each time it was stimulated by transiting Mars. This had been an eclipse with the Dragon's Tail in attendance. Having ended a job she loved to take a brand-new position that promised more clout (definitely a bad move with this particular eclipse), Darlene did not insist on a contract, which in hindsight she should have done. Once she had the new place up and running, Darlene was let go. Unable to get her old position back since it had been filled, she eventually felt forced to pay an agency to find her a job. The agency did of course find her a job, but it was not what she enjoyed and she didn't do well in her management capacity or in getting along with the other personnel. This led to a transfer, and then to being let go entirely. From there, Darlene went to another city and got a job at another franchise in the same capacity but ended up moving from one store to another over the next couple of years. At each of these job changes, it was always a transit of Mars over or opposite the eclipsed Mercury that timed the upheaval. Finally, Saturn came along to end this unfortunate cycle, and within three months of Saturn's pass, she was once again working in a capacity that she enjoyed.

Carla Loses Her Brother after an Eclipse to Her Mercury

Just three months following a South Node Solar eclipse to her Mercury, which rules siblings, Carla learned that her favorite brother was dying. He was an older brother and had been like a father to her and to the other younger children in the family for many years. She flew to be with him and stayed next to him until he died.

Janice Fights for Benefits and Then Wins Big
after Eclipses on Her Venus

Janice had a Lunar eclipse oppose her Venus, and this eclipse was of the influence of the Dragon's Tail. Having given notice to leave her job due to some company politics she wanted no part of, she had to fight to hang on to bonuses she'd earned over the several months preceding. Though she was emotionally miserable there and couldn't wait to get out, she had to extend her notice to avoid losing her benefits. Six months after the first eclipse, another Lunar eclipse fell on her Venus, this one accompanied by the North Node, or Dragon's Head. Within two weeks of this eclipse, her husband won a fair sum of money in a lottery, affording her a little peace and tranquility to regroup. As a result, she was able to create her own little moneymaking enterprise and didn't have to return to the rat race.

Arlene Is Duped after an Eclipse to Her Venus

Almost six months following a Lunar eclipse to her Venus, as Mars crossed the eclipse point, Arlene was taken advantage of by a romantic friend's daughter, one with a drug habit. Loaning the girl money on three occasions, Arlene finally discovered the truth but never recovered the money.

Dianne Marries with an Eclipse to Her Mars

Dianne married for the first time about one year following a Solar eclipse to her Mars. At the time of her marriage, the benevolent and ceremonial Jupiter was crossing the degree of the eclipse. This marriage ended when Saturn moved over the eclipse point several years later. Years later, Dianne experienced another Solar eclipse upon her Mars. Again, there were partnership themes. This time one relationship ended and a new one began that led to marriage some months later.

Darla and Bob Experience a Freak Accident with an Eclipse to His Mars

A young woman, separated from her husband and preparing for a divorce, had a Lunar eclipse fall on the Eighth House cusp of her nativity, associated with death and rebirth, which in the usual course of events would have sufficiently described her divorce. In this particular case, however, the eclipse also fell on her estranged husband's Mars. He accidentally shot and killed himself in a freak set of circumstances. He'd also experienced a Lunar eclipse opposite his Mars several months earlier. The relationship between them had been full of manipulation and jealous threats by him, and so it was many months before she was able to stop blaming herself for his death. She has since met someone else and built a new life.

Laura's Home Burns Down after an Eclipse to Her Mars

Laura had a South Node Solar eclipse fall on her Mars. About ten months later, as Jupiter and Uranus moved over the degree of the eclipse, her family's home burned due to a fire caused by faulty wiring. No one was seriously hurt, but most everything that did not burn was damaged by smoke and the home was unlivable. A previous Lunar eclipse had also fallen on her Fourth House cusp, announcing domestic changes.

Sue Meets Mate after Eclipses to Her Mars

Sue had two eclipses fall very nearly on her Mars. The first eclipse was a Solar eclipse with the North Node in attendance, and this one occurred almost two years prior to her meeting her future husband. The next eclipse on Mars was a Lunar eclipse, also with the Dragon's Head attending, and this one took place just a week before she met her husband-to-be. At the time of their meeting, the eclipse points were receiving stimulation from both Mars and Uranus.

Kay Makes Spiritual Progress with an Eclipse to Her Jupiter

Jupiter, as the Greater Fortune, rules spiritual beliefs. In the midst of one of the most difficult periods in her life, Kay had a North Node Solar eclipse fall on her Jupiter. In the year following, she felt she had made immense progress on her spiritual path, which helped a great deal in handling troubling issues. She even underwent a spiritual healing ceremony in a dream, which she says significantly reduced the amount of sleep she required thereafter. The planet Jupiter was actually depicted in her dream, and she knew enough astrology to understand its benevolent nature.

Earl Takes Severe Losses with an Eclipse to His Jupiter

Earl experienced a Solar eclipse with the South Node attending that fell on his Sixth House Jupiter, which usually provided him with job benefits. After thirty-one years on the job, Earl was forced by a company merger to take his retirement from his well-established company sooner than he had anticipated or planned. He got another job immediately. This contracting company did most of its work for the company he'd left, and soon the corporate and financial problems of his old company put a halt to all the work, forcing his new company into all but closing down and leaving him out of a job and with no work available

in his field. He could end up losing many of his retirement benefits if the company he originally worked for has to file for bankruptcy.

Sandra Has Bad Job Luck with an Eclipse to Her Jupiter

Another interesting example of an eclipsed Jupiter in the Sixth House of work comes from
Sandra. This happened many years ago when a pregnant woman could not perform certain
jobs. Sandra had a great job that she loved working in a restaurant inside of a large department store, but when she became pregnant she was moved to a retail department for safety
purposes. She hated it, and with this being her first pregnancy, she was tired all the time
and her energy was drained. As Uranus soon stimulated the degree of her eclipse, she simply went in and quit her job, giving no notice, something quite out of character for her.

Author Writes and Publishes Book with an Eclipse to Her Jupiter

In 1996, I had a Lunar eclipse fall on my natal Jupiter. As the Greater Fortune, it is the
planetary ruler of the zodiac sign Sagittarius, linked to things such as publishing.

Since an eclipse shows a place of stored-up energy, this eclipse was quite symbolic for
me, although I didn't fully understand the dynamics or the timing at work until later on.
What occurred, however, came almost effortlessly. I'd been keeping notes for an astrology
book for several years. Basically, the time had arrived to compile the book that I'd contem-
plated for so long. After all, the Lunar eclipse is about the culmination of something in
which we've invested time and energy. Two weeks following the Lunar eclipse, a Solar
eclipse fell on my natal Neptune and inspiration flowed.

With a certain sense of animation, I sat down to compile and refine my notes into a
book. A little less than four months later, it was completed and sent off to my publisher,
just as Saturn moved over the degree of my Jupiter where the first eclipse had fallen. Mars
was opposite the degree of the eclipse, where it would pass three times over the coming
months due to retrograde motion. As a planet that times activity and action, and related to
new enterprise, the Mars transits to the eclipsed Jupiter symbolized the lengthy publishing
process.

So, in this case, the window of opportunity was open for the precise amount of time it
took me to complete the task signified by an eclipsed Jupiter. Or, could it have been an
inner sense of timing that kept me synchronized with the cosmic energy forces so that the

work was completed on time?

Wendy Stabilizes Her Life after an Eclipse to Her Saturn

In her twenties, Wendy had multiple jobs, usually moving from one to the next every year or so. With an eclipse to her Saturn, she secured a better position than any she'd previously had and got a year's worth of experience under her belt. Then, utilizing a business connection from one of her previous jobs, she returned to work there, in a nicer environment and in a higher capacity, and she stayed happily for several years. In the process, her status increased and her income was the best and most stable ever, allowing her to get a much-needed new car and improve her standard of living.

Sharon Elopes Following an Eclipse to Her Uranus

About a year and a half following a North Node Lunar eclipse to her Uranus, Sharon eloped to Mexico with her boyfriend. At the time of their exciting and spontaneous elopement, Jupiter, planet of ceremonies, had just entered its 3-degree range to stimulate the eclipse.

Frank Learns of Untreatable Lung Cancer with an Eclipse to His Neptune

For Frank, a series of eclipses began to fall on personal planets three years preceding his death from lung cancer. The first was a Solar eclipse opposite his Sixth House Neptune, with the South Node attending. Following that, two eclipses spotlighted his Mercury—quite possibly a warning, for Mercury rules the lungs. The first eclipse to Mercury was a Lunar eclipse some two years before he even knew he had the cancer. Finally a Solar eclipse, with the South Node attending, also fell on his Mercury. Six months later, as the Sun opposed his eclipsed Mercury, he found out that he had inoperable advanced cancer and had only a few months to live. At the time of his death, Saturn and Mars were in opposition over his previously eclipsed Neptune.

Cheryl Has an Intense Affair Following an Eclipse to Her Pluto

Cheryl was the recipient of a Lunar eclipse that fell right on her Pluto. She was a young, married lady, but within a few months of that eclipse, Mars made one of its prolonged retrograde stations opposite the place of the eclipse, spending several weeks stimulating the eclipsed Pluto. Knowing it was wrong but unable to control her heightened sexual desires, Cheryl had an intense summer affair.

Julie's Dad Passes Away after an Eclipse to Her Pluto

Pluto, as the ruler of death and rebirth, usually affects a facet of the personality or of something in life like a relationship. Sometimes it actually does indicate the death of a close person in life, as it did for Julie. She experienced a Lunar eclipse that fell opposite her Pluto. A little more than a year later, her father fell ill when Mars moved over this eclipse. At the next pass of Mars to her eclipsed Pluto, her father passed away.

Maria Has an Epiphany and Reclaims Her Life after an Eclipse to Her Pluto

What started out as a really rough period for Maria turned out very well in the long run following a Lunar eclipse to her Pluto. This was a North Node eclipse, and many changes took place in the first few months after it. Stressed in her job, Maria gave her notice when she could no longer tolerate her working conditions. Not long after that, she and her husband got into a terrible row and she walked out. She finally came to the realization that her husband was never going to change. A second marriage for both of them, he was terribly jealous of her children. Up until the eclipse, she believed that if she treated his children well that he would eventually reciprocate with the same kind of caring and respect for hers. That never happened, and the marriage had deteriorated over the years. With a lot of property involved and a prenuptial agreement she'd signed (he was quite wealthy), the divorce was a grueling experience for her. Not only did it take a year and a half to receive the divorce decree, she lost half of her own retirement savings to him. Despite all this, she celebrates this eclipse because she says she's reclaimed her life and it raised her consciousness. She now has a home of her own, spends time doing things that are important to her, and has a happy brood of children that are supportive and loving and are providing her with grandchildren left and right!

End-of-Life Conditions & an Eclipse to the IC

The closing transit of Saturn to an eclipse on the IC, or Fourth House cusp, is sometimes linked to the closing epoch of life, especially in old age. One understands this synchronicity by Saturn representing old age and the IC signifying the end-of-life conditions. This was a feature in the horoscope and death of Grant Lewi, a famous astrologer and author who took out a life-insurance policy shortly before he died of a cerebral hemorrhage.[2]

Jim Morrison of The Doors also died when Saturn eventually transited an eclipse that had fallen on his IC some five years earlier.[3] In the case of author Barbara Cartland, she died just a few weeks prior to the 2000 eclipse at 10 degrees Cancer that fell on her IC, just before her ninety-ninth birthday.

---

1. When a person relocates following birth, the angles of the relocated chart for the new area are sensitive to eclipses in the same way as they are for eclipses to natal angles.

2. This eclipse fell on his relocated IC for Tucson, Arizona.

3. Celeste Teal, "Chapter 15: Eclipses & the Lunar Nodes," *Predicting Events with Astrology* (St. Paul, MN: Llewellyn Publishing, 1999).

Tables & Charts

Table 1: Master Eclipse & Planetary Transits for 2000–2015

This table furnishes many particulars about current eclipses as follows:

- The top line in the first column to the left gives the type of eclipse—Solar or Lunar— and its power-rating number, with 1 as the lowest power rating and 7 as the highest rating for any of the eclipses listed (higher-rated eclipses are italicized). "T" stands for a total eclipse that has increased the power rating.

- The date of the eclipse is given on the next line down.

- The degree and sign of the eclipse are shown below that. For practical purposes, the degree is enough to plot the eclipse into the personal horoscope, but the degree may be rounded up if the number of minutes is more than 30.

- Below the sign is indicated whether the eclipse is of the influence of the Dragon's Head or the Dragon's Tail.

- Columns two, three, four, five, and six provide dates of major stimulation to an eclipse by the Sun, Mars, Jupiter, Saturn, or any of the three outer planets.

- Column six occasionally contains a note about events that have corresponded with transits to an eclipse.

Eclipse Degree, Date & Power	Sun Transits	Mars Transits	Jupiter Transits	Saturn Transits	Outer Planet Transits
Solar Eclipse: 5 July 1, 2000 10 Cancer 14 Dragon's Head	09-30-2000 12-31-2000 07-01-2002 07-01-2003	09-26-2001 06-12-2002* 03-20-2003 05-23-2004	09-02-2001 01-04-2002 rx 04-26-2002	08-27-2003 12-26-2003 rx 05-14-2004	*Wildfires
T Lunar Eclipse: 4 July 16, 2000 24 Capricorn 19 Dragon's Tail	10-14-2000 01-14-2001 07-16-2001 07-16-2002	07-23-2000 10-19-2001 07-04-2002 04-12-2003 06-14-2004 03-12-2005	07-07-2002	09-09-2004 01-18-2005 rx 05-29-2005	
Solar Eclipse: 3 July 30, 2000 08 Leo 12 Dragon's Head	10-28-2000 01-28-2001 07-31-2001 07-31-2002 07-31-2003	08-13-2000 11-08-2001 07-26-2002 05-05-2003 07-06-2004 03-31-2005	09-09-2002 03-25-2003 rx 04-13-2003	09-22-2005 01-23-2006 rx 06-12-2006	Neptune: 03-25-2001 06-28-2001 rx 01-21-2002
Solar Eclipse: 3 Dec. 25, 2000 04 Capricorn 14 Dragon's Tail	03-25-2001 06-25-2001 12-25-2001 12-25-2002	09-16-2001 06-03-2002 03-11-2003 05-14-2004	08-01-2001	07-06-2003	
T Lunar Eclipse: 3 Jan. 9, 2001 19 Cancer 39 Dragon's Head	04-09-2001 07-11-2001 01-09-2002 01-09-2003	10-11-2001 06-27-2002 04-04-2003 06-07-2004	06-15-2002	07-30-2004	
T Solar Eclipse: 7 June 21, 2001 00 Cancer 10 Dragon's Head	09-19-2001 12-21-2001 06-21-2002 06-21-2003	09-08-2001* 05-28-2002 03-04-2003 05-07-2004		06-05-2003	*WTC & Pentagon attacks
Lunar Eclipse: 5 July 5, 2001 13 Capricorn 39 Dragon's Tail	10-03-2001 01-04-2002 07-05-2002 07-05-2003	10-02-2001 06-18-2002 03-26-2003 05-28-2004	09-27-2001 12-08-2001 rx 05-16-2002	Stations retro: 10-25-2003 Final pass: 06-13-2004	

Transit dates listed are for the exact contact of a planet to a previous eclipse; however, planetary energy usually operates within +/- 3 degrees. Thus, outer events may transpire within roughly three days of a transit by the Sun, within six days of a transit by Mars, within two weeks of a transit by Jupiter, and within a month or more of a transit of an outer planet. See chapter 4 for the kind of energy brought to the eclipse. Rx: Retrograde motion. The eclipse power rating is given on the top line. Higher-powered eclipses are italicized. "T" stands for a total eclipse that has increased the power rating.

Eclipse Degree, Date & Power	Sun Transits	Mars Transits	Jupiter Transits	Saturn Transits	Outer Planet Transits
T Solar Eclipse: 4 Dec. 14, 2001 22 Sagittarius 56 Dragon's Tail	03-14-2002 06-13-2002 12-14-2002	05-17-2002 02-21-2003		07-14-2002 01-23-2003 rx 03-23-2003	Pluto: 01-06-2005 06-23-2005 11-07-2005
Lunar Eclipse: 3 Dec. 30, 2001 08 Cancer 48 Dragon's Head	03-30-2002 06-30-2002 12-30-2002 12-30-2003	06-10-2002 03-18-2003	01-14-2002 04-16-2002	08-13-2003 01-12-2004 rx 04-30-2004	
Lunar Eclipse: 2 May 26, 2002 05 Sagittarius 04 Dragon's Tail	08-24-2002 11-27-2002 05-26-2003 05-26-2004	01-24-2003 03-29-2004 01-01-2005 02-27-2006	12-16-2006		
T Solar Eclipse: 5 June 10, 2002 19 Gemini 54 Dragon's Head	09-08-2002 12-11-2002 06-11-2003 06-11-2004	02-16-2003 04-21-2004 01-23-2005		06-20-2002	Pluto: 03-10-2003 04-04-2003 rx 12-16-2003 07-23-2004 rx 10-06-2004
Lunar Eclipse: 3 June 24, 2002 03 Capricorn 11 Dragon's Tail	09-22-2002 12-24-2002 06-24-2003	03-09-2003		06-28-2003	
Lunar Eclipse: 1 Nov. 19, 2002 27 Taurus 33 Dragon's Head	02-17-2003 05-18-2003 11-20-2003 11-20-2004	01-15-2003* 03-17-2004 12-21-2004 02-12-2006	11-12-2006		*Columbia launched 01-16-03 (disintegrated)
T Solar Eclipse: 2 Dec. 4, 2002 11 Sagittarius 58 Dragon's Tail	03-04-2003 06-02-2003 12-04-2003 12-04-2004 12-04-2005	02-04-2003 04-08-2004 01-11-2005 03-12-2006 12-22-2006 08-26-2007	01-20-2007 06-30-2007 rx 09-12-2007		

Eclipse Degree, Date & Power	Sun Transits	Mars Transits	Jupiter Transits	Saturn Transits	Outer Planet Transits
T Lunar Eclipse: 2 May 15, 2003 24 Scorpio 53 Dragon's Tail	08-13-2003 11-17-2003 05-15-2004 05-15-2005	03-13-2004 12-17-2004 02-07-2006 11-28-2006 07-30-2007	10-31-2006		
Solar Eclipse: 2 May 30, 2003 09 Gemini 20 Dragon's Head	08-28-2003 12-01-2003 05-30-2004 05-30-2005	04-04-2004 01-08-2005 03-07-2006 12-19-2006	01-06-2007		
T Lunar Eclipse: 2 Nov. 8, 2003 16 Taurus 13 Dragon's Head	02-06-2004 05-06-2004 11-08-2004 11-08-2005	02-28-2004 12-05-2004 08-29-2005 11-03-2005 01-17-2006	01-21-2006 04-16-2006 rx 09-18-2006		
T Solar Eclipse: 2 Nov. 23, 2003 01 Sagittarius 14 Dragon's Tail	02-21-2004 05-21-2004 11-23-2004	03-24-2004 12-27-2004			
Solar Eclipse: 1 April 19, 2004 29 Aries 49 Dragon's Head	07-18-2004 10-22-2004 04-20-2005 04-20-2006	11-10-2004 07-27-2005 10-23-2006 06-24-2007	10-25-2005		
T Lunar Eclipse: 2 May 4, 2004 14 Scorpio 42 Dragon's Tail	08-02-2004 11-06-2004 05-04-2005 05-04-2006	12-02-2004 08-25-2005 11-08-2005 rx 01-13-2006 11-14-2006 07-15-2007 10-25-2008	01-09-2006 04-28-2006 rx 09-09-2006		
Solar Eclipse: 2 Oct. 13, 2004 21 Libra 06 Dragon's Tail	01-11-2005 04-10-2005 10-13-2005 10-13-2006	10-28-2004 07-13-2005 10-10-2006 06-12-2007 09-20-2008	09-14-2005		

Transit dates listed are for the exact contact of a planet to a previous eclipse; however, planetary energy usually operates within +/- 3 degrees. Thus, outer events may transpire within roughly three days of a transit by the Sun, within six days of a transit by Mars, within two weeks of a transit by Jupiter, and within a month or more of a transit of an outer planet. See chapter 4 for the kind of energy brought to the eclipse. Rx: Retrograde motion. The eclipse power rating is given on the top line. Higher-powered eclipses are italicized. "T" stands for a total eclipse that has increased the power rating.

Eclipse Degree, Date & Power	Sun Transits	Mars Transits	Jupiter Transits	Saturn Transits	Outer Planet Transits
T Lunar Eclipse: 2 Oct. 27, 2004 05 Taurus 02 Dragon's Head	01-25-2005 04-24-2005 10-27-2005 10-27-2006	11-18-2004 08-05-2005 10-30-2006 07-01-2007 10-11-2008	11-18-2005		
T Solar Eclipse: 4 _April 8, 2005_ _19 Aries 06_ _Dragon's Head_	_07-07-2005_ _10-12-2005_ _04-08-2006_ _04-08-2007_	_07-10-2005_ _10-07-2006_ _06-09-2007_ _09-17-2008_	_09-03-2005_		
Lunar Eclipse: 2 April 24, 2005 04 Scorpio 20 Dragon's Tail	07-23-2005 10-27-2005 04-24-2006 04-24-2007	08-04-2005 10-29-2006 06-30-2007 10-10-2008	11-14-2005		
T Solar Eclipse: 2 Oct. 3, 2005 10 Libra 19 Dragon's Tail	01-01-2006 03-30-2006 10-03-2006 10-03-2007	09-23-2006 05-29-2007 09-04-2008			
Lunar Eclipse: 1 Oct. 17, 2005 24 Aries 13 Dragon's Head	01-15-2006 04-14-2006 10-17-2006 10-17-2007	10-14-2006 06-16-2007 09-25-2008			
Lunar Eclipse: 3 _March 14, 2006_ _24 Virgo 15_ _Dragon's Tail_	_06-12-2006_ _09-17-2006_ _03-14-2007_ _03-14-2008_	_08-30-2006_ _05-07-2007_ _08-10-2008_ _04-14-2009_	_05-03-2010_ _10-28-2010 rx_ _12-09-2010_	_09-11-2009_	_Uranus:_ _04-11-2009_ _09-27-2009 rx_ _02-01-2010_
T Solar Eclipse: 2 March 29, 2006 08 Aries 35 Dragon's Head	06-27-2006 10-01-2006 03-29-2007 03-29-2008	09-21-2006 05-26-2007 09-01-2008 05-03-2009			

Eclipse Degree, Date & Power	Sun Transits	Mars Transits	Jupiter Transits	Saturn Transits	Outer Planet Transits
Lunar Eclipse: 3 *Sept. 7, 2006* *15 Pisces 00* *Dragon's Head*	*12-06-2006* *03-05-2007* *09-07-2007* *09-07-2008*	*04-25-2007* *07-26-2008* *04-03-2009* *07-04-2010*	*03-22-2010*	*09-28-2008* *05-06-2009 rx* *05-27-2009*	*Uranus:* *03-11-2007* *10-31-2007 rx* *12-17-2007*
T Solar Eclipse: 3 *Sept. 22, 2006* *29 Virgo 20* *Dragon's Tail*	*12-21-2006* *03-20-2007* *09-22-2007* *09-22-2008*	*05-14-2007* *08-18-2008* *04-21-2009*	*06-01-2010* *09-14-2010 rx* *01-18-2011*	*10-23-2009* *04-17-2010 rx* *07-12-2010*	*Uranus:* *05-09-2010* *09-02-2010 rx* *02-27-2011*
T Lunar Eclipse: 4 *March 3, 2007* *13 Virgo 00* *Dragon's Tail*	*06-01-2007* *09-05-2007* *03-03-2008* *03-03-2009*	*04-23-2007* *07-22-2008* *03-31-2009* *06-30-2010*	*03-13-2010*	*09-12-2008*	*Uranus:* *04-12-2006* *08-30-2006 rx* *02-03-2007*
Solar Eclipse: 2 March 18, 2007 28 Pisces 07 Dragon's Head	06-16-2007 09-21-2007 03-18-2008 03-18-2009	05-12-2007 08-16-2008 04-19-2009 07-27-2010 03-30-2011	05-24-2010 09-23-2010 rx 01-11-2011	10-13-2009 05-12-2010 rx 06-17-2010	Uranus: 04-13-10 10-03-2010 rx 02-03-2011
T Lunar Eclipse: 3 *Aug. 28, 2007* *04 Pisces 45* *Dragon's Head*	*11-26-2007* *02-23-2008* *08-28-2008* *08-28-2009*	*07-09-2008* *03-21-2009* *06-16-2010* *02-28-2011* *11-20-2011* *03-31-2012 rx*	*02-07-2010*	*10-13-2007* *02-29-2008 rx* *07-03-2008*	
Solar Eclipse: 3 *Sept. 11, 2007* *18 Virgo 25* *Dragon's Tail*	*12-10-2007* *03-08-2008* *09-11-2008* *09-11-2009*	*07-31-2008* *04-07-2009* *07-10-2010* *03-18-2011*	*04-05-2010*	*10-29-2008* *03-08-2009 rx* *07-22-2009*	*Uranus is first* *to pass:* *03-04-2008*
T Solar Eclipse: 5 *Feb. 6, 2008* *17 Aquarius 44* *Dragon's Head*	*05-07-2008* *08-09-2008* *02-06-2009* *02-06-2010* *02-06-2011*	*06-10-2008* *02-27-2009* *10-02-2009* *01-06-2010 rx* *05-12-2010* *02-07-2011* *10-19-2011*	*03-24-2009* *09-24-2009 rx* *10-31-2909*		

Transit dates listed are for the exact contact of a planet to a previous eclipse; however, planetary energy usually operates within +/- 3 degrees. Thus, outer events may transpire within roughly three days of a transit by the Sun, within six days of a transit by Mars, within two weeks of a transit by Jupiter, and within a month or more of a transit of an outer planet. See chapter 4 for the kind of energy brought to the eclipse. Rx: Retrograde motion. The eclipse power rating is given on the top line. Higher-powered eclipses are italicized. "T" stands for a total eclipse that has increased the power rating.

Eclipse Degree, Date & Power	Sun Transits	Mars Transits	Jupiter Transits	Saturn Transits	Outer Planet Transits
T Lunar Eclipse: 3 Feb. 20, 2008 01 Virgo 53 Dragon's Tail	05-21-2008 08-24-2008 02-20-2009 02-20-2010	07-04-2008 03-17-2009 06-10-2010 02-25-2011 11-14-2011	01-26-2010	04-17-2008 rx 05-17-2008	
T Solar Eclipse: 4 Aug. 1, 2008 09 Leo 32 Dragon's Tail	10-30-2008 01-29-2009 08-01-2009 08-01-2010	02-16-2009 11-06-2009 01-30-2010 rx 04-23-2010 01-27-2011 10-04-2011	02-14-2009		
Lunar Eclipse: 2 Aug. 16, 2008 24 Aquarius 22 Dragon's Head	11-14-2008 02-12-2009 08-16-2009 08-16-2010	03-07-2009 05-26-2010 02-15-2011 10-31-2011	05-04-2009 07-27-2009 rx 12-21-2009		Neptune: 02-23-2009 09-14-2009 rx 12-23-2009
T Solar Eclipse: 4 Jan. 26, 2009 06 Aquarius 30 Dragon's Head	04-26-2009 07-29-2009 01-26-2010 01-26-2011 01-26-2012	02-12-2009 10-30-2009 02-07-2010 rx 04-14-2010 01-24-2011 09-29-2011 01-03-2013	02-12-2009		
Lunar Eclipse: 4 Feb. 9, 2009 21 Leo 00 Dragon's Tail	05-10-2009 08-13-2009 02-09-2010 02-09-2011	03-13-2009 05-19-2010 02-11-2011 10-24-2011 01-21-2013	04-11-2009 08-22-2009 rx 12-01-2009		
Lunar Eclipse: 3 July 7, 2009 15 Capricorn 24 Dragon's Head	10-04-2009 01-05-2010 07-07-2010 07-07-2011	09-19-2009 12-27-2010 08-26-2011 12-07-2012 08-05-2013	09-09-2013		
T Solar Eclipse: 3 July 21, 2009 29 Cancer 27 Dragon's Tail	10-19-2009 01-19-2010 07-21-2010 07-21-2011	10-15-2009 01-15-2011 09-17-2011 12-25-2012 08-27-2013			

Eclipse Degree, Date & Power	Sun Transits	Mars Transits	Jupiter Transits	Saturn Transits	Outer Planet Transits
Lunar Eclipse: 2 Aug. 5, 2009 13 Aquarius 43 Dragon's Head	11-03-2009 02-02-2010 08-05-2010 08-05-2011	11-17-2009 01-19-2010 rx 05-03-2010 02-02-2011 10-11-2011 01-12-2013			
Lunar Eclipse: 4 *Dec. 31, 2009* *10 Cancer 15* *Dragon's Tail*	*03-30-2010* *07-02-2010* *12-31-2010* *12-31-2011*	*12-21-2010* *08-18-2011* *11-30-2012* *07-28-2013*	*08-11-2013*		*Pluto:* *01-27-2013* *07-03-2013 rx* *12-02-2013*
T Solar Eclipse: 5 *Jan. 15, 2010* *25 Capricorn 01* *Dragon's Head*	*04-15-2010* *07-17-2010* *01-15-2011* *01-15-2012*	*01-09-2011* *09-10-2011* *12-19-2012* *08-20-2013*			
Lunar Eclipse: 5 *June 26, 2010* *04 Capricorn 46* *Dragon's Head*	*09-24-2010* *12-26-2010* *06-26-2011* *06-26-2012*	*12-14-2010* *08-10-2011* *11-23-2012* *07-20-2013*	*07-16-2013*		*Pluto:* *12-16-2010*
T Solar Eclipse: 2 July 11, 2010 19 Cancer 24 Dragon's Tail	10-09-2010 01-09-2011 07-11-2011 07-11-2012	01-02-2011 09-01-2011 12-12-2012 08-11-2013	10-11-2013 12-03-2013 rx 05-25-2014		
T Lunar Eclipse: 3 *Dec. 21, 2010* *29 Gemini 21* *Dragon's Tail*	*03-21-2011* *06-20-2011* *12-21-2011* *12-21-2012*	*08-02-2011* *11-16-2012* *07-12-2013* *10-25-2014*	*06-23-2013*		
Solar Eclipse: 4 *Jan. 4, 2011* *13 Capricorn 39* *Dragon's Head*	*04-04-2011* *07-05-2011* *01-04-2012* *01-04-2013*	*08-23-2011* *12-04-2012* *08-02-2013* *11-13-2014*	*08-28-2013* *01-19-2014 rx* *04-21-2014*		
Solar Eclipse: 2 June 1, 2011 11 Gemini 02 Dragon's Tail	08-30-2011 12-03-2011 06-01-2012 06-01-2013	07-06-2011 10-22-2012 06-15-2013 09-29-2014	08-05-2012 12-04-2012 rx 03-26-2013		

Transit dates listed are for the exact contact of a planet to a previous eclipse; however, planetary energy usually operates within +/- 3 degrees. Thus, outer events may transpire within roughly three days of a transit by the Sun, within six days of a transit by Mars, within two weeks of a transit by Jupiter, and within a month or more of a transit of an outer planet. See chapter 4 for the kind of energy brought to the eclipse. Rx: Retrograde motion. The eclipse power rating is given on the top line. Higher-powered eclipses are italicized. "T" stands for a total eclipse that has increased the power rating.

Eclipse Degree, Date & Power	Sun Transits	Mars Transits	Jupiter Transits	Saturn Transits	Outer Planet Transits
Lunar Eclipse: 2 June 15, 2011 24 Sagittarius 24 Dragon's Head	09-13-2011 12-16-2011 06-15 2012 06-15-2013	07-25-2011 11-09-2012 07 05-2013 10-18-2014	06-01-2013		
Solar Eclipse: 2† July 1, 2011 09 Cancer 12 Dragon's Tail	09-30-2011 12-31-2011 07-01-2012 07-01-2013	08-17-2011 11-29-2012 07-27-2013 11-07-2014	08-06-2013		Pluto: 03-04-12 05-18-12 rx 12-28-12 08-21-13 rx 10-19-13
Solar Eclipse: 2 Nov. 25, 2011 02 Sagittarius 37 Dragon's Head	02-23-2012 05-23-2012 11-25-2012 11-25-2013	10-10-2012 06-03-2013 09-17-2014 05-15-2015	06-23-2012	01-19-2015 05-09-2015 rx 10-17-2015	
T Lunar Eclipse: 3 *Dec. 10, 2011* *18 Gemini 11* *Dragon's Tail*	*03-10-2012* *06-08-2012* *12-10-2012* *12-10-2013*	*11-01-2012* *06-26-2013* *10-09-2014* *06-06-2015*	*05-04-2013*		
T Solar Eclipse: 3 *May 20, 2012* *00 Gemini 21* *Dragon's Tail*	*08-18-2012* *11-22-2012* *05-20-2013* *05-20-2014*	*10-07-2012* *05-31-2013* *09-14-2014* *05-12-2015* *03-06-2016*	*06-13-2012*	*12-26-2014* *06-09-2015 rx* *09-22-2015*	

† This eclipse may be worthy of three extra points. It falls nearly within 3 degrees of both the Sun and Jupiter in the USA chart, actually midway between the two.

Table 2: Eclipse Elements—Fire, Earth, Air & Water

Element	Sign	Ruler	People, Things, Events, Effects Signified
Fire	♈ Aries	♂ Mars	Police, Military, Firefighters, Heroes, Surgeons, Engineers, Athletes, Sportsmen, Agitators, War, Fire, Weaponry, Crime, Epidemics, Sudden, Angry, Dangerous, Infectious, Hot, Passionate
	♌ Leo	☉ Sun	Royals, King, President, Central Leaders, Men of Power, Executive Heads, Government, Noble Characters, Threat of Death/Overthrow, Gold, Vital, Prideful, Creative Will, Power, Egotistical
	♐ Sagittarius	♃ Jupiter	Clergy, Religious Leaders, Foreigners, Judiciary, World Travelers, Spiritual, Universities, Publishers, Journalists, International Finance, Assemblies, Expansive, Distant Vision, Acquisitive, Productive
Earth	♉ Taurus	♀ Venus	Builders, Bankers, Musicians, Textiles, Wages, Resources, Reserves, Paper Money and Coins, Property, Theaters, Festivals, Art Dealers, Plagues, Volcanoes, Avalanches, Earthquakes, Droughts
	♍ Virgo	☿ Mercury	Farmers, Growers, Nutritionists, Health Workers, Natural Resources, Environment, Harvests, Crops, Food Supply, Purity, Practical, Analyzing, Discretionary, Illness, Malnutrition, Famine, Feast
	♑ Capricorn	♄ Saturn	Statesmen, Elders, Law-Enforcement Authorities, Civil Service Employees, Industry, Business, Organizations, Public Buildings, Limits, Retards, Conserves, Scarcities, National Calamities
Air	♊ Gemini	☿ Mercury	Messengers, Mail Workers, News, Media, Youth, Communications, Transport, Teachers, Education, Marketplace, Trade, Internet, Mobility, Versatility, Debate, Dissent, Thievery, Communicable Ills
	♎ Libra	♀ Venus	Judges, Peace Preservers, Young Women, Artists, Courtship and Marriage, Social Issues, Divisions Among People, Religious Divisions, Turbulence Affecting Public Tranquility, Morals Jeopardized
	♒ Aquarius	♅ Uranus	Inventors, Technicians, Electricians, Labor Organizations, Aeronautics, Air and Rail Transport, Rebels, Revolutions, Strikes, Riots, Shocking, Spasmodic, Unexpected, Lightning, Explosive
Water	♋ Cancer	☽ Moon	Crowds, the Public, Working Classes, Women, Domestics, Homes, Land, Family Values, Country, Popular Subjects, Fertility, Fluctuation and Change, Silver, Liquids, Excessive Rain, Floods, Tides
	♏ Scorpio	♇ Pluto	Psychologists, Healers, Uniformed Workers, Miners, Reform Leaders, Underworld, Sex, Death, Taxes, Sewage, Refuse, Toxins, Porn, Coercive, Purging, Demolition, Reconstruction, Viruses
	♓ Pisces	♆ Neptune	Actors, Sailors, Prophets, Mystics, Social Movements, Charities, Medicine, Drugs, Oil, Gas, Chemicals, Alcohol, Liquids, Oceans, Seas, Fog, Clouds, Occluded, Dissolving, Widespread Unrest

An eclipse brings *change–emphasis–impact* to things shown by sign.

Table 3: Eclipse Life-Span Conversions

Here is a table of the first twenty millennium eclipses, with their suggested life-span conversions. For the four-year period from 2000 through 2003, there are twenty eclipses, ten Lunar and ten Solar. The average life span of these, including both types, is 3.75 years based on the shadow period. The average life span of the Lunar eclipses is 4.75 years, and the average life span of the Solar eclipses is 3 years, including two Solar eclipses in 2003 with a life span of one year or less.[1] (For practical purposes, a 3.5-year life span can be assigned to all eclipses.)

The italicized eclipses are subject to important and intense planetary stimulation while they are still active, providing greater scope for changes.

Date of the Eclipse	Zodiac Degree	Eclipse Type	Shadow Period	Life Span to Year
Jan. 20, 2000	1 Leo	Lunar	5 hours 00 minutes	5.00 years–2005
Feb. 5, 2000	16 Aquarius	Solar	3 hours 48 minutes	3.75 years–2004
July 1, 2000	*10 Cancer*	*Solar*	*2 hours 50 minutes*	*3.00 years–2003*
July 16, 2000	*24 Capricorn*	*Lunar*	*5 hours 59 minutes*	*6.00 years–2006*
July 30, 2000	8 Leo	Solar	3 hours 11 minutes	3.25 years–2003
Dec. 25, 2000	*4 Capricorn*	*Solar*	*4 hours 17 minutes*	*4.25 years–2005*
Jan. 9, 2001	*20 Cancer*	*Lunar*	*5 hours 14 minutes*	*5.25 years–2006*
June 21, 2001	*0 Cancer*	*Solar*	*2 hours 54 minutes*	*3.00 years–2004*
July 5, 2001	*13 Capricorn*	*Lunar*	*5 hours 29 minutes*	*5.50 years–2007*
Dec. 14, 2001	*23 Sagittarius*	*Solar*	*3 hours 28 minutes*	*3.50 years–2005*
Dec. 30, 2001	*9 Cancer*	*Lunar*	*4 hours 8 minutes*	*4.00 years–2005*
May 26, 2002	5 Sagittarius	Lunar	3 hours 41 minutes	3.75 years–2006
June 10, 2002	*20 Gemini*	*Solar*	*3 hours 47 minutes*	*3.75 years–2006*
June 24, 2002	*3 Capricorn*	*Lunar*	*2 hours 17 minutes*	*2.25 years–2004*
Nov. 20, 2002	27 Taurus	Lunar	4 hours 29 minutes	4.50 years–2007
Dec. 4, 2002	12 Sagittarius	Solar	3 hours 21 minutes	3.25 years–2006
May 15, 2003	25 Scorpio	Lunar	5 hours 9 minutes	5.00 years–2008
May 30, 2003	9 Gemini	Solar	0 hours 47 minutes	0.75 year–2004
Nov. 9, 2003	16 Taurus	Lunar	6 hours 6 minutes	6.00 years–2009
Nov. 23, 2003	1 Sagittarius	Solar	1 hour 0 minutes	1.00 year–2004

---

1. The eclipse duration is from beginning to end of the eclipse shadow phases, as given on Fred Espenak's astronomy website, http://sunearth.gsfc.nasa.gov/eclipse/eclipse.html. His information is published in the *Observer's Handbook* and reported for NASA.

Catalog of Annotated Eclipse Charts for 1999–2012

Here, you'll see some brief observations of the general planetary influences in play during each eclipse to 2012. Remember that an eclipse is an entity in its own right, with a birth, a rise to maturity, a decline, and a death, and each carries its own vibration or personality. These condensed sketches give the more prominent characteristics of each eclipse using short descriptive phrases based on the concept that the eclipse points to a place of crisis, emphasis, or change—where attention is focused in terms of mundane affairs. However, an eclipse has multiple manifestations, which vary by region, so the key phrases may connect to more than one event.

Oftentimes, certain themes overlap from one eclipse to the next, reflective of concerns that remain focal. If an event will have a major impact upon the people (the masses) and at a national level, there are often similar indicators in sequential Lunar and Solar eclipses. Lunar eclipses seem especially reflective of conditions affecting the masses and the "common people," including natural disasters.

As this book goes to press, two notable events have happened since the eclipse annotations were done. The huge killer earthquake and tsunami of late 2004 and Hurricane Katrina of 2005 both appear to be most conspicuously linked to previous Lunar eclipses, falling in the signs Scorpio and Taurus, respectively. The earthquake that caused the tsunami was of such tremendous force that it actually caused the earth to wobble on its axis.

The names of the eclipses in this catalog are just my best attempt to name them. I'm sure that more descriptive names might be given to many of them as we look at things in retrospect.

If your city or country is listed as one of those for which the eclipse is of emphasis, turn to the Annotated Catalog of National Figures to find the planet the eclipse is spotlighting. Then, using Table 4: Planetary Keys, you can find the people and affairs associated with the planet to see those coming into focus in your area.

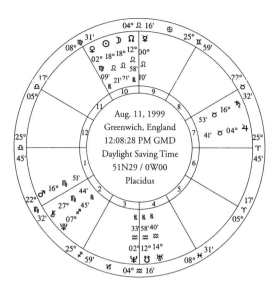

Solar Eclipse in Leo

Universal Eclipse Chart, Name: The Great Divide, Date: Aug. 11, 1999.

Eclipse ruled by the Sun: accents ruling powers. Features a Grand Cross involving the Sun, Moon, Uranus, Mars, and Saturn: tension, conflict, and anxieties that are difficult to appease. Chart ruler (Venus) is retrograde and squared by Pluto in the Second House: financial repercussions. Grand Cross planets are angular and in fixed signs; world stress relative to money and supremacy. Major theme: individual ego versus brotherhood of man = terrorism. Eclipse leads to a whole new world order. Eclipse opposes USA Moon: affects the public.

Solar Eclipse in Cancer

Washington, D.C. Eclipse Chart, Name: Summers of Fire, Date: July 1, 2000.

Cancer eclipse: A group of planets in Cancer emphasizes the Water element. Mars is Lord of the eclipse: water dangers of all kinds. Danger of water shortage as Mars heat and fire dries up the available supply. Indicative of excessive heat, drought, and fires. Eclipse on USA Sun. Chart ruler is Pluto: costly adjustments. Uranus in Fourth House: unexpected elements affecting land and homes such as floods or forest fires. Excessive wildfires in West due to the eclipse falling directly overhead, with extreme fire seasons for four years. Shark attacks also escalated coincident with this eclipse. Consummating Saturn transit comes with Mars in spring of 2004, nearing the fourth anniversary of the eclipse. After this fire season, brittle forests left to heal.

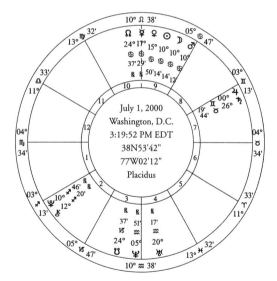

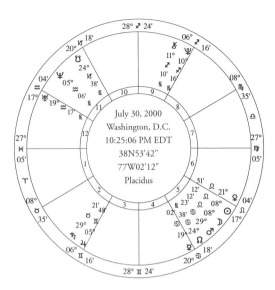

Solar Eclipse in Leo

Washington, D.C. Eclipse Chart, Name: Fight for Power, Date: July 30, 2000.

Eclipse ruled by the Sun: accents world leaders. Features Neptune opposite eclipse: deceptive opposition to a world power. Saturn in degree of Pleiades: something to cry about. In Second House: financial tears. Venus in critical degree: well-being of public is grave. Saturn square Venus: sadness. Uranus on U.S. Moon: sudden upset to public tranquility. Separations. This eclipse tied to the U.S. Dragon's Head, George W. Bush's Ascendant, and Osama bin Laden's Sun. This eclipse was also of emphasized importance for the Twin Towers, Manhattan, the NYSE, Afghanistan, Iraq, and Russia.

Solar Eclipse in Cancer

Washington, D.C. Eclipse Chart, Name: Homeland Security, Date: June 21, 2001.

Eclipse in Aries Point degree: strongly emphasizing events of worldwide importance, accenting all countries and Mother Earth. For the USA, an emphasis in Twelfth House suggested covert enemies. U.S. Pluto on Seventh House cusp: power struggles. Mars with Pluto in Fifth House opposite Saturn and Jupiter: conflicts and events affect stock market. Midheaven and IC in critical degrees: national crisis makes impact on citizens. Terrorist attacks coincided with Mars stimulation to this eclipse almost three months later. This eclipse gets a final pass from Saturn on June 5, 2003, bringing increased wisdom about defending the Homeland. This eclipse was also of exceptional import for Japan, Vatican City, Manhattan, North Korea, Palestine, New York City, Los Angeles, the United Nations, and the Twin Towers.

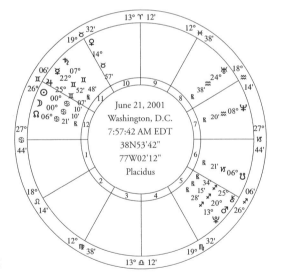

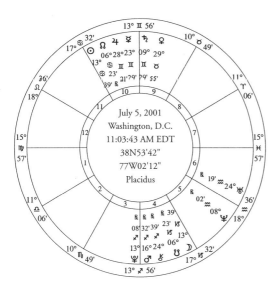

Lunar Eclipse in Capricorn

Washington, D.C. Eclipse Chart, Name: National Calamity, Date: July 5, 2001.

Eclipse in critical degree, angular, and ruled by Saturn. Accents business and national crisis. Eclipse falls across the USA Sun and Bush's Sun. Features Venus in Ninth House: foreign influences and long-distance travel. Venus in degree of the Pleiades: something to weep about. Pluto and Mars on IC: terrible trouble at home. Neptune in Fifth House: dissolving stocks (collapse of WTC). This eclipse is prone to stimulation through fall of 2004. From fall of 2003 to fall of 2004, Bush and USA under severe testing. This eclipse is emphasized in importance also for Cuba, Japan, Russia, the NYSE, and the Twin Towers.

Solar Eclipse in Sagittarius

Washington, D.C. Eclipse Chart, Name: Holy War, Date: Dec. 14, 2001.

Accent on foreign affairs and religious issues. For the U.S., eclipse opposes Mars and emphasis is in Seventh House of open enemies. Pluto in Seventh opposite Saturn in First: power struggle for command and authority. Mars and Uranus are both in critical degrees in Tenth House: activities of president and government are serious, grave, and critical. Neptune in Ninth: uncertainties in foreign affairs. U.S. Uranus rising: surprising events, liberty and freedom at stake. Jupiter on U.S. Sun: protecting the U.S. Strikes in Afghanistan at time of eclipse. Strikes on Iraq in March 2003, when eclipse was restimulated by both Mars and Saturn. This eclipse was of emphasis for Australia, Cuba, France, Iraq, Israel, Iran, Mexico, North Korea, the United Nations, NASA, Phoenix, Roswell, New York City, and Manhattan.

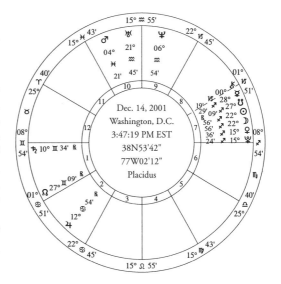

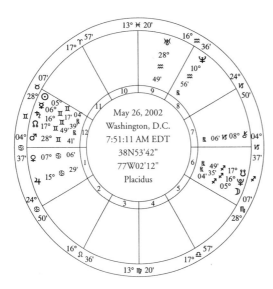

Lunar Eclipse in Sagittarius

Washington, D.C. Eclipse Chart, Name: Call to Arms, Date: May 26, 2002.

Sagittarius accents foreign and religious affairs. Retrograde Mercury in Gemini is Lord: need for reviews of intelligence and documents. For U.S., Mercury in Twelfth House of CIA. Eclipse in Sixth House: affects military and civil workers. Pluto in Sixth: use of force. Venus and Jupiter in First House: protecting U.S. citizens. First pass of Mars in January 2003 coincided with major troops sent into Iraq. Turbulence there and/or connected to this eclipse could continue until 2006. This eclipse is of emphasis for China, Cuba, Iran, Mexico, North Korea, Palestine, Roswell, Afghanistan, Russia, the United Kingdom, New York City, and the White House.

Solar Eclipse in Gemini

Washington, D.C. Eclipse Chart, Name: Thieves, Pirates, and Murderers, Date: June 10, 2002.

Gemini eclipse accents transport, communication, and the marketplace. Saturn is Lord of the eclipse: restriction, delays. Eclipse on U.S. Mars, threatening commerce. Eclipse in Seventh House of open enemies. Pluto opposite eclipse: war-on-terror effects. Pluto on Ascendant: public terrorized. South Node is rising in a critical degree: sacrifice, misjudgment. Critical degree on cusp of Sixth: crisis involves military. Struggle relating to economy and market activity. Efforts are blocked. The decline in the DJIA was worsened by Saturn crossing this eclipse in June 2002. Eclipse fell on Iraq's Moon, Venus, and Saturn: change in regime leads to turbulence affecting its citizens. This eclipse was also of significance for Canada, Cuba, France, Iran, Iraq, North Korea, Vatican City, NASA, the United Nations, New York City, the United Kingdom, Roswell, and the White House.

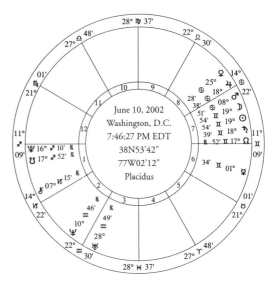

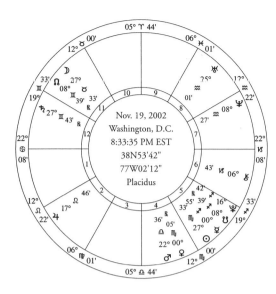

Lunar Eclipse in Taurus

Washington, D.C. Eclipse Chart, Name: Material Discomforts, Date: Nov. 19, 2002.

Eclipse in Taurus, ruled by Venus: accents banking, finances, and earth changes. For U.S., Venus in Fourth with Mars in mutual reception: real estate is saving grace for U.S. Following this eclipse, a focus on U.S. economics, real estate. Earthquakes, volcanoes, avalanches escalated, followed by the SARS outbreak in China, which was spotlighted by eclipse. Shuttle Columbia launched when Mars opposed this eclipse, disintegrating upon reentry. Challenger disaster also coincided with shuttle launch when Mars opposed an earlier eclipse near same degree in Taurus that falls on the Eighth House cusp (associated with death) of the NASA chart. Eclipse also of emphasis for New York City.

Solar Eclipse in Sagittarius

Washington, D.C. Eclipse Chart, Name: Casualties of Journalists, Date: Dec. 4, 2002.

Ruling Jupiter accents foreign affairs, religion, and journalists. Change affects communication, transportation, imports and exports. For U.S., Saturn in Ninth: long-distance travel advisories and restrictions. Critical degree on Eleventh House cusp: situations grave with allies. Jupiter trine Pluto: loyal support. Uranus in Fifth: unusual entertainment. Mars' first pass to eclipse coincided with debate among U.N. members about military action into Iraq. Great Britain loyal to U.S. Air travel affected by war and SARS. Many journalists were lost in Iraq, and embedded reporters furnish close-up view of war. Eclipse linked to mad cow disease in Canada and ban on exports. Eclipse also of emphasis for Australia, Egypt, France, Israel, Mexico, Vatican City, Los Angeles, New York City, and Manhattan.

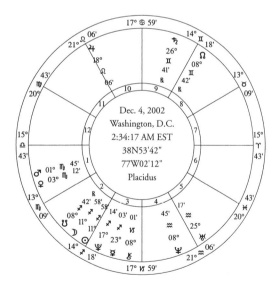

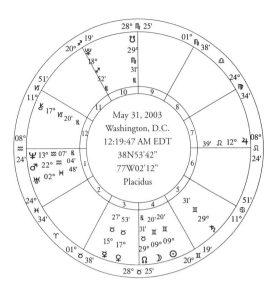

Solar Eclipse in Gemini

Washington, D.C. Eclipse Chart, Name: Winds and Party Splits, Date: May 31, 2003.

Accents transport, communications, education, and documents. Disputes affecting religion. Debating journalists. Eclipse in degree of Aldebaran: warmongering. Charges of treachery. Travel misfortunes. For USA, eclipse on Uranus, ruling electricity, computer technology. Homeland security tested. Public unrest: in the dark on some matter; unexpected developments. Mysterious crimes or fraud. Unfavorable for land and house property. Ill feelings between people and government. Criticism, discrepancies, and scandal. Potential downfall of well-known person. This eclipse is emphasized for Australia, Egypt, Israel, Iran, Mexico, Russia, NASA, Los Angeles, New York City, and Manhattan.

Lunar Eclipse in Taurus

Washington, D.C. Eclipse Chart, Name: Money Matters and Taxes, Date: Nov. 8, 2003.

Eclipse accents finances and agriculture. Religious disputes and travel hazards. Reputation of prominent person in jeopardy, crimes or scandal. For the USA, the nation's popularity abroad fluctuates. Issues of food and humanitarian aid. Developments with allies. Accent on commerce and shipping. Education disputes and strikes, lawsuits involving entertainment figures. Venus, ruling comforts, is disturbed by Mars, suggesting problems for workers, high expenditure of military, and potential illnesses. Coastal storms. Benefits to those in need. Earthquake potential. Eclipse falls on China's Venus: perhaps an encore of SARS. The eclipse falls on the White House Neptune, planet of intrigue and mystery. This eclipse is of emphasis for Australia, Canada, Cuba, the United Kingdom, Israel, Palestine, the United Nations, Los Angeles, Manhattan, Phoenix, and NASA.

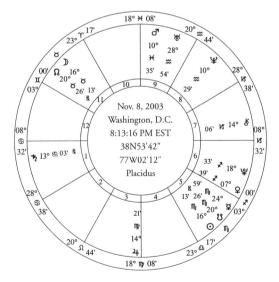

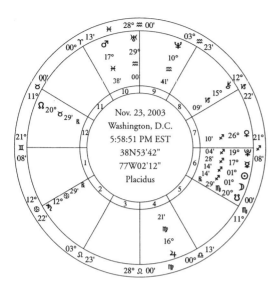

Solar Eclipse in Sagittarius

Washington, D.C. Eclipse Chart, Name: Brewing Dissension, Date: Nov. 23, 2003.

Accents religion, courts of law, foreign affairs, and distant travel. Jupiter and Mars square Mercury: religious disputes, travel hazards, bad for trade, difficulties for journalists. Uranus square eclipse: strikes, riots, technology problems. For USA, affairs are critical for employment, civil workers, and health care. Labor disputes, worker discontent, military movement, and strategies tested; conflict with enemy. Surprise elements surround president, and government may take false step. Global travel raises potential for spread of viruses. This eclipse is emphasized for Vatican City, Australia, China, France, North Korea, Mexico, Palestine, NASA, New York City, Roswell, and the White House.

Solar Eclipse in Aries

Washington, D.C. Eclipse Chart, Name: Apprehension, Date: April 19, 2004.

Eclipse ruled by Mars: warlike tones, conflict, accidents, or sickness. Eclipse in degree of fixed star Mirach: okay for martial matters but bad for domestic affairs. For USA, trouble in the religious world, dissensions and/or failed legislations. Political excitement and angry debates. Risky position for leaders; popularity abroad in question, possible loss of ally. Mars and Pluto opposition: secret enemies, viruses. A potentially powerful enemy comes to light. Crime increases, many captures are made. Aid to the needy. Aids literature and education. (Cattle problems?) Peak of stimulation in the fall of 2004. This eclipse is of emphasis for Iraq, Japan, the United Nations, the NYSE, New York City, Los Angeles, France, Vatican City, Phoenix, and the Twin Towers (activity around Ground Zero?).

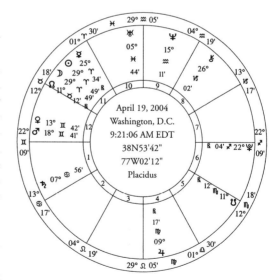

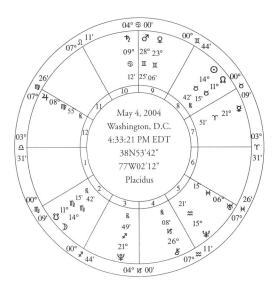

Lunar Eclipse in Scorpio

Washington, D.C. Eclipse Chart, Name: Sex, Death and Taxes, Date: May 4, 2004.

Rulers Pluto and Mars: feverish, bad for health, questions of mortality. Trouble for laboring classes and occupations connected with water, liquids, and the sea. Earthquakes. Threat to prominent person. Mysterious crimes and scandals. Sex crimes. For USA, money matters critical. Government has deep concerns; removes obstacles and makes reforms. Treaties and talks with foreign countries. Negotiations regarding imports, exports, and foreign trade. Restoring sociability. Literature and publishing enhanced. Legal and religious disputes. Breach of promises. Failed legislation. Eclipse emphasized for Canada, Cuba, Palestine, the United Nations, Manhattan, Israel, Vatican City, NASA, and the White House.

Solar Eclipse in Libra

Washington, D.C. Eclipse Chart, Name: High Society Disturbances, Date: Oct. 13, 2004.

Changes affect public tranquility. Libra spotlights judges, peacekeeping; complicated court cases and scandals. Issues of equality. Unfortunate for social life and marriage. Military movement, increase and expansion. Benefits to charities and hospitals. For USA, eclipse emphasizes entertainment, stock market, birth rate, children's interests, and issues of morality. Bad for schools and children's education; legislation unpopular. Hinders transit and communications. Storms at sea. Finance suffers; failure to meet expectations. Social and family life adversely affected. Unexpected or mysterious deaths. Public funeral. First peak: Halloween of 2004. Emphasized for Egypt, Israel, Iraq, Japan, Afghanistan, Russia, Mexico, Palestine, Phoenix, NASA, the NYSE, the United Nations, and the Twin Towers (activity at Ground Zero?).

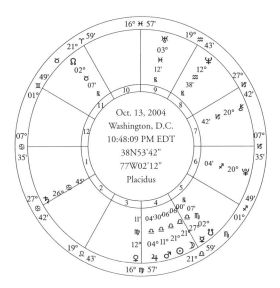

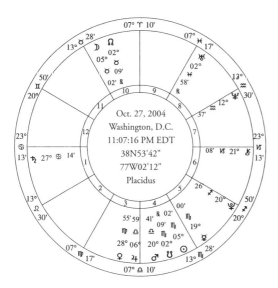

Lunar Eclipse in Taurus

Washington, D.C. Eclipse Chart, Name: Culminations, Date: Oct. 27, 2004.

Eclipse in Taurus: emphasizing money, comfort, and material needs. Agricultural concerns, possible cattle disease. For USA, eclipse in Tenth House tends to be unfortunate for government; troubles of one kind or another. Law and order are preserved, and Venus shows an increase of peace and goodwill following. Country infused with spirit. Could be social scandals, public ceremony. Improvements in education, new military strategies. A lady of eminence may suffer. Eclipse emphasized in importance for Iran, Cuba, France, Japan, Mexico, North Korea, Vatican City, Russia, New York City, the NYSE, and NASA.

Solar Eclipse in Aries

Washington, D.C. Eclipse Chart, Name: Seeking New Solutions, Date: April 8, 2005.

Aries eclipse: new enterprises. Venus is Lord (Lady) of eclipse, ruling material and creature comforts. Venus in degree of fixed star Baten Kaitos; associated with shipwreck and isolation. Threat of imprisonment or death of a leader and/or a notable woman. For U.S.: questions of mortality and changes in nation's earning power, assets in property, stocks, and bonds and/or receipt of benefits, insurance, pensions. Saturn afflicts eclipse: loss or delayed benefits. Encourages medical and health discoveries; new programs. Peak: July 5, 2005 (Mars), and Sept. 3, 2005 (Jupiter; gains/losses). This eclipse emphasized in importance for Egypt, Afghanistan, Iran, Japan, Mexico, Phoenix, the United Nations, the NYSE, Manhattan, the Twin Towers (activity at Ground Zero?), and the White House.

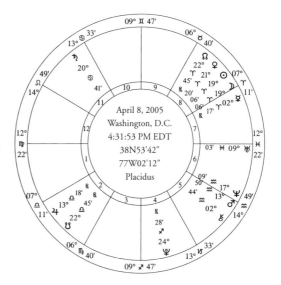

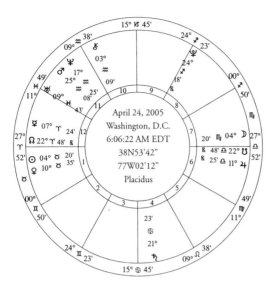

Lunar Eclipse in Scorpio

Washington, D.C. Eclipse Chart, Name: Repairs and Renovations, Date: April 24, 2005.

Ruled by Pluto: thunder, lightning, and earthquakes. For USA, an accent on financial relations with foreign nations. Mars in beneficial contact to Pluto: power for reform; opportunities in foreign relations, shipping, imports, exports, and religious matters. Government shows strength in spite of problems, and legislation progresses. Trouble affecting working classes or health of citizens. Wet and cold weather. Land and property restrictions. Jupiter over U.S. Saturn: growing within structure of limitations. This eclipse is of emphasized importance for Cuba, France, Iraq, Mexico, North Korea, Russia, Vatican City, NASA, and the NYSE.

Solar Eclipse in Libra

Washington, D.C. Eclipse Chart, Name: International Relations, Date: Oct. 3, 2005.

Social issues; outer circumstances and turbulence affect public tranquility. Eclipse in degree of fixed stars Caphir and Vindemiatrix: poor health or difficulties; associated with widowhood. Issues of foreign finance. Changes in international relations. Material agitation or scarcity. For USA, eclipse denotes activity, tension, adjustments, moving through crisis affecting public health and welfare. Removal of obstacles, new regulations. Questions of mortality and death. Health peculiarities, morality and drug concerns. Potential virus-outbreak concerns. Changes affect post office, mail workers, transport, communications, and borders. This eclipse is emphasized for Palestine, the United Kingdom, China, Egypt, France, Iran, Israel, Japan, North Korea, Vatican City, the United Nations, NASA, New York City, Los Angeles, and Phoenix.

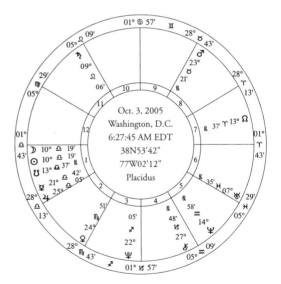

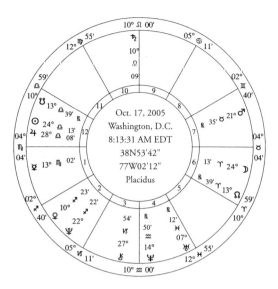

Lunar Eclipse in Aries

Washington, D.C. Eclipse Chart, Name: Aborted Births, Date: Oct. 17, 2005.

Military operations: Reviews and revisions are in order. For U.S., unfortunate for government; an official may die, suffer loss or disgrace. High national spending. Trade and communications disturbances. Bad press. Health, civil workers, and/or employment suffer. Needed adjustments in health care and hospitalization. Funding improves issue of central focus. May revolve around better pay or relief for civil workers, nursing care. Dragon's Tail on U.S. Saturn: concerns elderly. General dangers for women with Lunar eclipse in Aries. This eclipse is emphasized in importance for Russia, Iraq, Israel, Japan, Manhattan, New York City, Los Angeles, Phoenix, NASA, and the NYSE.

Lunar Eclipse in Virgo

Washington, D.C. Eclipse Chart, Name: Environment and Health, Date: March 14, 2006.

Mercury rules and is retrograde in Pisces: environmental and health concerns; reviews, research, and programs involving hospitals, aid, and institutions. Mercury trine Jupiter: optimism and faith; success in faith healings. Mars square Uranus: unexpected events, innovative enterprise, medical breakthroughs. Mars square Mercury: accident potential, especially travel-related or mechanical. For U.S., eclipse on Neptune: accents welfare, places of recovery, drugs, oil, and oceans. Discontent, distress, or sorrow among working class. Civil workers may deal with emergency situation. May show stormy weather, destruction of property, changes in domestics, general turbulence. This eclipse is emphasized for Canada, Egypt, Iran, Mexico, Manhattan, and NASA.

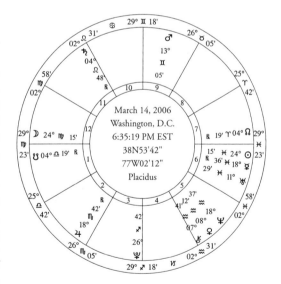

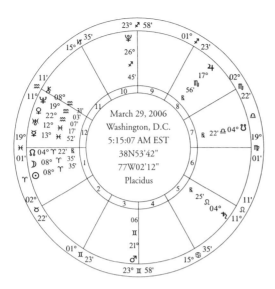

Solar Eclipse in Aries

Washington, D.C. Eclipse Chart, Name: Progress through Tumult, Date: March 29, 2006.

Signifies heat, fires, accidents. Death of noble, royal, or high-ranking officer. Saturn trines this eclipse: favorable for timely rescue and saving graces. For USA, fire in public buildings possible. Mars trine Venus and Neptune: restoring harmony, helping others, charitable works. Jupiter square Neptune: fraud, crimes, scandal. Success and reforms in municipal matters, military, aid to needy. Building prospers. Jupiter and Pluto in reception: spiritual renewal, religious healing. Complications for president. This eclipse is of emphasized importance for France, China, Egypt, Israel, Palestine, the United Kingdom, Iran, Japan, Mexico, North Korea, Vatican City, Los Angeles, New York City, Phoenix, NASA, and the United Nations.

Lunar Eclipse in Pisces

Washington, D.C. Eclipse Chart, Name: Shipping and Water Concerns, Date: Sept. 7, 2006.

Eclipse influenced by Neptune, and Uranus is Lord: uncertainties, confusion, and unexpected events cause unrest, perhaps relating to water or environmental issues. Delays, setbacks, or losses abroad. Death of famous star. For USA, travel and transit hazards. Impact on communications, utilities, and shipping. Discontent of postal workers, crimes, and discredit to municipal officers. Generally disruptive for transport and communications. Trade disputes. Legal and religious upsets. Fortunate discovery or invention, sudden opportunities. Jupiter and Pluto in reception: increases depth of investigative work. This eclipse is emphasized for Canada, China, Iran, Mexico, North Korea, Russia, Los Angeles, Manhattan, and the Twin Towers (activity at Ground Zero?).

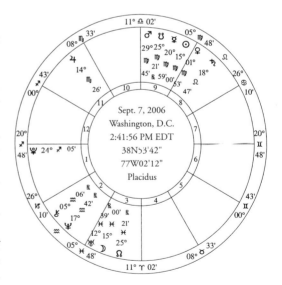

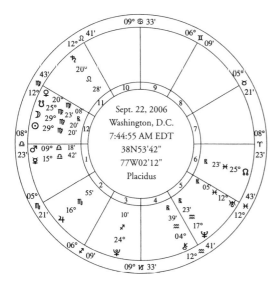

Solar Eclipse in Virgo

Washington, D.C. Eclipse Chart, Name: Parting with the Past, Date: Sept. 22, 2006.

Virgo accents health and civil-service workers. Adversities, warlike tones, hostilities directed toward officials. For USA, there are disadvantages or liabilities; some misfortune. There may be secret hostilities abroad or an increase of secret crimes. Political and religious misunderstandings, social struggles. Military or civil-service activities attract attention. Military successes. Work and trade increase. Changes affecting finances. Problems with shipping. Trouble for theaters, amusements, and social entertainment; losses from financial speculation. Concerns and activity surrounding charitable programs and institutions, prison systems, and places of rehab. Eclipse of emphasis for Afghanistan, the White House, Roswell, the NYSE, Canada, Iran, and NASA.

Lunar Eclipse in Virgo

Washington, D.C. Eclipse Chart, Name: Health and Recovery, Date: March 3, 2007.

Mercury rules Virgo, denoting health concerns, but Uranus becomes Lord, emphasizing surprising factors, perhaps including solutions, breakthrough discoveries. Mercury is retrograde: reviews, research, and refining details. Confusion and delays. For U.S., focus on public health, activities surrounding civil workers and laboring classes. Strikes, riots, and discontent among workers, problems for the navy. Drug experimentation, peculiar disorders. Hospitals and charities may lack funds or resources. Humanitarian movements. Changes in land and property markets. Activity surrounding entertainers. Eclipse of emphasis for Australia, China, Egypt, Mexico, North Korea, Palestine, Russia, and Los Angeles.

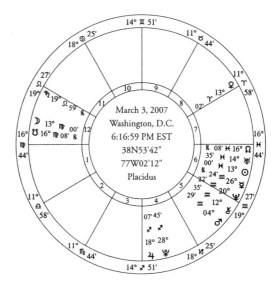

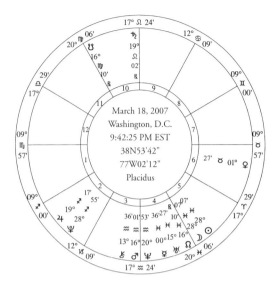

Solar Eclipse in Pisces

Washington, D.C. Eclipse Chart, Name: Lifestyle Changes, Date: March 18, 2007.

Neptune rules: accents popular movements, oil, actors, sickness abroad. Pluto squares this eclipse: breakdowns, decay, war tones, power struggles. For USA, concerns over children's interests and pursuits of pleasure; affects upper classes. Children's interests suffer. Death of a theatrical artist. Stock and investment losses. Problems in government; new methods cause trouble. Wasted resources. Peace and order disturbed but devotional religious movements grow. Crime toward prominent person. Discontent and difficulties among civil servants, military, and police—discredits them. Expenses. Trouble for water companies and turbulence in the land. Fires and/or explosions in public buildings, earthquakes. Eclipse of emphasis for Canada, Iran, Vatican City, the White House, NASA, and the NYSE.

Lunar Eclipse in Pisces

Washington, D.C. Eclipse Chart, Name: Public Excitement, Date: Aug. 28, 2007.

Ruled by Neptune: social movements. Grand Cross: widespread unrest, separations, religious sorrows, and grief for priests. Saturn in degree of Regulus: tremendous power or sudden downfall of someone in high office. For USA, unexpected disturbance and complications in international affairs. Trouble affecting churches and religion. Motoring or aviation accidents. Disturbances in government, excitement, military questions arise. Prominent person in royal or political circles may die. This eclipse of emphasis for Canada, the United Kingdom, the White House, France, Iran, Mexico, Vatican City, Phoenix, the Twin Towers (activity at Ground Zero?), and NASA.

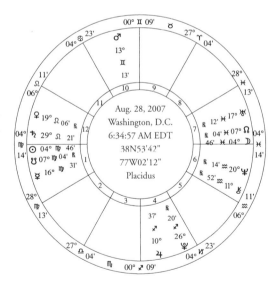

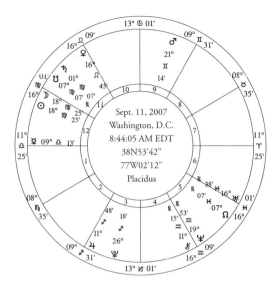

Solar Eclipse in Virgo

Washington, D.C. Eclipse Chart, Name: Fruits of the Earth, Date: Sept. 11, 2007.

Virgo emphasizes health and environmental concerns. Grand Cross and Uranus in opposition to eclipse suggest social unrest and unusual emergencies, perhaps food shortages, crop problems, a virus or fever. For USA, focus is on public health and welfare, hospitals and charitable institutions. Concerns and uncertainties about loved ones. Hazardous conditions in shipping and travel, accidents or explosions on warships, death of sailors, clerics. Drugs, oil, or alcohol issues and/or handling peculiar health problems or an emergency. Potential strikes or rioting. This eclipse is of emphasis for Canada, Iran, North Korea, Mexico, the NYSE, and the Twin Towers (activity at Ground Zero?).

Solar Eclipse in Aquarius

Washington, D.C. Eclipse Chart, Name: Attaining Group Ideals, Date: Feb. 6, 2008.

Eclipse in Aquarius, sign of the brotherhood fraternity. Retrograde Mercury is Lord: emphasizes messengers, travelers, thieves, and bandits. Group spokesperson in the spotlight, whose ego identifies with own ideas: dislike of hypocrisy; may have hidden agenda. Eclipse falls on the USA Moon: changes affect "the common people" and working classes. Home, land, and domestic concerns; taxation. Government troubles. Pluto in Aries Point degree suggests turning points regarding nuclear or atomic energy, war on terror, reform leaders, sexual issues. Coastal and shipping focus. Changeable weather and air. Foggy condition. Eclipse of emphasis for Afghanistan, China, Cuba, the United Kingdom, Israel, Iran, Iraq, Japan, North Korea, Manhattan, the NYSE, and NASA.

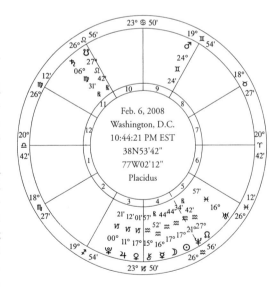

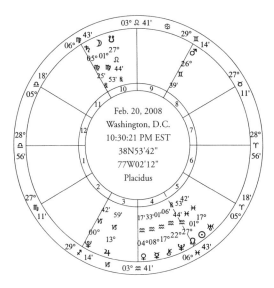

Lunar Eclipse in Virgo

Washington, D.C. Eclipse Chart, Name: Practical Solutions, Date: Feb. 20, 2008.

Accents public health and welfare. Cases of want and social dissatisfaction. Trade suffers. For USA, difficulties for government, dissension, or delayed legislation. Crop or employment problems, worker discontent and strife. New military undertakings, increasing strength of army and navy. Benefits to charities. Coastal storms and potential shipping accidents. Travel- and transit-related dangers and concerns. Pluto in Aries Point degree and trine to eclipse: opportunity for changes to vehicles and transport systems to aid environmental efforts. Jupiter in critical degree: church or foreign dignitary makes news. This eclipse is of emphasis for the United Kingdom, Cuba, Phoenix, NASA, Iran, Iraq, and the White House.

Solar Eclipse in Leo

Washington, D.C. Eclipse Chart, Name: Sensational Events, Date: Aug. 1, 2008.

Leo spotlights royalty, world leaders, and central figures. Poses threats. Lord Mercury accents a youthful leader of dramatic speech. For USA, eclipse falls on Dragon's Head: ambitious offensive action often follows events happening here. Great deal of activity at the Capitol. Political and public excitement, discussions, speeches, printed news, crime and court cases. Secret plots by foreign powers. Financial frauds and/or bad for marriages. Separations, crimes toward women. Country's finances squeezed by unexpected expenses. Shipping accidents and unusual deaths. This eclipse is also emphasized for Israel, Iraq, Afghanistan, France, Russia, the United Nations, Manhattan, the NYSE, and the Twin Towers (activity at Ground Zero?).

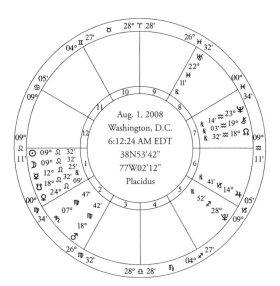

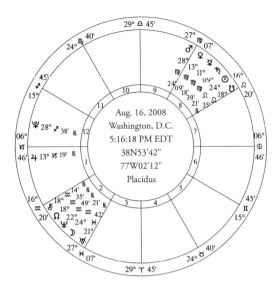

Lunar Eclipse in Aquarius

Washington, D.C. Eclipse Chart, Name: Changes in All Things, Date: Aug. 16, 2008.

Eclipse in Aquarius. Neptune is Lord of the eclipse: dissolve, illusion, mystery. Since Neptune is in reception with Uranus, a combination of influences makes for unpredictable and strange potentials. Bizarre estrangements, separations, and culminations. Charitable works and goodwill. For USA, changes pertaining to mortality or death of a statesman and transitions in national wealth and earning potential; taxes, pensions, interest rates, and foreign stocks and bonds. Extravagances. Problems in shipping, travel, and foreign affairs. Eclipse emphasized for Egypt, Iraq, Los Angeles, Phoenix, the United Kingdom, Japan, Mexico, Manhattan, the NYSE, and the White House.

Solar Eclipse in Aquarius

Washington, D.C. Eclipse Chart, Name: Reform and Resistance, Date: Jan. 26, 2009.

Eclipse in humanitarian sign. Jupiter is Lord of the eclipse, emphasizing foreign affairs, religious and judicial matters. Jupiter expands themes suggesting global and universal values. For USA, eclipse falls on Dragon's Tail (to serve and transcend) and in house of national wealth, banks, financial transactions, and decisions of legislature that cost the public. There are major transitions taking place with potential for new corporate enterprises and financial organizations and group goals. Potential dissension from landowners to government plans, but many progressive influences and ability to overcome differences. Travel and transport changes. Turbulent weather. This eclipse is also of emphasis for Afghanistan, China, Canada, France, Israel, Russia, Los Angeles, Manhattan, NASA, the White House, and the Twin Towers (activity or ceremony at Ground Zero?).

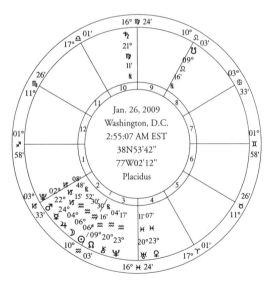

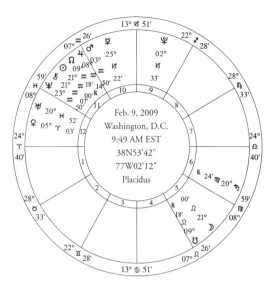

Lunar Eclipse in Leo

Washington, D.C. Eclipse Chart, Name: Stirs Insurrection, Date: Feb. 9, 2009.

Leo brings world leaders into view: threats are posed. Eclipse in degree of fixed star Algenubi: "he who rends," suggests focus upon, or pressure from, someone of artistic expression, yet of potentially brutish influence. Neptune is Lord of the eclipse: social movements. Unrest abroad. For USA, public opinion fluctuates regarding work conditions, health services, and children's welfare. The government is beset by troubles, legislation is confused; failure of measures. Financial fluctuations. Nutrition and health concerns. Hospital resources in question. This eclipse of emphasis for Afghanistan, Iraq, Egypt, the United Kingdom, Japan, Mexico, Manhattan, the NYSE, and the White House.

Lunar Eclipse in Capricorn

Washington, D.C. Eclipse Chart, Name: National Concerns, Date: July 7, 2009.

Eclipse brings state executives, law enforcement authorities, and business matters to the fore. Eclipse in degree of fixed star Wega: public disgrace, losses through writings or forgery, gains through pensions and annuities. For the USA with emphasis to Sun: challenges, but with good chances for successes to follow. Situations are uncertain, mysterious, and surprising regarding issues abroad. Changes in international affairs. Shipping disputes and discontent of sailors. Political excitement. The president is subject to surprising developments, unpopularity, and/or intrigue. Spread of mysticism, religious disputes. This eclipse is of emphasis for Cuba, Russia, Japan, Phoenix, Vatican City, Los Angeles, Manhattan, Roswell, the NYSE, and the Twin Towers (activity at Ground Zero?).

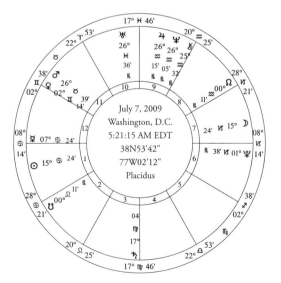

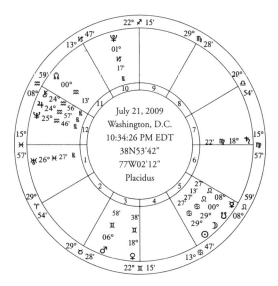

Solar Eclipse in Cancer

Washington, D.C. Eclipse Chart, Name: Desire for Reforms, Date: July 21, 2009.

Eclipse ruled by the Moon, emphasizes domestic issues, women's interests, home and family matters. Fluctuations of public opinion. For USA, eclipse falls opposite Pluto: need for purging and reform. National dispute. Upper classes disturbed, desire reform. Charges of treachery. Outrage against authority. Change of status for president, who goes behind the scenes. Also, focus on children's interests, birth rate, amusements, and speculation. Increases in communications, transport, and aviation. Benefits inventions, discoveries, and technology. Hindrances in money matters. Expenses. This eclipse also of emphasis for Afghanistan, Iran, North Korea, Phoenix, Cuba, the United Kingdom, Palestine, Los Angeles, Manhattan, and New York City.

Lunar Eclipse in Aquarius

Washington, D.C. Eclipse Chart, Name: Humanitarian Deeds, Date: Aug. 5, 2009.

Eclipse ruled by the revolutionary Uranus and in degree of fixed star Dorsum: an unfortunate influence. Danger of strikes, riots, and rebellion. For the USA, there's an infusion of energy but discontent with government. Sociological turbulence and excitement, ill temper, or lawlessness. Eclipse accents concerns over secret crimes and criminals, places of rehab and charitable works. The president deeply immersed in such matters. May be concerns for excessive expenses in regard to these or for bettering prison or hospital conditions and/or virtual healing centers. This eclipse of emphasis for Cuba, Egypt, France, China, Iran, the United Kingdom, Israel, Iraq, North Korea, Vatican City, the United Nations, NASA, and the NYSE.

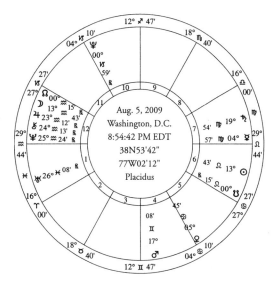

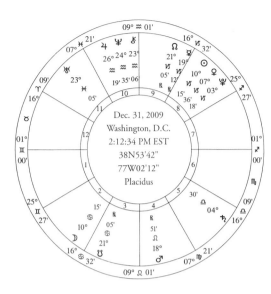

Lunar Eclipse in Cancer

Washington, D.C. Eclipse Chart, Name: Burdens and Sorrows, Date: Dec. 31, 2009.

Sensitivities heightened. Venus is Lord (Lady) of the eclipse: changes affecting social harmony or monetary affairs. There may be trouble in trade, delays or obstructions in legislation. Activity and troubles abroad. Accents a much-loved authority figure. For the USA, the eclipse falls on the Sun, bringing the president front and center after a period of obscurity; handling power, accepting or relinquishing responsibilities. Some misfortune may overshadow the social side of the nation. A focus on values: death and rebirth. Benefits to science. This eclipse of emphasis for Australia, Canada, Egypt, France, the United Kingdom, Japan, Palestine, Russia, the United Nations, and New York City.

Solar Eclipse in Capricorn

Washington, D.C. Eclipse Chart, Name: Ceremony Fit for a King, Date: Jan. 15, 2010.

Focus on national affairs. Venus and Saturn share Lordship of the eclipse: engagement or marriage of royalty or other religious ceremonials. Travel of royalty. For the USA, a ceremony involving a prominent person. People are well-disposed toward the government. National expenses may be high. May be the death of a wealthy person or someone in the legal, religious, or scientific world. The eclipse falling in the Third House brings increase in publications, excitable opinions, and neighboring nations are friendly. Power and vigor infused into the country. Science and education benefit. Eclipse across both Mercury and Pluto: brings changes to trade, inland transit, communication, and transport sectors. Possible breakdowns and reconstruction. This eclipse is also of emphasis for Afghanistan, China, Israel, New York City, Phoenix, Cuba, and the United Nations.

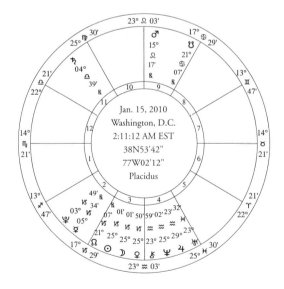

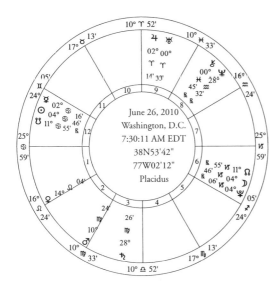

Lunar Eclipse in Capricorn

Washington, D.C. Eclipse Chart, Name: A Rough Patch, Date: June 26, 2010.

Focus on national and domestic business. Eclipse features a Grand Cross involving seven planets and two Lords—Pluto and Mercury: obstructions in transport and communications. For the USA, focus is on health, employment, and civil servants. Discontent affects public harmony. Changes involve jobs, health, civil servants, rehab centers. Uranus in an Aries Degree point: historical marker for science. Research on secret projects, but potential indiscretions lead to danger. There are themes of obsession and mutually coercive tactics to win domination. Conspiracies among men. This eclipse is also of emphasis for Afghanistan, Australia, Canada, China, Los Angeles, Roswell, and the United Nations.

Solar Eclipse in Cancer

Washington, D.C. Eclipse Chart, Name: Victory over Obstacles, Date: July 11, 2010.

Cancer eclipse spotlights interests relating to domestic issues, homes, land, and crops. Eclipse falls in degree of fixed star Castor: of a wicked influence; associated with decapitation, fevers, rape, and murder. For the USA, eclipse brings emphasis to foreign affairs, long-distance travel, higher education, publishing, and religion. There is practical problem solving. Financial stress present with delay of new opportunity for expansion and growth. Banks and markets subject to fluctuations. Unusual trends in the pursuit of pleasure, romance, and entertainment; restrictions apply. New educational programs are costly. This eclipse is of emphasis for Iraq, the White House, the United Kingdom, Vatican City, Los Angeles, Manhattan, New York City, and Roswell.

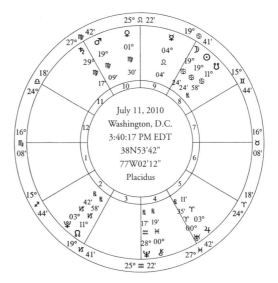

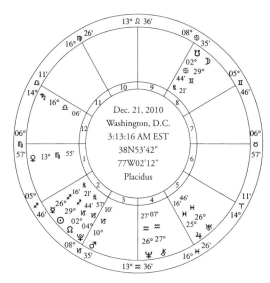

Lunar Eclipse in Gemini

Washington, D.C. Eclipse Chart, Name: Intellectual Values, Date: Dec. 21, 2010.

As Lord of the eclipse, retrograde Mercury signifies youthful persons; the witty, the jokester, or the thief. It emphasizes communications, travel and transit, literary and educational persons. May be the loss or death of a renowned writer, professor, or illustrious person. Eclipse in last degree of sign: resolving old issues; foreign agreements, religious or educational matters. Fortunate for publications of mysticism. For the USA, focus in financial sectors. Erratic pace of incoming information. Nerves high-strung. May be mechanical malfunctions. Imaginative movements in music and entertainment. This eclipse of emphasis for Afghanistan, Japan, North Korea, Palestine, Vatican City, Phoenix, Australia, Cuba, Israel, Manhattan, and New York City.

Solar Eclipse in Capricorn

Washington, D.C. Eclipse Chart, Name: The Balance of Power, Date: Jan. 4, 2011.

Focus on business and national affairs. Eclipse in a critical degree: denoting potential for a central event having wide-range impact. Eclipse in degree of fixed star Manubrium: flaring heat. A turbulent spirit against those in high places. For the USA, the eclipse falls over the Sun: U.S. administration and government crucially linked to larger world affairs. There is potentially powerful opposition to overcome. For U.S., eclipse in house of earning power and expenditures: obstacles, legislative delays. Trade and labor restricted. Meditation, yoga, and/or self-indulgences to cope with discontent. Eclipse of emphasis for Japan, Russia, the United Nations, Cuba, New York City, Phoenix, and the NYSE.

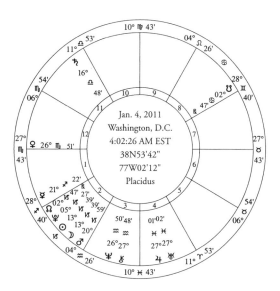

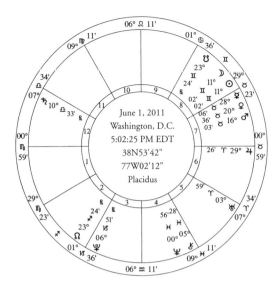

Solar Eclipse in Gemini

Washington, D.C. Eclipse Chart, Name: Something to Cry About, Date: June 1, 2011.

Mercury rules eclipse: focus on communications and transit. For the USA, eclipse falls on Uranus: surprising developments. Government may deal with a loss of support. Eclipse in Eighth House: attention and discussions on taxation, imports, sanitation, mortality, burial laws, or contagion. Potential death or resignation of a statesman and/or a literary figure, writer, educator, or travelers. Treaties, agreements may be strained in foreign relations. Potential workers strikes, military moves, and/or urgent health situation. Dealing with hospital or prison conditions and mysterious crimes. Eclipse of emphasis for Australia, Egypt, France, Israel, Mexico, Vatican City, Los Angeles, Manhattan, and New York City.

Lunar Eclipse in Sagittarius

Washington, D.C. Eclipse Chart, Name: Restoring Peace and Prosperity, Date: June 15, 2011.

Jupiter-ruled eclipse puts focus on foreign, religious, and judicial matters as well as world travel and travelers. For the USA, Mercury closely aligns with eclipse, and its position in Eighth House continues talks and discussions regarding taxation on imports, sanitation, burials, hospital conditions. Chart features very similar to last eclipse, however new information comes to light, allowing some matters to improve. Foreign relations improve, becoming more prosperous. Some adjustments possible only through high-spirited arguments and disputes. Potential travel accidents, attention on crime, rehab, hospitals. The marriage rate increases and someone of high profile marries. This eclipse is of emphasis for Afghanistan, Phoenix, Australia, France, Israel, the United Nations, Manhattan, and Roswell.

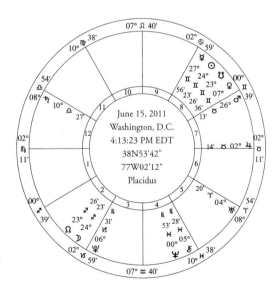

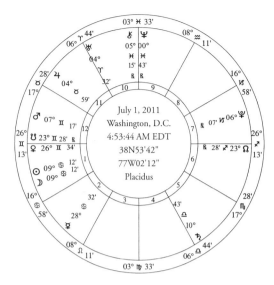

Solar Eclipse in Cancer

Washington, D.C. Eclipse Chart, Name: Democratic Spirit, Date: July 1, 2011.

Cancer eclipse: fluctuations affecting domestic harmony, emotional security; accents home, real estate, and family matters. Grand Cross involving the Sun, Moon, Saturn, Uranus, and Pluto: restrictions, need for flexibility, and power struggles. For the USA, the eclipse falls near the U.S. Sun and Jupiter: potential difficulties for government. Eclipse in First House: accents issues regarding health and welfare of citizens with benefits for those in need. Power to conquer. Potential disturbance in trade and commerce and unfortunate for building and land. Eclipse of emphasis for Afghanistan, Australia, Canada, Egypt, France, the United Kingdom, Japan, Palestine, Russia, the United Nations, and New York City.

Solar Eclipse in Sagittarius

Washington, D.C. Eclipse Chart, Name: Blazing New Trails, Date: Nov. 25, 2011.

Jupiter-ruled eclipse: accents publishing, travel, religion, and foreign relations. Potential for grand and useful reforms. For the USA, eclipse in Third House shows travel of president and/or focus on travel conditions and transport workers. Potential for accidents and/or discontent of workers. Extension of power of nation in world, although some complications to overcome. Concerns over secret enemies and/or prison or hospital conditions. A mysterious crime and/or scandal emerges. May increase divorce rate. May be death of noble. This eclipse is of emphasis for Afghanistan, China, Australia, France, Mexico, North Korea, Palestine, Roswell, New York City, NASA, and the White House.

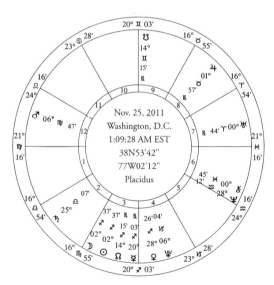

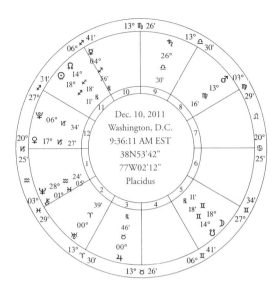

Lunar Eclipse in Gemini

Washington, D.C. Eclipse Chart, Name: Solicitations, Date: Dec. 10, 2011.

Mercury-ruled eclipse: accents messengers and speakers, youth, transport, communications, and education. For the USA, the eclipse falls on Mars, ruler of military, and affecting activity in the marketplace. Focus on speculation, stock market, children's interests, birth rate, and places of amusement. Falling birth rate. Deaths of soldiers or those engaged in Mars occupations. Health concerns. Mercury retrograde: reviews of legislation regarding education, transport, and communication. Spirited debates. Could be good for literary projects, scientific discoveries, inventions, and beneficial strides in motoring and aviation. Eclipse of emphasis for Australia, Canada, Cuba, France, the United Kingdom, Iran, Iraq, North Korea, Russia, Vatican City, New York City, Roswell, NASA, and the United Nations.

Solar Eclipse in Gemini

Washington, D.C. Eclipse Chart, Name: Property Agreements, Date: May 20, 2012.

Mercury-ruled eclipse: accents communications, mobility, and transport. There is contention and potential for deceptions. For the USA, a treaty may be involved. Visiting ambassadors. There are troublesome uncertainties and unsettling times. An underestimation of efforts risks failure. Mars overhead shows quarrels and conflicts, warlike themes, and/or military involvement. Mercury shows complicated situations and communication obstacles over high-cost matters: prosperous potential. Concerns: finance and material. Crime rate changes, railway or mechanical accidents. Risky speculations. Unusual effects to entertainment venues. This eclipse is of emphasis for Australia, Cuba, the White House, France, Mexico, North Korea, Palestine, Vatican City, New York City, Roswell, and NASA.

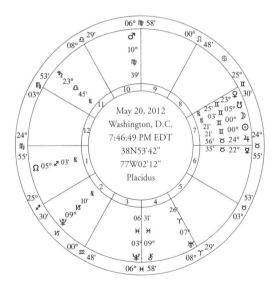

Annotated Catalog of National Figures

In this annotated catalog of national figures, you will find the horoscopes for a sampling of countries and U.S. cities. The catalog includes some anecdotal information surrounding previous and coming eclipses that are of emphasis for each of the entries. This helps give an idea of how to judge the meaning or message of an eclipse falling on important places in the chart of a national figure. For example, an eclipse to France's Mars, ruling such things as heat, preceded the killer heat wave in France in 2003. SARS brought problems for both Canada and China following eclipses that impacted Venus in those national charts, with Venus suggesting changes having an effect on public tranquility. As one more example, similar eclipse patterns were in force in NASA's horoscope preceding both the Challenger and the Columbia tragedies.

While an eclipse chart indicates mundane events both large and small, it may prove even more informative to track the eclipse as it falls on important places in the charts of national figures. All of those listings are given for the entries included here, with the planets or points that receive specific eclipse stimulation in each national figure through 2011. An eclipse falling on the Sun of a national figure is among the most important.

USA cities include Los Angeles, Manhattan, New York City, Phoenix, and Roswell. The Twin Towers horoscope is included, although we now call the area Ground Zero. Eclipses falling in that chart may continue to show activity around Ground Zero until there is a new structure and memorial in place.

Other enterprises and horoscopes include the New York Stock Exchange, NASA, the White House, the United Nations, and Vatican City.

Other countries besides the USA are Afghanistan, Australia, Canada, China, Cuba, Egypt, France, Iran, Iraq, Israel, Japan, Mexico, North Korea, Palestine, Russia, and the United Kingdom.

If your country or city is listed, you can follow the important eclipses taking place through 2011.

Every effort has been made to furnish accurate horoscopes for the national figures, with data double- and triple-checked against the most reputable sources. Sources are included.

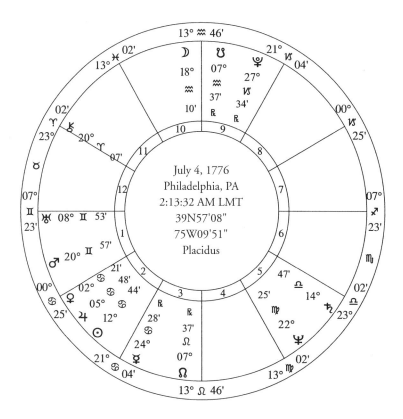

July 4, 1776
Philadelphia, PA
2:13:32 AM LMT
39N57'08"
75W09'51"
Placidus

USA

The birth of the nation took place when the Declaration of Independence was signed. The First House describes an entity, and here we see Gemini rising, the sign of declarations. Mars in the First House describes a fight (against Britain) to achieve independence, ruled by Mars. Though Uranus had not yet been discovered, it is rising in the chart, appropriately reflecting a revolt for freedom. Eclipses falling on planets in the USA chart identify important happenings for the USA. Due to its status as the # 1 world power, those same eclipses often identify important developments affecting the rest of the world. An example would be the 2001 eclipses on important U.S. placements that reverberated around the world following the terror attacks on September 11. The timing of events often coincides with transits to eclipses, as noted in that case. As another example, transiting Mars' later stimulation to the 2002 eclipse across the USA Ascendant closely coincided with the launch and disappearance of the shuttle Columbia, the latter event more precisely timed by a New Moon on the USA MC opposed by Jupiter, and with additional stress to Mars and Uranus. The 2008 eclipse falling on the U.S. Dragon's Head shall most assuredly stir the dragon to action. These eclipses are often followed by offensive action and military moves.

To find the people and things emphasized by eclipses listed on the next page, refer to table 4. To find the power rating of an eclipse, refer to table 1. This table also lists dates of major planetary stimulation to each eclipse, which may closely coincide with notable events traceable to the eclipse. Though there are a few versions of the U.S. chart with slight variations, the list of eclipses given here will be accommodating no matter the chart of choice. Data for this popular all-time favorite can be verified at AstroDatabank.com. Source notes: Ray Allen Billington, Bert James Loewenborg, and Samuel Hugh Brockunier, *The United States* (New York: Rinehart and Co., 1947), p. 15: "The symbolic first breath, or birth hour, of the nation occurred in the early morning hours of July 4, 1776."

Eclipse Emphasis for the USA through 2011

July 1, 2000, Solar Eclipse emphasizes—The Sun

July 16, 2000, Lunar Eclipse emphasizes—Mercury

July 30, 2000, Solar Eclipse emphasizes—The Dragon's Head

Dec. 25, 2000, Solar Eclipse emphasizes—Venus and Jupiter

June 21, 2001, Solar Eclipse emphasizes—Venus

July 5, 2001, Lunar Eclipse emphasizes—The Sun

Dec. 14, 2001, Solar Eclipse emphasizes—Mars

Dec. 30, 2001, Lunar Eclipse emphasizes—Jupiter

May 26, 2002, Lunar Eclipse emphasizes—The Ascendant

June 10, 2002, Solar Eclipse emphasizes—Mars

June 24, 2002, Lunar Eclipse emphasizes—Venus and Jupiter

May 30, 2003, Solar Eclipse emphasizes—The Ascendant and Uranus

Oct. 13, 2004, Solar Eclipse emphasizes—Chiron (Wounded Healer)

April 8, 2005, Solar Eclipse emphasizes—Chiron (Wounded Healer)

March 14, 2006, Lunar Eclipse emphasizes—Neptune

Feb. 6, 2008, Solar Eclipse emphasizes—The Moon

Aug. 1, 2008, Solar Eclipse emphasizes—The Dragon's Head

Jan. 26, 2009, Solar Eclipse emphasizes—The Dragon's Tail

Feb. 9, 2009, Lunar Eclipse emphasizes—The Moon

July 7, 2009, Lunar Eclipse emphasizes—The Sun

July 21, 2009, Solar Eclipse emphasizes—Pluto

Aug. 5, 2009, Lunar Eclipse emphasizes—The Midheaven

Dec. 31, 2009, Lunar Eclipse emphasizes—The Sun

Jan. 15, 2010, Solar Eclipse emphasizes—Pluto and Mercury

June 26, 2010, Lunar Eclipse emphasizes—Venus and Jupiter

Jan. 4, 2011, Solar Eclipse emphasizes—The Sun

June 1, 2011, Solar Eclipse emphasizes—Uranus

July 1, 2011, Solar Eclipse emphasizes—The Sun

Dec. 10, 2011, Lunar Eclipse emphasizes—Mars

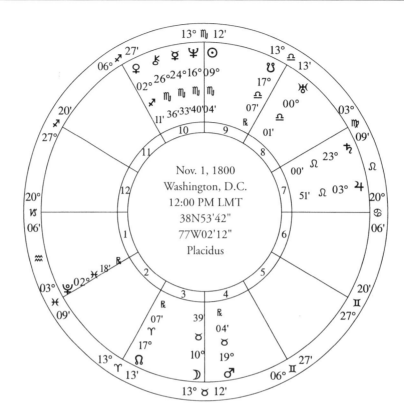

White House

The true birth of the White House came when a U.S. president first took up residency, reflected in the chart above. Eclipses falling prominently in this chart reflect activities at the White House as it functions as home to the First Family, with the president as head of household, and as headquarters where some of the most important decisions are made. To cite an example, the Lunar Eclipse of May 15, 2003, fell on the White House Mercury, ruling communicators. Press Secretary Ari Fleischer, representative for the White House, resigned from his post shortly following. That same eclipse would spotlight all things connected to communications and intelligence into and out of the White House for some time.

To find the people and things emphasized by eclipses listed here, refer to table 4. To find the raw power rating of any eclipse, refer to table 1. That table also gives the dates of planetary stimulation to the eclipse, which may coincide closely with notable events traceable to the eclipse. Eclipse power increases by the number of contacts it makes to planets in the White House chart, an indication of its importance for the White House family and staff. See more definition of future eclipses in the Catalog of Annotated Eclipse Charts. The White House chart forms many significant connections to the First Cornerstone chart of Oct. 13, 1792. Data source: Freidel & Pencak, *The White House: The First Two Hundred Years* (Boston, MA: Northeastern University Press, 1994).

Eclipse Emphasis for the White House through 2011

Jan. 9, 2001, Lunar Eclipse emphasizes—The Ascendant

May 26, 2002, Lunar Eclipse emphasizes—Venus

Nov. 19, 2002, Lunar Eclipse emphasizes—Chiron (Wounded Healer)

May 15, 2003, Lunar Eclipse emphasizes—Mercury

Nov. 8, 2003, Lunar Eclipse emphasizes—Neptune and Mars

Nov. 23, 2003, Solar Eclipse emphasizes—Venus

May 4, 2004, Lunar Eclipse emphasizes—The Midheaven and Neptune

April 8, 2005, Solar Eclipse emphasizes—The Dragon's Head

Sept. 22, 2006, Solar Eclipse emphasizes—Uranus

March 18, 2007, Solar Eclipse emphasizes—Uranus

Aug. 28, 2007, Lunar Eclipse emphasizes—Pluto

Feb. 20, 2008, Lunar Eclipse emphasizes—Pluto

Aug. 16, 2008, Lunar Eclipse emphasizes—Saturn

Jan. 26, 2009, Solar Eclipse emphasizes—Jupiter

Feb. 9, 2009, Lunar Eclipse emphasizes—Saturn

July 11, 2010, Solar Eclipse emphasizes—The Ascendant

Nov. 25, 2011, Solar Eclipse emphasizes—Venus

May 20, 2012, Solar Eclipse emphasizes—Venus

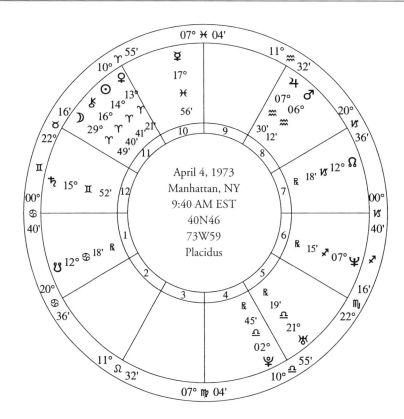

07° ♓ 04'

10° ♈ 55'
☿ 17°
11° ♒ 32'

☉ 13°
♀ 14°
♓ 56'
♃ 07°
♂ 06°

♉
16° 16°
☽ 29° ♈
♈ 41 21
40' 49'
11

30' 12'
♒

20° ♑ 36'

22° ♉

April 4, 1973
Manhattan, NY
9:40 AM EST
40N46
73W59
Placidus

℞ 18' ♑ 12° ☊

♄ 15° ♊ 52' 12

7
00° ♑ 40'

00° ♋ 40'
Ⅱ

1

6
℞ 15' ♐ 07° ♆ ♐

☋ 12° ♋ 18' ℞

2
16' ♏

5

3   4   ℞ 19' ♎

20° ♋ 36'

℞ 45' ♎

21° ♎

22° ♏

02°
♇ ♋
10° ♎ 55'

11° ♌ 32'

☿ ♎ 55'

07° ♍ 04'

Twin Towers

The Twin Towers are no more, collapsing as Mars stimulated the powerful eclipse of June 21, 2001, which fell on the Tower's Ascendant, representative of the structure itself. The Twin Towers birth chart is cast for the ribbon-cutting ceremony, unveiling the towers as a world trading center. The chart shows one of the powerful world point degrees rising, also called an Aries Point degree, to symbolize such worldly status. The construction of the towers was a highly debated project, proposed to bring prosperity to a deteriorating area. It was gray and rainy the morning it was dedicated, the attendees of the ribbon-cutting ceremony protecting themselves with umbrellas. (Source: 2002 History Channel documentary *World Trade Center: Rise and Fall of an American Icon*.) The symbolism is chilling. On September 11, 2001, the area around where the towers stood became referred to as Ground Zero. Because there remains a strong patriotic connection to the towers and what they stood for, they remain in memory and perhaps remain standing in a ghostly way. Eclipses listed here that follow 9/11 may continue to reflect activity at Ground Zero for some time.

To find the people and things emphasized by coming eclipses, refer to table 4. To find the raw power rating of an eclipse, refer to table 1. That table also gives the dates of stimulation to the eclipse, which may closely coincide with notable events that are traceable to the eclipse. Watch for the ribbon-cutting ceremony for the new structure, at which time a new chart can be constructed. That new chart will undoubtedly make strong connections to this one and to the USA chart. Note connections from this chart to the USA chart.

Eclipse Emphasis for the Twin Towers Area through 2011

July 1, 2000, Solar Eclipse emphasizes—The Dragon's Tail

July 30, 2000, Solar Eclipse emphasizes—Mars and Jupiter

June 21, 2001, Solar Eclipse emphasizes—The Ascendant

July 5, 2001, Lunar Eclipse emphasizes—The Dragon's Head

May 26, 2002, Lunar Eclipse emphasizes—Neptune

June 24, 2002, Lunar Eclipse emphasizes—The Ascendant

May 30, 2003, Solar Eclipse emphasizes—Neptune

April 19, 2004, Solar Eclipse emphasizes—The Moon

Oct. 13, 2004, Solar Eclipse emphasizes—Uranus

April 8, 2005, Solar Eclipse emphasizes—Uranus

Sept. 7, 2006, Lunar Eclipse emphasizes—Mercury

Aug. 28, 2007, Lunar Eclipse emphasizes—The Midheaven

Sept. 11, 2007, Solar Eclipse emphasizes—Mercury

Aug. 1, 2008, Solar Eclipse emphasizes—Mars

Jan. 26, 2009, Solar Eclipse emphasizes—Mars and Jupiter

July 7, 2009, Lunar Eclipse emphasizes—The Dragon's Head

Dec. 31, 2009, Lunar Eclipse emphasizes—The Dragon's Tail

Jan. 4, 2011, Solar Eclipse emphasizes—The Dragon's Head

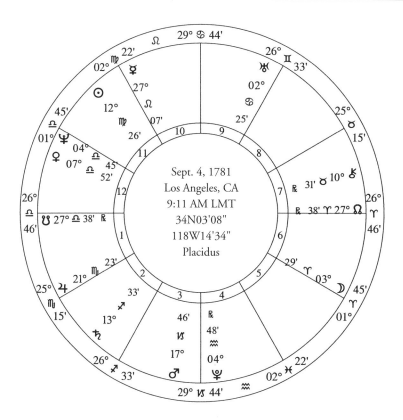

Chart data:
Sept. 4, 1781
Los Angeles, CA
9:11 AM LMT
34N03'08"
118W14'34"
Placidus

Los Angeles

Under the orders of King Carlo III of Spain, a pueblo was founded in 1781, on the site now known as Los Angeles, to grow food for the soldiers guarding this remote Spanish territory. The name Los Angeles is Spanish for "the angels." The chart shown here reflects L.A.'s birth. Eclipses making contact with L.A.'s planets are of extra importance for the city, and are usually followed by events of the nature of the planet stimulated. An eclipse in 2001 on L.A.'s Uranus, ruling electricity, was a good representative of the energy crisis and electrical brownouts affecting the state. In 2006–2007, eclipses to L.A.'s Sun suggest that the mayor or an important city official comes strongly into view, with attending changes and transitions. Central issues for the city come into focus.

To find the people and things emphasized by coming eclipses, refer to table 4. To find the raw power rating of an eclipse, refer to table 1. That table also gives the dates of stimulation to the eclipse, which may closely coincide with notable events that are traceable to the eclipse. See more definition of future eclipses in the Catalog of Annotated Eclipse Charts. L.A. chart data source: Marc Penfield, *Horoscopes of the Western Hemisphere* (San Diego, CA: ACS Publications, 1984). Chart rectified by Penfield.

Eclipse Emphasis for Los Angeles through 2011

Dec. 25, 2000, Solar Eclipse emphasizes—Uranus

Jan. 9, 2001, Lunar Eclipse emphasizes—Mars

June 21, 2001, Solar Eclipse emphasizes—Uranus

June 24, 2002, Lunar Eclipse emphasizes—Uranus

Dec. 4, 2002, Solar Eclipse emphasizes—Saturn

April 19, 2004, Solar Eclipse emphasizes—The Dragon's Head

Oct. 3, 2005, Solar Eclipse emphasizes—Venus

Oct. 17, 2005, Lunar Eclipse emphasizes—The Ascendant

March 29, 2006, Solar Eclipse emphasizes—Venus

Sept. 7, 2006, Lunar Eclipse emphasizes—The Sun

March 3, 2007, Lunar Eclipse emphasizes—The Sun

Aug. 16, 2008, Lunar Eclipse emphasizes—Mercury

Jan. 26, 2009, Solar Eclipse emphasizes—Pluto

July 7, 2009, Lunar Eclipse emphasizes—Mars

July 21, 2009, Solar Eclipse emphasizes—The Midheaven

June 26, 2010, Lunar Eclipse emphasizes—Uranus

July 11, 2010, Solar Eclipse emphasizes—Mars

June 1, 2011, Solar Eclipse emphasizes—Saturn

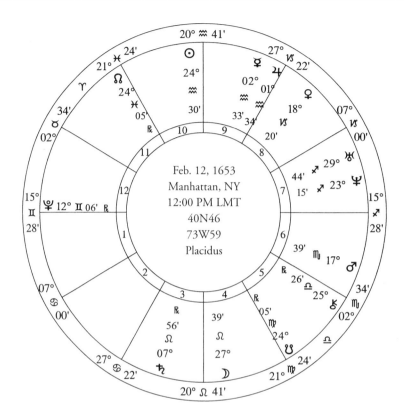

Manhattan

Manhattan was born 247 years before New York City, which came into being when the several boroughs combined to form greater New York. Pluto shares nearly the same zodiacal position in the birth charts for NYC and Manhattan. Pluto is the slowest-moving planet and had just completed one revolution through the zodiac from the time Manhattan was incorporated until NYC was formed. An eclipse making contact with one of Manhattan's planets is of extra importance for the city, bringing events according to the nature of the planet stimulated and often timed by transits to the eclipse. Centrally located, a similar trend of important eclipses affects Manhattan at the same time as New York City. The year 2009 will be important for Manhattan and its residents, with multiple eclipses of note.

To find the people and things emphasized by the coming eclipses listed here, refer to table 4. To find the raw power rating of any eclipse, refer to table 1. That table also gives the dates of planetary stimulation to the eclipse, which may closely coincide with notable events traceable to the eclipse. See more definition of future eclipses in the Catalog of Annotated Eclipse Charts. Chart data source: Maggie Hyde, "Tomorrow's News," *American Astrology* (Sept. 2002): p. 57.

Eclipse Emphasis for Manhattan through 2011

July 30, 2000, Solar Eclipse emphasizes—Saturn

Jan. 9, 2001, Lunar Eclipse emphasizes—Venus

June 21, 2001, Solar Eclipse emphasizes—Uranus

Dec. 14, 2001, Solar Eclipse emphasizes—Neptune

Dec. 4, 2002, Solar Eclipse emphasizes—Pluto

May 30, 2003, Solar Eclipse emphasizes—Pluto

Nov. 8, 2003, Lunar Eclipse emphasizes—Mars

May 4, 2004, Lunar Eclipse emphasizes—Mars

Oct. 17, 2005, Lunar Eclipse emphasizes—Chiron (Wounded Healer)

March, 14 2006, Lunar Eclipse emphasizes—The Dragon's Tail

Feb. 6, 2008, Solar Eclipse emphasizes—The Midheaven

Aug. 1, 2008, Solar Eclipse emphasizes—Saturn

Aug. 16, 2008, Lunar Eclipse emphasizes—The Sun and Moon

Jan. 26, 2009, Solar Eclipse emphasizes—Saturn

Feb. 9, 2009, Lunar Eclipse emphasizes—The Midheaven

July 7, 2009, Lunar Eclipse emphasizes—Venus

July 21, 2009, Solar Eclipse emphasizes—Jupiter

July 11, 2010, Solar Eclipse emphasizes—Venus

Dec. 21, 2010, Lunar Eclipse emphasizes—Uranus

June 1, 2011, Solar Eclipse emphasizes—Pluto

June 15, 2011, Lunar Eclipse emphasizes—Neptune

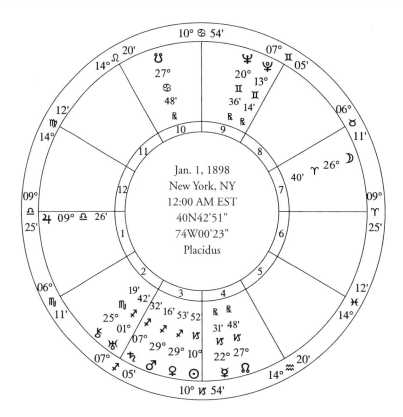

New York City

In New York City's horoscope, Mars and Venus in Sagittarius together in the Third House show the diversity in neighborhoods, with men and women from all backgrounds and cultures. A long series of eclipses touched on important places in the New York City nativity from 2000 through 2001, indicating a period in which that city would be in higher focus. Although a great many eclipses fall on important places in the NYC map, corresponding with its general business and eventful happenings, the number of eclipses spotlighting the Big Apple decreases between 2006 and 2009, rising again from there. By the end of 2009, the city comes into prominent view, with a focus on the mayor and other city leaders. Come 2010–2011, there could be a major shift in the reputation of an important NYC official, as in 2001 with Mayor Rudy Giuliani, who before 9/11 had less than the shining-star status he won for his superb handling of that catastrophic emergency.

To find the people and things emphasized by coming eclipses, refer to table 4. To find the raw power rating of any eclipse, refer to table 1. That table also gives the dates of planetary stimulation to the eclipse, which may closely coincide with notable events traceable to the eclipse. See more definition of current and coming eclipses in the Catalog of Annotated Eclipse Charts. Chart data source: Maggie Hyde, "Tomorrow's News," *American Astrology* (Sept. 2002): p. 56.

Eclipse Emphasis for New York City through 2011

July 1, 2000, Solar Eclipse emphasizes—The Sun and Midheaven

July 16, 2000, Lunar Eclipse emphasizes—Mercury

Jan. 9, 2001, Lunar Eclipse emphasizes—Mercury

June 21, 2001, Solar Eclipse emphasizes—Venus and Mars

July 5, 2001, Lunar Eclipse emphasizes—The Sun and Midheaven

Dec. 14, 2001, Solar Eclipse emphasizes—Neptune

Dec. 30, 2001, Lunar Eclipse emphasizes—The Sun and Midheaven

May 26, 2002, Lunar Eclipse emphasizes—Saturn

June 10, 2002, Solar Eclipse emphasizes—Neptune

Nov. 19, 2002, Lunar Eclipse emphasizes—Chiron (Wounded Healer)

Dec. 4, 2002, Solar Eclipse emphasizes—Pluto

May 15, 2003, Lunar Eclipse emphasizes—Chiron (Wounded Healer)

May 30, 2003, Solar Eclipse emphasizes—Saturn

Nov. 23, 2003, Solar Eclipse emphasizes—Uranus

April 19, 2004, Solar Eclipse emphasizes—The Moon

Oct. 3, 2005, Solar Eclipse emphasizes—The Ascendant and Jupiter

Oct. 17, 2005, Lunar Eclipse emphasizes—The Moon

March 29, 2006, Solar Eclipse emphasizes—The Ascendant and Jupiter

July 21, 2009, Solar Eclipse emphasizes—The Dragon's Tail

Dec. 31, 2009, Lunar Eclipse emphasizes—The Sun and Midheaven

Jan. 15, 2010, Solar Eclipse emphasizes—Mercury and the Dragon's Head

July 11, 2010, Solar Eclipse emphasizes—Mercury

Dec. 21, 2010, Lunar Eclipse emphasizes—Venus and Mars

Jan. 4, 2011, Solar Eclipse emphasizes—The Sun and Midheaven

June 1, 2011, Solar Eclipse emphasizes—Pluto

July 1, 2011, Solar Eclipse emphasizes—The Sun and Midheaven

Nov. 25, 2011, Solar Eclipse emphasizes—Uranus

Dec. 10, 2011, Lunar Eclipse emphasizes—Neptune

May 20, 2012, Solar Eclipse emphasizes—Uranus

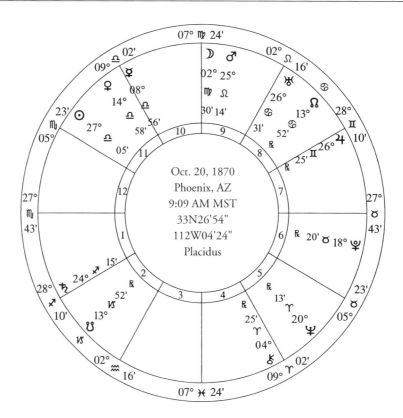

Phoenix, Arizona

Phoenix was established on the site of an ancient American Indian irrigation system. As a new town arising from an old habitation, the city was named for the mythical bird, the Phoenix. Pioneers in 1868 capitalized on the irrigation-system remains, diverting water from the Salt River to begin farming. An eclipse falling prominently in the Phoenix nativity is of extra importance for the city. The eclipse of December 14, 2001, in the sign of Sagittarius, bringing focus to religious leaders, fell on Saturn in the Phoenix chart, suggesting discipline and emphasizing elders. A Catholic crisis followed. Phoenix Bishop O'Brien became the subject of scrutiny and judgment over the next couple of years for his knowledge of sexual abuse by priests. Finally, in the spring of 2003, the elderly bishop resigned from his position after being caught leaving the scene of a hit-and-run accident. His resignation came just as Saturn completed its final stimulation to the eclipse. As another example, the eclipse of May 18, 2003, on Phoenix's Ascendant was receiving planetary stimulation in August 2003 when a ruptured pipeline created a gas shortage.

To find the people and things emphasized by coming eclipses, refer to table 4. To find the raw power rating of any eclipse, refer to table 1, which also gives dates of stimulation. Chart data source: Marc Penfield, *Horoscopes of the Western Hemisphere* (San Diego, CA: ACS Publications, 1984). Chart rectified by Penfield. A chart for the incorporation of Phoenix (shared by Phil Sedgwick) on February 25, 1881, shows the Sun in the same degree as the IC of the founding chart, both transited by retrograde Mars when the pipeline broke.

Eclipse Emphasis for Phoenix through 2011

July 16, 2000, Lunar Eclipse emphasizes—Uranus

July 5, 2001, Lunar Eclipse emphasizes—The Dragon's Tail

Dec. 14, 2001, Solar Eclipse emphasizes—Saturn

Nov. 19, 2002, Lunar Eclipse emphasizes—The Ascendant

May 18, 2003, Lunar Eclipse emphasizes—The Ascendant

Nov. 8, 2003, Lunar Eclipse emphasizes—Pluto

April 19, 2004, Solar Eclipse emphasizes—The Sun

Oct. 13, 2004, Solar Eclipse emphasizes—Neptune

April 8, 2005, Solar Eclipse emphasizes—Neptune

Oct. 3, 2005, Solar Eclipse emphasizes—Mercury

Oct. 17, 2005, Lunar Eclipse emphasizes—The Sun

March 29, 2006, Solar Eclipse emphasizes—Mercury

Aug. 28, 2007, Lunar Eclipse emphasizes—The Moon and Midheaven

Feb. 20, 2008, Lunar Eclipse emphasizes—The Moon

Aug. 16, 2008, Lunar Eclipse emphasizes—Mars

July 7, 2009, Lunar Eclipse emphasizes—The Dragon's Tail

July 21, 2009, Solar Eclipse emphasizes—Uranus

Jan. 15, 2010, Solar Eclipse emphasizes—Uranus

Dec. 21, 2010, Lunar Eclipse emphasizes—Jupiter

Jan. 4, 2011, Solar Eclipse emphasizes—The Dragon's Tail

June 15, 2011, Lunar Eclipse emphasizes—Jupiter and Saturn

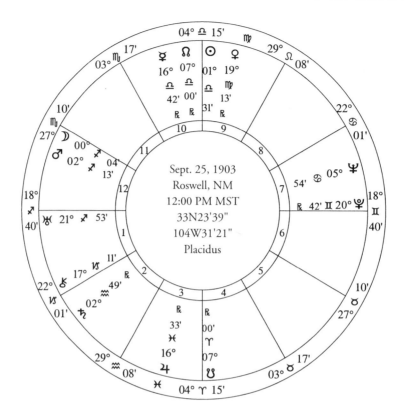

Roswell, New Mexico

In 1946, several eclipses touched upon planets in the Roswell birth chart. A highly significant one fell on November 24, 1946, upon the Moon and Mars and in the most secretive area of the Roswell horoscope. Just as Mars transited this eclipse by opposition in early July 1947, the controversial alien sightings by residents and military followed an apparent accident by an alien spacecraft during a lightning storm. The government later insisted that the incident could be explained by crash test dummies and weather balloons, although many who were at the scene or had firsthand information maintain this was a cover-up. Will the eclipses of 2011and 2012 to those same planets bring the potential for another alien contact in Roswell, and will people be more prepared, or might these eclipses bring light to the truth of that first encounter? Whatever is going on, the Roswell chart shows excitable eclipse stimulation.

    To find the people and things emphasized by coming eclipses, refer to table 4. To find the raw power rating of any eclipse, refer to table 1. That table also gives the dates of planetary stimulation to the eclipse, which may closely coincide with notable events traceable to the eclipse. See more definition of coming eclipses in the Catalog of Annotated Eclipse Charts. Chart data source: Donna Cunningham, "The UFO Cover Up," *Dell Horoscope* (Sept. 1996): p. 55. Her stated reference was Carolyn M. Dodson, *Horoscopes of U.S. States & Cities* (San Diego, CA: ACS Publications, 1975).

Eclipse Emphasis for Roswell through 2011

Dec. 25, 2000, Solar Eclipse emphasizes—Neptune

Dec. 14, 2001, Solar Eclipse emphasizes—Uranus and Pluto

Dec. 30, 2001, Lunar Eclipse emphasizes—Neptune

May 26, 2002, Lunar Eclipse emphasizes—Mars

June 10, 2002, Solar Eclipse emphasizes—Pluto

June 24, 2002, Lunar Eclipse emphasizes—Neptune

Nov. 23, 2003, Solar Eclipse emphasizes—The Moon and Mars

April 8, 2005, Solar Eclipse emphasizes—Mercury

March 29, 2006, Solar Eclipse emphasizes—The Dragon's Tail

Sept. 7, 2006, Lunar Eclipse emphasizes—Jupiter

Sept. 22, 2006, Solar Eclipse emphasizes—The Sun

Sept. 11, 2007, Solar Eclipse emphasizes—Venus

July 7, 2009, Lunar Eclipse emphasizes—Chiron (Wounded Healer)

June 26, 2010, Lunar Eclipse emphasizes—Neptune

July 11, 2010, Solar Eclipse emphasizes—Chiron (Wounded Healer)

June 15, 2011, Lunar Eclipse emphasizes—Uranus

Nov. 25, 2011, Solar Eclipse emphasizes—The Moon and Mars

Dec. 10, 2011, Lunar Eclipse emphasizes—Pluto and Uranus

May 20, 2012, Solar Eclipse emphasizes—The Moon and Mars

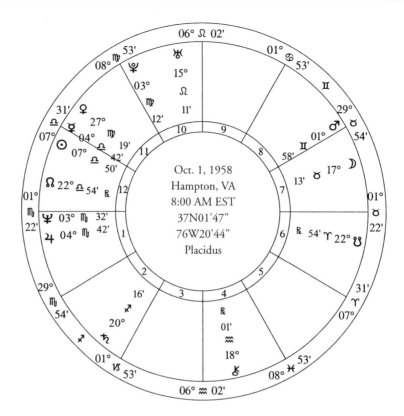

NASA

An eclipse that occurred on November 19, 2002, fell on the Eighth House cusp of the NASA chart, a point associated with death. Soon after, the Columbia space shuttle launched as Mars transited that November eclipse, ending in tragedy days later upon Columbia's reentry. A nearly identical set of eclipse patterns prevailed when the Challenger launched and exploded within minutes in 1986: Mars was transiting a previous Lunar eclipse in late Taurus. NASA has an outstanding number of eclipses in the years ahead, suggesting much activity and many projects. Similar to the previous ones to the Eighth House cusp, eclipses to NASA's Mars are significant of potential accidents and mechanical malfunctions. It would be a preventive step to forego launches during Mars transits to those eclipses. Those eclipse periods are better for mechanical makeovers and fleet overhauls and excellent for exploration of the planet Mars itself. (While only eclipses to major planets and points are given in these listings due to space consideration, eclipses falling on house cusps are also significant and informative.)

To find the people and things emphasized by these coming eclipses, refer to table 4. To find the raw power rating of any eclipse, refer to table 1. That table also gives the dates of planetary stimulation to the eclipse, which may closely coincide with notable events traceable to the eclipse. See more definition of coming eclipses in the Catalog of Annotated Eclipse Charts. Chart data made available by Lois Rodden (AstroDatabank.com) through a friend who worked at NASA.

Eclipse Emphasis for NASA through 2011

Dec. 14, 2001, Solar Eclipse emphasizes—Saturn

June 10, 2002, Solar Eclipse emphasizes—Saturn

Nov. 19, 2002, Lunar Eclipse emphasizes—Eighth House cusp

Nov. 8, 2003, Lunar Eclipse emphasizes—The Moon

Nov. 23, 2003, Solar Eclipse emphasizes—Mars

May 4, 2004, Lunar Eclipse emphasizes—The Moon

Oct. 13, 2004, Solar Eclipse emphasizes—The Dragon's Head

Oct. 27, 2004, Lunar Eclipse emphasizes—Jupiter and Neptune

April 24, 2005, Lunar Eclipse emphasizes—Jupiter and Neptune

Oct. 3, 2005, Solar Eclipse emphasizes—The Sun

Oct. 17, 2005, Lunar Eclipse emphasizes—The Dragon's Tail

March 14, 2006, Lunar Eclipse emphasizes—Venus

March 29, 2006, Solar Eclipse emphasizes—The Sun

Sept. 22, 2006, Solar Eclipse emphasizes—Venus

March 18, 2007, Solar Eclipse emphasizes—Venus

Aug. 28, 2007, Lunar Eclipse emphasizes—Pluto

Feb. 6, 2008, Solar Eclipse emphasizes—Uranus and Chiron (Wounded Healer)

Feb. 20, 2008, Lunar Eclipse emphasizes—Pluto

Jan. 26, 2009, Solar Eclipse emphasizes—The Midheaven

Aug. 5, 2009, Lunar Eclipse emphasizes—Uranus

Nov. 25, 2011, Solar Eclipse emphasizes—Mars

Dec. 10, 2011, Lunar Eclipse emphasizes—Saturn

May 20, 2012, Solar Eclipse emphasizes—Mars

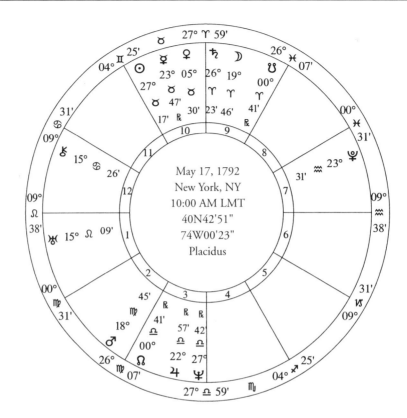

New York Stock Exchange

The powerful Solar eclipse of July 2000 fell upon the Ascendant of the New York Stock Exchange chart, bringing emphasis to the organization and suggesting changes in the general situation. That year saw its record high, an extreme point jump followed by an extreme point slide. This shows how an eclipse tends to shake things up, and the dates of the records that were set illustrate how an eclipse sometimes starts to manifest even before the eclipse occurs. Later, just prior to the terrorist attacks, an eclipse fell upon NYSE's Chiron, often associated with pain and wounding. Closing for four days, it reopened on September 17 and set a record volume of 2.37 billion shares traded, with stock prices plummeting. The years 2008–2009 appear to be highlighted, with several significant eclipses on important places. The organization comes into the spotlight, perhaps especially in early 2009 with transits to the eclipse on the Ascendant.

To find the people and things emphasized by coming eclipses, refer to table 4. To find the raw power rating of any eclipse, refer to table 1. That table also gives the dates of planetary stimulation to the eclipse, which may closely coincide with notable events traceable to the eclipse. See more definition of coming eclipses in the Catalog of Annotated Eclipse Charts. Chart data source: Maggie Hyde, "Tomorrow's News," *American Astrology* (Oct. 2002): p. 56. She states that although there are various times used for this chart, the 9 degrees Leo rising version is the most radical now, with a Midheaven of 27 Aries 59.

Eclipse Emphasis for the NYSE through 2011

July 30, 2000, Solar Eclipse emphasizes—The Ascendant

July 5, 2001, Lunar Eclipse emphasizes—Chiron (Wounded Healer)

Nov. 19, 2002, Lunar Eclipse emphasizes—The Sun

May 15, 2003, Lunar Eclipse emphasizes—Mercury

April 19, 2004, Solar Eclipse emphasizes—Neptune and the Midheaven

Oct. 13, 2004, Solar Eclipse emphasizes—The Moon and Jupiter

Oct. 27, 2004, Lunar Eclipse emphasizes—Venus

April 8, 2005, Solar Eclipse emphasizes—The Moon

April 24, 2005, Lunar Eclipse emphasizes—Venus

Oct. 17, 2005, Lunar Eclipse emphasizes—Saturn and Jupiter

Sept. 22, 2006, Solar Eclipse emphasizes—The Dragon's Head

March 18, 2007, Solar Eclipse emphasizes—The Dragon's Tail

Sept. 11, 2007, Solar Eclipse emphasizes—Mars

Feb. 6, 2008, Solar Eclipse emphasizes—Uranus

Aug. 1, 2008, Solar Eclipse emphasizes—The Ascendant

Aug. 16, 2008, Lunar Eclipse emphasizes—Pluto

Feb. 9, 2009, Lunar Eclipse emphasizes—Pluto

July 7, 2009, Lunar Eclipse emphasizes—Chiron (Wounded Healer)

Aug. 5, 2009, Lunar Eclipse emphasizes—Uranus

Jan. 4, 2011, Solar Eclipse emphasizes—Chiron (Wounded Healer)

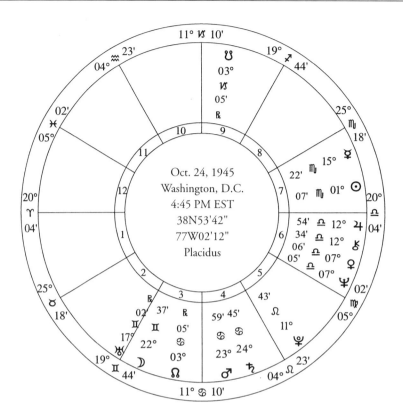

United Nations

The extreme number of eclipses falling on conspicuous places in the chart of the United Nations is indicative of the number of countries and interests that are represented by that body. In June of 2002, the Gemini Solar eclipse touching off both the Moon and Uranus, which together sometimes denote sudden separations, was followed by separations and disagreement among UN members about the handling of the threat of weapons of mass destruction in Iraq. In 2004–2005, the general situation and body of the UN are slated for some transitions. Membership changes and/or changes of attitudes of members are suggested. The 2010–2011period is strongly highlighted for activity and changes.

To find the people and things emphasized by coming eclipses, refer to table 4. To find the raw power rating of any eclipse, refer to table 1. That table also gives the dates of planetary stimulation to the eclipse, which may closely coincide with notable events traceable to the eclipse. See more definition of coming eclipses in the Catalog of Annotated Eclipse Charts. Chart data source: Stephen Erlewine, *The Circle Book of Charts* (Tempe, AZ: American Federation of Astrologers, 1991), p. 261.

Eclipse Emphasis for the United Nations through 2011

July 1, 2000, Solar Eclipse emphasizes—The Midheaven

July 16, 2000, Lunar Eclipse emphasizes—Mars and Saturn

Dec. 25, 2000, Solar Eclipse emphasizes—The Dragon's Tail

June 21, 2001, Solar Eclipse emphasizes—The Dragon's Head

Dec. 14, 2001, Solar Eclipse emphasizes—The Moon

Dec. 30, 2001, Lunar Eclipse emphasizes—The Midheaven

June 10, 2002, Solar Eclipse emphasizes—The Moon and Uranus

June 24, 2002, Lunar Eclipse emphasizes—The Dragon's Tail

Nov. 8, 2003, Lunar Eclipse emphasizes—Mercury

April 19, 2004, Solar Eclipse emphasizes—The Sun

May 4, 2004, Lunar Eclipse emphasizes—Mercury

Oct. 13, 2004, Solar Eclipse emphasizes—The Ascendant

April 8, 2005, Solar Eclipse emphasizes—The Ascendant

Oct. 3, 2005, Solar Eclipse emphasizes—Jupiter

March 29, 2006, Solar Eclipse emphasizes—Venus and Neptune

Aug. 1, 2008, Solar Eclipse emphasizes—Pluto

Aug. 5, 2009, Lunar Eclipse emphasizes—Pluto

Dec. 31, 2009, Lunar Eclipse emphasizes—The Midheaven

Jan. 15, 2010, Solar Eclipse emphasizes—Mars and Saturn

June 26, 2010, Lunar Eclipse emphasizes—The Dragon's Tail

Jan. 4, 2011, Solar Eclipse emphasizes—The Midheaven

June 15, 2011, Lunar Eclipse emphasizes—The Moon

July 1, 2011, Solar Eclipse emphasizes—The Midheaven

Dec. 10, 2011, Lunar Eclipse emphasizes—Uranus

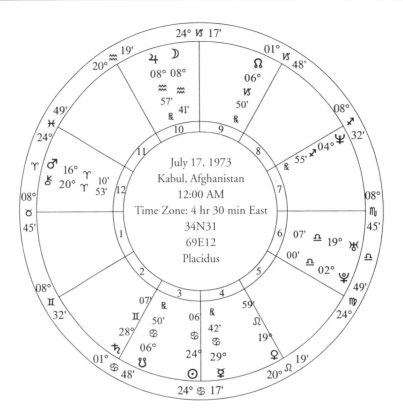

Afghanistan

An eclipse to Afghanistan's Dragon's Tail in 2001 illustrates the sacrifice of that country's people through another war—this one to bring powerlessness to the oppressive Taliban and al-Qaeda. Important transitional periods are often noted with eclipses to the Lunar Nodes. When a new permanent governing body is elected and begins to function, that will mark a new birth for Afghanistan. That chart will undoubtedly show connections to this one, and the eclipses listed here to this chart should continue to reflect increased activity for the country according to the nature of the planet or point eclipsed. The Solar Eclipse of January 15, 2010, brings quite a spotlight to the country for a year or more.

To find the people and things emphasized by coming eclipses, refer to table 4. To find the raw power rating of any eclipse, refer to table 1. That table also gives the dates of planetary stimulation to the eclipse, which may closely coincide with notable events traceable to the eclipse. See more definition of coming eclipses in the Catalog of Annotated Eclipse Charts. Chart data from Stephanie Clement, who cited her source as Nicholas Campion, *The Book of World Horoscopes* (Bristol, England: Cinnabar Books, 1999).

Eclipse Emphasis for Afghanistan through 2011

July 16, 2000, Lunar Eclipse emphasizes—The Sun and Midheaven

July 30, 2000, Solar Eclipse emphasizes—The Moon and Jupiter

Dec. 25, 2000, Solar Eclipse emphasizes—The Dragon's Head

June 21, 2001, Solar Eclipse emphasizes—Saturn

Dec. 30, 2001, Lunar Eclipse emphasizes—The Dragon's Tail

May 26, 2002, Lunar Eclipse emphasizes—Neptune

Oct. 13, 2004, Solar Eclipse emphasizes—Uranus

April 8, 2005, Solar Eclipse emphasizes—Uranus

Sept. 22, 2006, Solar Eclipse emphasizes—Pluto

Feb. 6, 2008, Solar Eclipse emphasizes—Venus

Aug. 1, 2008, Solar Eclipse emphasizes—The Moon and Jupiter

Jan. 26, 2009, Solar Eclipse emphasizes—The Moon and Jupiter

Feb. 9, 2009, Lunar Eclipse emphasizes—Venus

July 21, 2009, Solar Eclipse emphasizes—Mercury

Jan. 15, 2010, Solar Eclipse emphasizes—The Sun and Midheaven

June 26, 2010, Lunar Eclipse emphasizes—The Dragon's Head

Dec. 21, 2010, Lunar Eclipse emphasizes—Saturn

June 15, 2011, Lunar Eclipse emphasizes—Saturn

July 1, 2011, Solar Eclipse emphasizes—The Dragon's Tail

Nov. 25, 2011, Solar Eclipse emphasizes—Neptune

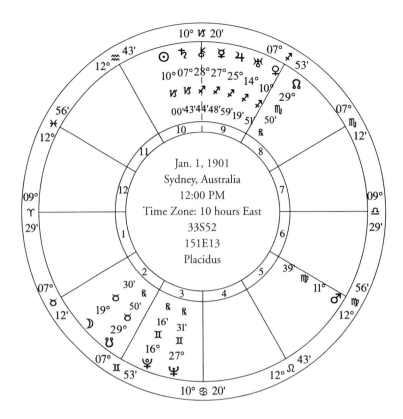

Australia

Australia became a federated nation in 1901, with the first Commonwealth ceremony held in Sydney's Centennial Park on January 1, when the first inauguration was also held. Later, the capital moved to Canberra. An eclipse falling on a planet in Australia's horoscope is of some importance for the continent. Australia has many planets grouped together so that eclipses falling in the signs Gemini or Sagittarius often tend to impact two or more planets at once. In May 2003, a Solar eclipse in Gemini opposed Australia's Venus, which rules young ladies and their interests. Following that eclipse, attention in Australia was drawn to the extraordinary number of young women with anorexic eating disorders. The youngest was only four years old. Venus also rules social harmony, pleasure pursuits, and a variety of related things, so the same eclipse will continue to highlight these for some time.

To find the people and things emphasized by coming eclipses, refer to table 4. To find the raw power rating of any eclipse, refer to table 1. That table also gives the dates of planetary stimulation to the eclipse, which may closely coincide with notable events traceable to the eclipse. See more definition of coming eclipses in the Catalog of Annotated Eclipse Charts. This chart is calculated for noon based on this data source: *Documenting a Democracy*, The National Archives of Australia, http://www.foundingdocs.gov.au/default.asp.

Eclipse Emphasis for Australia through 2011

July 1, 2000, Solar Eclipse emphasizes—The Sun and Saturn

Dec. 14, 2001, Solar Eclipse emphasizes—Jupiter

Dec. 30, 2001, Lunar Eclipse emphasizes—The Sun and Saturn

Nov. 19, 2001, Lunar Eclipse emphasizes—The Dragon's Tail

Dec. 4, 2002, Solar Eclipse emphasizes—Venus and Uranus

May 30, 2003, Solar Eclipse emphasizes—Venus

Nov. 8, 2003, Lunar Eclipse emphasizes—The Moon

Nov. 23, 2003, Solar Eclipse emphasizes—The Dragon's Head

March 3, 2007, Lunar Eclipse emphasizes—Mars

Dec. 31, 2009, Lunar Eclipse emphasizes—The Sun and Saturn

June 26, 2010, Lunar Eclipse emphasizes—Saturn

Dec. 21, 2010, Lunar Eclipse emphasizes—Mercury and Neptune

June 1, 2011, Solar Eclipse emphasizes—Venus and Uranus

June 15, 2011, Lunar Eclipse emphasizes—Jupiter

July 1, 2011, Solar Eclipse emphasizes—The Sun and Saturn

Nov. 25, 2011, Solar Eclipse emphasizes—The Dragon's Head

Dec. 10, 2011, Lunar Eclipse emphasizes—Pluto

May 20, 2012, Solar Eclipse emphasizes—The Dragon's Tail

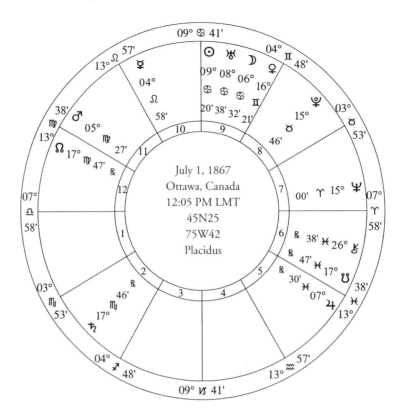

Canada

The horoscope for Canada is cast for when the British North American Act went into effect and the new dominion of Canada came into existence. This chart reflects the time of the official announcement and celebrations. An eclipse that falls conspicuously upon one of Canada's planets represents eventful happenings of greater importance for the county. Following eclipses to Canada's Venus and Moon in 2002, the arrival of SARS to the country had an impact on residents, with many under quarantine and a lengthy period to contain the spread of the deadly virus. The first case of SARS was reported in mid-February 2003, as Mars transited the eclipse to Venus. By May 2003, Canada was also coping with mad cow disease, quarantining herds and facing bans on its meat. Many worries and restrictions were dealt with as transiting Saturn contacted previous eclipses to Canada's Moon in mid-2003.

To find the various people and things emphasized by coming eclipses, refer to table 4. To find the raw power rating of any eclipse, refer to table 1. That table also gives the dates of planetary stimulation to the eclipse, which may closely coincide with notable events traceable to the eclipse. See more definition of coming eclipses in the Catalog of Annotated Eclipse Charts. Chart data from *Astrology Weekly*, http://www.astrology-weekly.com/countries/canada.php. Source: astrologer Rab Wilkie.

Eclipse Emphasis for Canada through 2011

July 1, 2000, Solar Eclipse emphasizes—The Sun and Uranus

Dec. 25, 2000, Solar Eclipse emphasizes—The Moon

Dec. 30, 2001, Lunar Eclipse emphasizes—The Sun and Uranus

June 10, 2002, Solar Eclipse emphasizes—Venus

June 24, 2002, Lunar Eclipse emphasizes—The Moon

Nov. 8, 2003, Lunar Eclipse emphasizes—Pluto and Saturn

May 4, 2004, Lunar Eclipse emphasizes—Saturn and Pluto

March 14, 2006, Lunar Eclipse emphasizes—Chiron (Wounded Healer)

Sept. 7, 2006, Lunar Eclipse emphasizes—The Dragon's Tail

Sept. 22, 2006, Solar Eclipse emphasizes—Chiron (Wounded Healer)

March 18, 2007, Solar Eclipse emphasizes—Chiron (Wounded Healer)

Aug. 28, 2007, Lunar Eclipse emphasizes—Jupiter and Mars

Sept. 11, 2007, Solar Eclipse emphasizes—The Dragon's Head

Jan. 26, 2009, Solar Eclipse emphasizes—Mercury

Dec. 31, 2009, Lunar Eclipse emphasizes—The Sun and Uranus

June 26, 2010, Lunar Eclipse emphasizes—The Moon

July 1, 2011, Solar Eclipse emphasizes—The Sun and Uranus

Dec. 10, 2011, Lunar Eclipse emphasizes—Venus

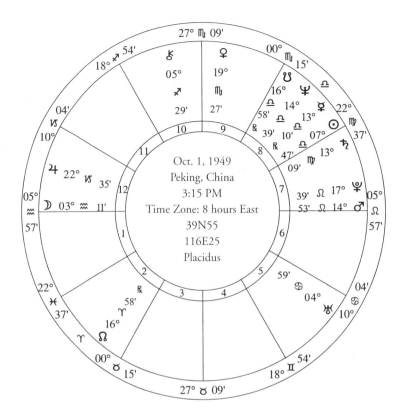

China

The People's Republic of China was formed on November 7, 1931. A later change in government entailed a new birth on October 1, 1949, as shown here. The positions of Venus and Mercury in the old chart become the Midheaven in the new chart, so that the Lunar Eclipse of November 19, 2002, fell on conspicuous places in both charts, bringing China into the spotlight and coinciding with the outbreak of SARS. The emphasis of that eclipse to Venus and Mercury in the old chart was especially indicative of the changes in social interaction, transport, marketplace activity, etc., as the virus was being contained.

To find the people and things emphasized by coming eclipses, refer to table 4. To find the raw power rating of any eclipse, refer to table 1. That table also gives the dates of planetary stimulation to the eclipse, which may closely coincide with notable events traceable to the eclipse. See more definition of coming eclipses in the Catalog of Annotated Eclipse Charts. Chart data from Judy Collins, education director for the Arizona Society of Astrologers. She cites her source as Nicholas Campion's *World Horoscopes* software program.

Eclipse Emphasis for China through 2011

Dec. 25, 2000, Solar Eclipse emphasizes—Uranus
May 26, 2002, Lunar Eclipse emphasizes Chiron (Wounded Healer)

June 24, 2002, Lunar Eclipse emphasizes—Uranus

Nov. 19, 2002, Lunar Eclipse emphasizes—The Midheaven

May 15, 2003, Lunar Eclipse emphasizes—The Midheaven

Nov. 8, 2003, Lunar Eclipse emphasizes—Venus

Oct. 3, 2005, Solar Eclipse emphasizes—The Sun and Mercury

March 29, 2006, Solar Eclipse emphasizes—The Sun

Sept. 7, 2006, Lunar Eclipse emphasizes—Saturn

March 3, 2007, Lunar Eclipse emphasizes—Saturn

Feb. 6, 2008, Solar Eclipse emphasizes—Pluto and Mars

Jan. 26, 2009, Solar Eclipse emphasizes—The Ascendant

Aug. 5, 2009, Lunar Eclipse emphasizes—Mars and Pluto

Jan. 15, 2010, Solar Eclipse emphasizes—Jupiter

June 26, 2010, Lunar Eclipse emphasizes—Uranus

Nov. 25, 2011, Solar Eclipse emphasizes—Chiron (Wounded Healer)

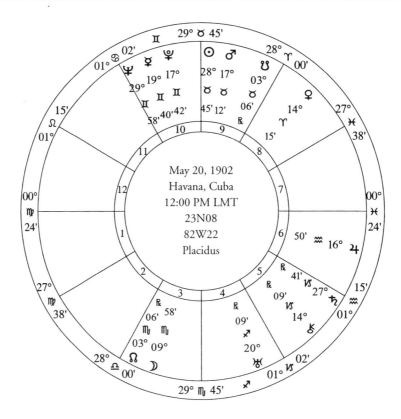

Cuba

Cuba gained independence from the U.S. in May of 1902, reflected in the chart shown here. An eclipse falling upon a planet in the Cuba nativity is of some significance for the country. As an example, in 2002, an eclipse to Cuba's Sun brought the country's leader into the spotlight, and there were concerns for Castro's apparently deteriorating health. In late 2003, an eclipse falls on Cuba's Mars, followed by another in early 2004, an indication of potential conflicts, turbulence, and unrest to follow in the country. These may be especially notable in late 2005 as transiting Mars stimulates those eclipses. The year 2011 is also likely to produce some noise and eventful times with an eclipse falling on three of Cuba's planets.

To find the people and things emphasized by coming eclipses, refer to table 4. To find the raw power rating of any eclipse, refer to table 1. That table also gives the dates of planetary stimulation to the eclipse, which may closely coincide with notable events traceable to the eclipse. See more definition of coming eclipses in the Catalog of Annotated Eclipse Charts. Chart data source: Maggie Hyde, "Tomorrow's News," *American Astrology* (March 2003): p. 56.

Eclipse Emphasis for Cuba through 2011

July 5, 2001, Lunar Eclipse emphasizes—Chiron (Wounded Healer)

Dec. 14, 2001, Solar Eclipse emphasizes—Uranus

June 10, 2002, Solar Eclipse emphasizes—Mercury, Pluto, and Uranus

Nov. 19, 2002, Lunar Eclipse emphasizes—The Sun and Midheaven

Nov. 8, 2003, Lunar Eclipse emphasizes—Mars

May 4, 2004, Lunar Eclipse emphasizes—Mars

Oct. 27, 2004, Lunar Eclipse emphasizes—The Dragon's Tail

April 24, 2005, Lunar Eclipse emphasizes—The Dragon's Head

Feb. 6, 2008, Solar Eclipse emphasizes—Jupiter

Feb. 20, 2008, Lunar Eclipse emphasizes—The Ascendant

July 7, 2009, Lunar Eclipse emphasizes—Chiron (Wounded Healer)

July 21, 2009, Solar Eclipse emphasizes—Saturn

Aug. 5, 2009, Lunar Eclipse emphasizes—Jupiter

Jan. 15, 2010, Solar Eclipse emphasizes—Saturn

Dec. 21, 2010, Lunar Eclipse emphasizes—Neptune

Jan. 4, 2011, Solar Eclipse emphasizes—Chiron (Wounded Healer)

Dec. 10, 2011, Lunar Eclipse emphasizes—Mercury, Pluto, and Uranus

May 20, 2012, Solar Eclipse emphasizes—The Sun and Midheaven

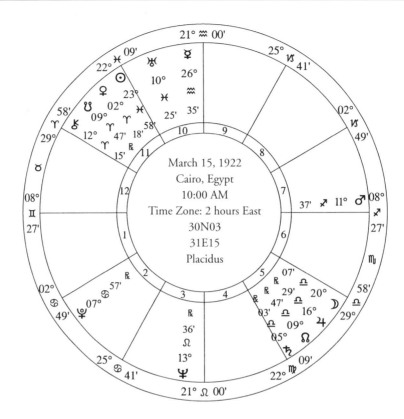

Egypt

The Proclamation of Independence for Egypt was issued by the Sultan just one day after the British Parliament declared Egypt to be a sovereign state. Then, almost thirty years later (June 18, 1953, 11:30 p.m., Cairo) an independence declaration by President Nassar for the Republic of Egypt results in a birth chart with planetary connections to the original, which is the one illustrated here. When an eclipse falls conspicuously on a planet in Egypt's chart, it is of increased importance for the country. For example, in 2004 and 2005, eclipses touch upon Egypt's Moon. The Moon is representative of the working classes, the common people, and women and crowds, so these eclipses will be quite important for the citizens of Egypt for some time following. The eclipse of early 2006 on the Sun is also important, often bringing changes affecting central leaders.

To find the people and things emphasized by coming eclipses, refer to table 4. To find the raw power rating of any eclipse, refer to table 1. That table also gives the dates of planetary stimulation to the eclipse, which may closely coincide with notable events traceable to the eclipse. See more definition of coming eclipses in the Catalog of Annotated Eclipse Charts. Chart data source: Maggie Hyde, "Tomorrow's News," *American Astrology* (Dec. 2002): p. 56. Her stated source: Nicholas Campion, *The Book of World Horoscopes* (Bristol, England: Cinnabar Books, 1999).

Eclipse Emphasis for Egypt through 2011

July 1, 2000, Solar Eclipse emphasizes—Pluto

Dec. 25, 2000, Solar Eclipse emphasizes—Pluto

Dec. 30, 2001, Lunar Eclipse emphasizes—Pluto

Dec. 4, 2002, Solar Eclipse emphasizes—Mars

May 30, 2003, Solar Eclipse emphasizes—The Ascendant and Mars

Oct. 13, 2004, Solar Eclipse emphasizes—The Moon

April 8, 2005, Solar Eclipse emphasizes—The Moon

Oct. 3, 2005, Solar Eclipse emphasizes—The Dragon's Head and Chiron (Wounded Healer)

March 14, 2006, Lunar Eclipse emphasizes—The Sun

March 29, 2006, Solar Eclipse emphasizes—The Dragon's Tail

Sept. 22, 2006, Solar Eclipse emphasizes—Venus

March 3, 2007, Lunar Eclipse emphasizes—Uranus

Aug. 16, 2008, Lunar Eclipse emphasizes—Mercury

Feb. 9, 2009, Lunar Eclipse emphasizes—The Midheaven

Aug. 5, 2009, Lunar Eclipse emphasizes—Neptune

Dec. 31, 2009, Lunar Eclipse emphasizes—Pluto

June 1, 2011, Solar Eclipse emphasizes—The Ascendant and Mars

July 1, 2011, Solar Eclipse emphasizes—Pluto

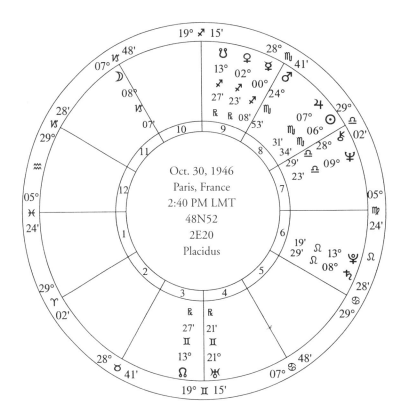

France

When an eclipse makes contacts to planets in France's horoscope, it is of some great importance for the country. In 2002, an eclipse fell on the Dragon's Tail of France's horoscope. The Dragon's Tail is associated with sacrifice and selfless service. Demonstrating a cautious stance, France refused to go along with the U.S. for war on Iraq. France was severely shunned by the U.S., with restaurants changing the name of french fries to freedom fries, feeling that France owed the U.S. its loyalty. These repercussions for France show how sacrifice is rightly attributed to eclipses on the Dragon's Tail, often unavoidable. In another example, the Lunar eclipse of May 2003 fell on France's Mars, associated with fire and heat. Following that eclipse, an extreme heat wave caused the deaths of more than 10,000 residents as the eclipse was stimulated by the transiting Sun in mid-August.

To find the people and things emphasized by coming eclipses, refer to table 4. To find the raw power rating of any eclipse, refer to table 1. That table also gives the dates of planetary stimulation to the eclipse, which may closely coincide with notable events traceable to the eclipse. See more definition of coming eclipses in the Catalog of Annotated Eclipse Charts. Chart data source: Stephen Erlewine, *The Circle Book of Charts* (Tempe, AZ: American Federation of Astrologers, 1991), p. 262, citing Charles E. O. Carter in his *Introduction to Political Astrology*. Conflicting data surrounding the official start of the Fifth Republic prevented a use of that chart. Nicholas Campion recommends October 6, 1958, 6:30 p.m. CET, Paris, resulting in a chart that does show many connections to this one, with duplications of important degrees.

Eclipse Emphasis for France through 2011

July 1, 2000, Solar Eclipse emphasizes—The Moon

Dec. 14, 2001, Solar Eclipse emphasizes—Uranus

Dec. 30, 2001, Lunar Eclipse emphasizes—The Moon

May 26, 2002, Lunar Eclipse emphasizes—Venus

June 10, 2002, Solar Eclipse emphasizes—The Midheaven and Uranus

Nov. 19, 2002, Lunar Eclipse emphasizes—Mars

Dec. 4, 2002, Solar Eclipse emphasizes—The Dragon's Tail

May 15, 2003, Lunar Eclipse emphasizes—Mars

Nov. 23, 2003, Solar Eclipse emphasizes—Venus and Mercury

April 19, 2004, Solar Eclipse emphasizes—Chiron (Wounded Healer)

Oct. 27, 2004, Lunar Eclipse emphasizes—The Sun and Jupiter

April 24, 2005, Lunar Eclipse emphasizes—The Sun

Oct. 3, 2005, Solar Eclipse emphasizes—Neptune

March 29, 2006, Solar Eclipse emphasizes—Neptune

Aug. 28, 2007, Lunar Eclipse emphasizes—The Ascendant

Aug. 1, 2008, Solar Eclipse emphasizes—Saturn

Jan. 26, 2009, Solar Eclipse emphasizes—Saturn

Aug. 5, 2009, Lunar Eclipse emphasizes—Pluto

Dec. 31, 2009, Lunar Eclipse emphasizes—The Moon

June 1, 2011, Solar Eclipse emphasizes—The Dragon's Head

June 15, 2011, Lunar Eclipse emphasizes—Uranus

July 1, 2011, Solar Eclipse emphasizes—The Moon

Nov. 25, 2011, Solar Eclipse emphasizes—Venus and Mercury

Dec. 10, 2011, Lunar Eclipse emphasizes—The Midheaven

May 20, 2012, Solar Eclipse emphasizes—Mercury and Venus

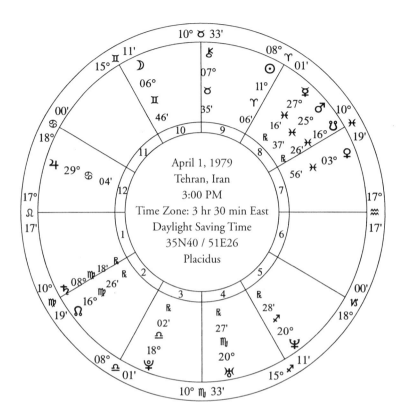

Iran

An eclipse that falls on a planet in the horoscope of Iran is of some importance for the country. For example, on May 30, 2003, the Solar eclipse in the sign Gemini, the sign of the twins, fell on the Moon of Iran's chart, signaling that women of note would come into the spotlight. Soon after the eclipse, the Siamese twins Laleh and Ladan Bijani underwent an unprecedented surgery to the head and brain in order to be separated from one another. By age twenty-nine, they felt it worth the risk to be able to lead separate lives, the two having distinct interests, personalities, likes and dislikes. They schooled in law to follow the dedication of the more extroverted and dominant of the two. The other wanted to be a journalist. The country mourned the loss when both twins died during surgery. That same eclipse would show a general emphasis on women's interests for some time as well as increased fluctuation in the public mood on important issues.

To find the various people and things emphasized by coming eclipses, refer to table 4. To find the raw power rating of any eclipse, refer to table 1. That table also gives the dates of planetary stimulation to the eclipse, which may closely coincide with notable events traceable to the eclipse. See more definition of coming eclipses in the Catalog of Annotated Eclipse Charts. Chart data source: Maggie Hyde, "Tomorrow's News," *American Astrology* (April 2003): p. 56.

Eclipse Emphasis for Iran through 2011

Dec. 14, 2001, Solar Eclipse emphasizes—Neptune

May 26, 2002, Lunar Eclipse emphasizes—The Moon

June 10, 2002, Solar Eclipse emphasizes—Neptune

May 30, 2003, Solar Eclipse emphasizes—The Moon

Oct. 27, 2004, Lunar Eclipse emphasizes—Chiron (Wounded Healer)

April 8, 2005, Solar Eclipse emphasizes—Pluto

Oct. 3, 2005, Solar Eclipse emphasizes—The Sun

March 14, 2006, Lunar Eclipse emphasizes—Mars and Mercury

March 29, 2006, Solar Eclipse emphasizes—The Sun

Sept. 7, 2006, Lunar Eclipse emphasizes—The Dragon's Tail

Sept. 22, 2006, Solar Eclipse emphasizes—Mercury

March 18, 2007, Solar Eclipse emphasizes—Mercury

Aug. 28, 2007, Lunar Eclipse emphasizes—Venus

Sept. 11, 2007, Solar Eclipse emphasizes—The Dragon's Head

Feb. 6, 2008, Solar Eclipse emphasizes—The Ascendant

Feb. 20, 2008, Lunar Eclipse emphasizes—Venus

July 21, 2009, Solar Eclipse emphasizes—Jupiter

Aug. 5, 2009, Lunar Eclipse emphasizes—The Ascendant

Dec. 10, 2011, Lunar Eclipse emphasizes—Neptune

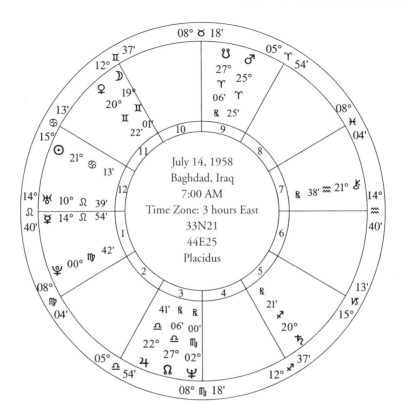

Iraq

An eclipse falling upon a planet in Iraq's chart is of some significance for the country. In 2000 and again in early 2001, Lunar eclipses fell upon the Sun in the Iraq chart, bringing the Iraqi leader, Saddam Hussein, into the spotlight. Another eclipse also indicated major changes for Iraqi citizens. It fell squarely across Iraq's Moon, Venus, and Saturn in 2002. A new authority was suggested, as well as a turbulent period affecting public tranquility. During transits to those eclipses by Mars in April of 2003, U.S. forces helped citizens destroy statues of Hussein, symbolic of toppling Saddam Hussein and his regime. Turmoil, looting, and uprisings continued through power shortages and other hardships that greatly impinged upon the quality of life of the average citizen.

To find the people and things emphasized by coming eclipses, refer to table 4. To find the raw power rating of any eclipse, refer to table 1. That table also gives the dates of planetary stimulation to the eclipse, which may closely coincide with notable events traceable to the eclipse. See more definition of coming eclipses in the Catalog of Annotated Eclipse Charts. When the Iraqi people vote on a new constitution and a new permanent government is established and commences to operate, that will mark a new birth and a new birth chart for Iraq. There will undoubtedly be strong ties between the old and new charts. Chart data from Nicholas Campion, *The Book of World Horoscopes* (Bristol, England: Cinnabar Books, 1999), chart 162.

Eclipse Emphasis for Iraq through 2011

July 16, 2000, Lunar Eclipse emphasizes—The Sun

July 30, 2000, Solar Eclipse emphasizes—Uranus

Jan. 9, 2001, Lunar Eclipse emphasizes—The Sun

Dec. 14, 2001, Solar Eclipse emphasizes—Saturn and Venus

June 10, 2002, Solar Eclipse emphasizes—The Moon, Venus, and Saturn

April 19, 2004, Solar Eclipse emphasizes—The Dragon's Tail

Oct. 13, 2004, Solar Eclipse emphasizes—Jupiter

April 24, 2005, Lunar Eclipse emphasizes—Neptune

Oct. 17, 2005, Lunar Eclipse emphasizes—Mars and Jupiter

Feb. 6, 2008, Solar Eclipse emphasizes—The Ascendant and Mercury

Feb. 20, 2008, Lunar Eclipse emphasizes—Pluto

Aug. 1, 2008, Solar Eclipse emphasizes—Uranus

Aug. 18, 2008, Lunar Eclipse emphasizes—Chiron (Wounded Healer)

Feb. 9, 2009, Lunar Eclipse emphasizes—Chiron (Wounded Healer)

Aug. 5, 2009, Lunar Eclipse emphasizes—The Ascendant and Mercury

July 11, 2010, Solar Eclipse emphasizes—The Sun

Dec. 10, 2011, Lunar Eclipse emphasizes—The Moon, Venus, and Saturn

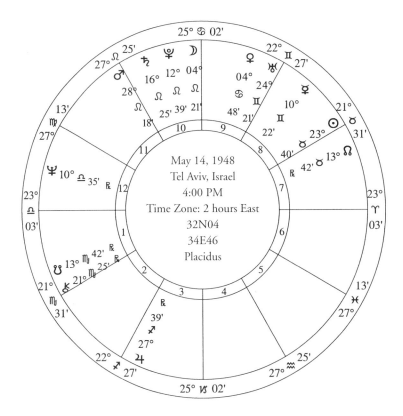

Israel

The eclipses listed below fall on conspicuous places in the Israel birth chart, and are of some importance for the nation. In May of 2003, two eclipses fell in the chart of Israel—the first on Israel's Sun, bringing leader Ariel Sharon to the forefront, and the second on Israel's Mercury, which coincided closely with the beginning of talks for a peacekeeping agreement with Palestine, a roadmap for peace set forth by U.S. President Bush to help resolve long-standing disputes between the two nations, including dual claims to the Holy City. These eclipses will be open to stimulation for some time, during which the peace process will proceed or be deterred.

To find the people and things emphasized by coming eclipses, refer to table 4. To find the raw power rating of any eclipse, refer to table 1. That table also gives the dates of planetary stimulation to the eclipse, which may closely coincide with notable events traceable to the eclipse. See more definition of coming eclipses in the Catalog of Annotated Eclipse Charts. Chart data source: Maggie Hyde, "Tomorrow's News," *American Astrology* (Aug. 2002): p. 56.

Eclipse Emphasis for Israel through 2011

July 16, 2000, Lunar Eclipse emphasizes—The Midheaven
Dec. 25, 2000, Solar Eclipse emphasizes—Venus

Dec. 14, 2001, Solar Eclipse emphasizes—Uranus

June 24, 2002, Lunar Eclipse emphasizes—Venus

Dec. 4, 2002, Solar Eclipse emphasizes—Mercury

May 15, 2003, Lunar Eclipse emphasizes—The Sun

May 30, 2003, Solar Eclipse emphasizes—Mercury

Nov. 8, 2003, Lunar Eclipse emphasizes—The Dragon's Head

May 4, 2004, Lunar Eclipse emphasizes—The Dragon's Tail

Oct. 13, 2004, Solar Eclipse emphasizes—The Ascendant

Oct. 3, 2005, Solar Eclipse emphasizes—Neptune

Oct. 17, 2005, Lunar Eclipse emphasizes—The Ascendant

March 29, 2006, Solar Eclipse emphasizes—Neptune

Feb. 6, 2008, Solar Eclipse emphasizes—Saturn

Aug. 1, 2008, Solar Eclipse emphasizes—Pluto

Jan. 26, 2009, Solar Eclipse emphasizes—The Moon

Aug. 5, 2009, Lunar Eclipse emphasizes—Saturn and Pluto

Jan. 15, 2010, Solar Eclipse emphasizes—The Midheaven

June 26, 2010, Lunar Eclipse emphasizes—Venus

Dec. 21, 2010, Lunar Eclipse emphasizes—Jupiter

June 1, 2011, Solar Eclipse emphasizes—Mercury

June 15, 2011, Lunar Eclipse emphasizes—Uranus and Jupiter

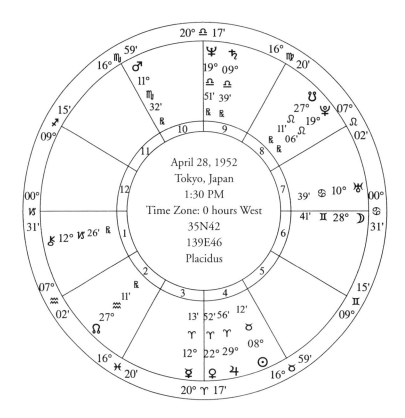

Japan

This horoscope for Japan shows planetary links to its previous chart of 1868 and the restoration of imperial authority at that time. Both charts show planets in the middle degrees of the cardinal signs—Aries, Cancer, Libra, and Capricorn—appropriately reflecting Japan's status as a major world power. This chart is especially outstanding by having a world point rising at the Ascendant, sometimes called an Aries Point degree, associated with worldly connections. Coming eclipses to important planets or points in Japan's chart will reflect events of significance for the nation and its people. The Lunar Eclipse of October 27, 2004, will be of importance for its governmental leaders. In fact there are several eclipses in 2004 and 2005 that will remain sensitive to transits for some time to come.

To find the people and things emphasized by coming eclipses, refer to table 4. To find the raw power rating of any eclipse, refer to table 1. That table also gives the dates of planetary stimulation to the eclipse, which may closely coincide with notable events traceable to the eclipse. See more definition of coming eclipses in the Catalog of Annotated Eclipse Charts. Chart data from Judy Collins, education director for the Arizona Society of Astrologers. She cites her source as Nicholas Campion's *World Horoscopes* software program.

Eclipse Emphasis for Japan through 2011

July 1, 2000, Solar Eclipse emphasizes—Uranus

June 21, 2001, Solar Eclipse emphasizes—The Ascendant and Moon

July 5, 2001, Lunar Eclipse emphasizes—Uranus and Chiron (Wounded Healer)

Dec. 30, 2001, Lunar Eclipse emphasizes—Uranus

June 24, 2002, Lunar Eclipse emphasizes—The Ascendant

April 19, 2004, Solar Eclipse emphasizes—Jupiter

Oct. 13, 2004, Solar Eclipse emphasizes—Venus, Neptune, and the Midheaven

Oct. 27, 2004, Lunar Eclipse emphasizes—The Sun

April 8, 2005, Solar Eclipse emphasizes—Venus and Neptune

Oct. 3, 2005, Solar Eclipse emphasizes—Mercury and Saturn

Oct. 17, 2005, Lunar Eclipse emphasizes—Venus

March 29, 2006, Solar Eclipse emphasizes—Saturn

Feb. 6, 2008, Solar Eclipse emphasizes—Pluto

Aug. 16, 2008, Lunar Eclipse emphasizes—The Dragon's Head

Feb. 9, 2009, Lunar Eclipse emphasizes—Pluto

July 7, 2009, Lunar Eclipse emphasizes—Chiron (Wounded Healer)

Dec. 31, 2009, Lunar Eclipse emphasizes—Uranus and Chiron (Wounded Healer)

Dec. 21, 2010, Lunar Eclipse emphasizes—The Moon

Jan. 4, 2011, Solar Eclipse emphasizes—Uranus and Chiron (Wounded Healer)

July 1, 2011, Solar Eclipse emphasizes—Uranus

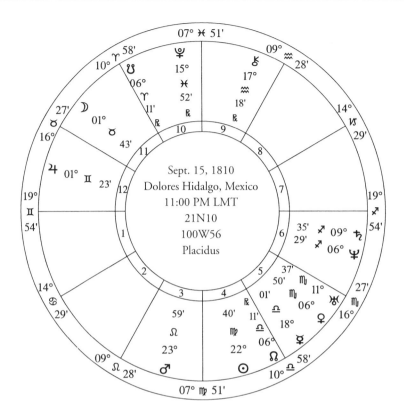

Mexico

Mexico's revolt against Spain in achieving its independence began on the evening of September 15, 1810, when the leading revolutionary, Priest Hidalgo, rang the church bell in Mexico City at 11 p.m. to signal the start of the uprising. Each year on September 15 the same church bell rings at 11 p.m. to commemorate Mexico's independence. Eclipses that fall on conspicuous places in the Mexico horoscope are of heightened importance for the country. Early in 2006, an eclipse highlights Mexico's central leadership figure and several eclipses fall on important places. These are likely to bring the country into the spotlight for an extended period as change, transformations, and reforms take place.

To find the various people and things emphasized by future eclipses listed here, refer to table 4. To find the raw power rating of any eclipse, refer to table 1. That table also gives the dates of planetary stimulation to the eclipse, which may closely coincide with notable events traceable to the eclipse. See more definition of coming eclipses in the Catalog of Annotated Eclipse Charts. Chart data source: Maggie Hyde, "Tomorrow's News," *American Astrology* (June 2002): p. 56.

Eclipse Emphasis for Mexico through 2011

Dec. 14, 2001, Solar Eclipse emphasizes—The Ascendant

May 26, 2002, Lunar Eclipse emphasizes—Neptune

Dec. 4, 2002, Solar Eclipse emphasizes—Saturn

May 30, 2003, Solar Eclipse emphasizes—Saturn

Nov. 23, 2003, Solar Eclipse emphasizes—Jupiter

Oct. 13, 2004, Solar Eclipse emphasizes—Mercury

Oct. 27, 2004, Lunar Eclipse emphasizes—Venus

April 8, 2005, Solar Eclipse emphasizes—Mercury

April 24, 2005, Lunar Eclipse emphasizes—Venus

March 14, 2006, Lunar Eclipse emphasizes—The Sun

March 29, 2006, Solar Eclipse emphasizes—The Dragon's Tail

Sept. 7, 2006, Lunar Eclipse emphasizes—Pluto

March 3, 2007, Lunar Eclipse emphasizes—Pluto

Aug. 28, 2007, Lunar Eclipse emphasizes—The Midheaven

Sept. 11, 2007, Solar Eclipse emphasizes—Pluto

Aug. 16, 2008, Lunar Eclipse emphasizes—Mars

Feb. 9, 2009, Lunar Eclipse emphasizes—Mars

June 1, 2011, Solar Eclipse emphasizes—Saturn

Nov. 25, 2011, Solar Eclipse emphasizes—Jupiter

May 20, 2012, Solar Eclipse emphasizes—Jupiter

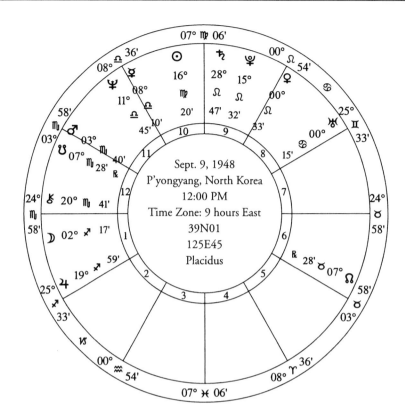

North Korea

An eclipse that touches upon a planet in North Korea's horoscope is of important note for the country. In 2001 and 2002, eclipses brought emphasis to North Korea's Jupiter, associated with an urge to expand one's sphere of influence. Soon after, Kim Jong II announced nuclear-weapons plans that caused the world to sit up and take notice. Jupiter is also associated with exaggeration, boasting, propaganda, and thinking big, and this example illustrates how the qualities of a planet can become distorted by the influence of an eclipse. Coming in 2004 and 2005, North Korea's Mars is eclipsed, denoting potential conflicts, either initiated by or directed toward the country, and while those eclipses remain sensitive to transits for some time, they may not be nearly as impressive as the later time period in 2006–2007 when North Korea's Sun receives three eclipses within a year's time. An eclipse to the Sun is one of the most important because it brings the leaders and decision makers of a nation into the limelight.

To find the various people and things emphasized by coming eclipses, refer to table 4. To find the raw power rating of any eclipse, refer to table 1. That table also gives the dates of planetary stimulation to the eclipse, which may closely coincide with notable events traceable to the eclipse. See more definition of coming eclipses in the Catalog of Annotated Eclipse Charts. Chart data source: *U.S. Department of State,* www.state.gov/www/background_notes/north_korea_0696_bgn.html, under the "Korean War" subheading. In his *Book of World Horoscopes*, Nicholas Campion offers different data: noontime one day later, changing little but the Moon position.

Eclipse Emphasis for North Korea through 2011

June 21, 2001, Solar Eclipse emphasizes—Uranus

Dec. 14, 2001, Solar Eclipse emphasizes—Jupiter

May 26, 2002, Lunar Eclipse emphasizes—The Moon

June 10, 2002, Solar Eclipse emphasizes—Jupiter

June 24, 2002, Lunar Eclipse emphasizes—Uranus

Nov. 19, 2002, Lunar Eclipse emphasizes—The Ascendant

May 15, 2003, Lunar Eclipse emphasizes—The Ascendant

Nov. 23, 2003, Solar Eclipse emphasizes—The Moon

Oct. 27, 2004, Lunar Eclipse emphasizes—The Dragon's Head and Mars

April 24, 2005, Lunar Eclipse emphasizes—Mars

Oct. 3, 2005, Solar Eclipse emphasizes—Neptune and Mercury

March 29, 2006, Solar Eclipse emphasizes—Mercury

Sept. 7, 2006, Lunar Eclipse emphasizes—The Sun

March 3, 2007, Lunar Eclipse emphasizes—The Sun

Sept. 11, 2007, Solar Eclipse emphasizes—The Sun

Feb. 6, 2008, Solar Eclipse emphasizes—Pluto

July 21, 2009, Solar Eclipse emphasizes—Venus

Aug. 5, 2009, Lunar Eclipse emphasizes—Pluto

Dec. 21, 2010, Lunar Eclipse emphasizes—Uranus

Nov. 25, 2011, Solar Eclipse emphasizes—The Moon

Dec. 10, 2011, Lunar Eclipse emphasizes—Jupiter

May 20, 2012, Solar Eclipse emphasizes—The Moon

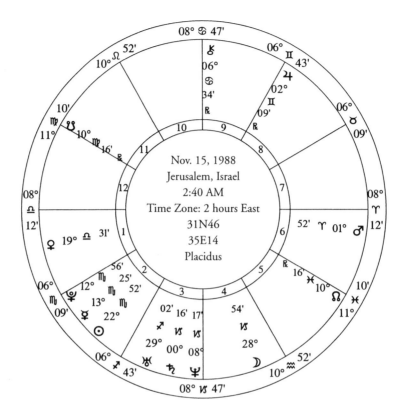

Palestine

An eclipse falling upon a planet in the Palestine chart signifies an eclipse process of importance for its citizens and leaders. The same eclipse of May 2003 that fell upon Israel's Sun also fell opposite Palestine's Sun, bringing the leaders of Israel and Palestine to the fore and depicting central issues for both sides. Coincident with the time of this eclipse, U.S. President George W. Bush proposed a roadmap plan for peace that would give Palestine statehood by 2005. Also similar to Israel, an eclipse in 2003 emphasizes Palestine's Mercury, connected to agreements and roadmap plans. Still, in looking ahead to 2006, an eclipse falling on Palestine's Mars suggests a final conflict in gaining statehood or another Mars-related event.

To find the people and things emphasized by coming eclipses, refer to table 4. To find the raw power rating of any eclipse, refer to table 1. That table also gives the dates of planetary stimulation to the eclipse, which may closely coincide with notable events traceable to the eclipse. See more definition of coming eclipses in the Catalog of Annotated Eclipse Charts. Chart data from Nicholas Campion, *The Book of World Horoscopes* (Bristol, England: Cinnabar Books, 1999), chart 240. With new statehood for Palestine, a new chart can be cast. That chart will make ties to this one, but a brighter outlook might be anticipated if it removes Chiron, the Wounded Healer, from the Midheaven.

Eclipses for Palestine through 2011

July 1, 2000, Solar Eclipse emphasizes—The Midheaven and Neptune

June 21, 2001, Solar Eclipse emphasizes—Saturn

Dec. 30, 2001, Lunar Eclipse emphasizes—The Midheaven and Neptune

May 26, 2002, Lunar Eclipse emphasizes—Jupiter

June 24, 2002, Lunar Eclipse emphasizes—Saturn

May 15, 2003, Lunar Eclipse emphasizes—The Sun

Nov. 8, 2003, Lunar Eclipse emphasizes—Mercury

Nov. 23, 2003, Solar Eclipse emphasizes—Jupiter

May 4, 2004, Lunar Eclipse emphasizes—Mercury

Oct. 13, 2004, Solar Eclipse emphasizes—Venus

Oct. 3, 2005, Solar Eclipse emphasizes—The Ascendant

March 29, 2006, Solar Eclipse emphasizes—The Ascendant

Sept. 22, 2006, Solar Eclipse emphasizes—Mars

March 3, 2007, Lunar Eclipse emphasizes—The Dragon's Tail

July 21, 2009, Solar Eclipse emphasizes—The Moon

Dec. 31, 2009, Lunar Eclipse emphasizes—The Midheaven and Neptune

Dec. 21, 2010, Lunar Eclipse emphasizes—Uranus

July 1, 2011, Solar Eclipse emphasizes—The Midheaven and Neptune

Nov. 25, 2011, Solar Eclipse emphasizes—Jupiter

May 20, 2012, Solar Eclipse emphasizes—Jupiter

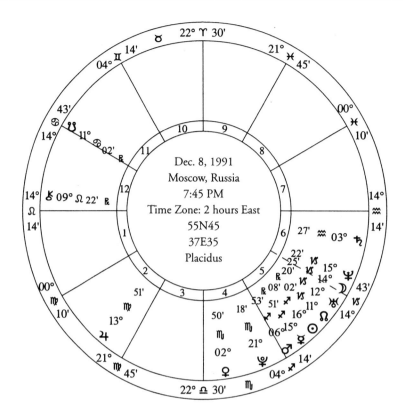

Dec. 8, 1991
Moscow, Russia
7:45 PM
Time Zone: 2 hours East
55N45
37E35
Placidus

Russia

An eclipse falling upon a planet in Russia's chart is of special significance for the country. In 2002 and 2003, eclipses emphasized Russia's Mars, associated with arms and weapons. Arms trades with Iran became a highlighted topic, as well as defense-plan cooperatives with other countries. Those eclipses and related activities continue to receive stimulation until early 2007. Eclipse potential also increases by the number of planets it contacts. In 2011, an eclipse falls upon four conspicuous places in Russia's chart, representing a period of some complexity and importance. Russia's space program may be one hot topic, in the limelight as early as 2009, with increased activity, transformations, and changes to follow.

To find the people and things emphasized by coming eclipses, refer to table 4. To find the raw power rating of any eclipse, refer to table 1. That table also gives the dates of planetary stimulation to the eclipse, which may closely coincide with notable events traceable to the eclipse. See more definition of coming eclipses in the Catalog of Annotated Eclipse Charts. Chart data for Russia's Independence Proclamation: Arizona Society of Astrologers newsletter, Feb. 2000; column by Judy Collins, education director for the Arizona Society of Astrologers. Her source: Nicholas Campion's *World Horoscopes* software program.

Eclipse Emphasis for Russia through 2011

July 1, 2000, Solar Eclipse emphasizes—The Sun, the Dragon's Tail, and Uranus

July 30, 2000, Solar Eclipse emphasizes—Chiron (Wounded Healer)

July 5, 2000, Lunar Eclipse emphasizes—The Moon, the Dragon's Head, Uranus, and Neptune

Dec. 30, 2001, Lunar Eclipse emphasizes—The Dragon's Tail

May 26, 2002, Lunar Eclipse emphasizes—Mars

May 30, 2003, Solar Eclipse emphasizes—Mars

Oct. 13, 2004, Solar Eclipse emphasizes—The Midheaven

Oct. 27, 2004, Lunar Eclipse emphasizes—Venus

April 24, 2005, Lunar Eclipse emphasizes—Venus

Oct. 17, 2005, Lunar Eclipse emphasizes—The Midheaven

Sept. 7, 2006, Lunar Eclipse emphasizes—Jupiter

March 3, 2007, Lunar Eclipse emphasizes—Jupiter

Aug. 1, 2008, Solar Eclipse emphasizes—Chiron (Wounded Healer)

Jan. 26, 2009, Solar Eclipse emphasizes—Saturn

July 7, 2009, Lunar Eclipse emphasizes—The Moon, Neptune, and Uranus

Dec. 31, 2009, Lunar Eclipse emphasizes—The Dragon's Head and Uranus

Jan. 4, 2011, Solar Eclipse emphasizes—The Dragon's Head, the Moon, Uranus, and Neptune

July 1, 2011, Solar Eclipse emphasizes—The Dragon's Tail and Uranus

Dec. 10, 2011, Lunar Eclipse emphasizes—The Sun and Mercury

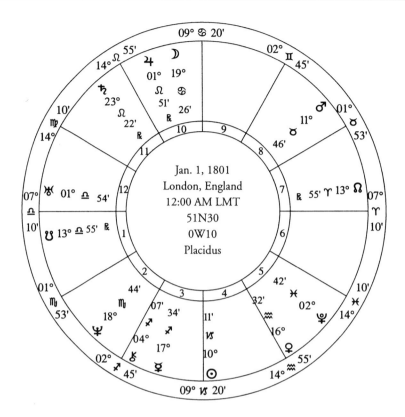

United Kingdom

The horoscope for the United Kingdom is cast for the Union of Great Britain and Ireland. When an eclipse highlights a planet in this chart, it shows an eclipse of note for the UK. Three notable eclipses occurred between 2000 and 2001. Two of the three stimulated both the Sun and Midheaven, bringing a focus to central leaders and to the reputation of the country. Either of these will often bring a nation into the world spotlight. Another eclipse fell on the Moon, spotlighting public opinion. Following these eclipses, the UK became the U.S.'s strongest ally in fighting the war on terror, with cooperative efforts between Prime Minister Tony Blair and U.S. President George W. Bush that eventually generated opinions from other nations as well as from its own citizens about Britain's stance on the matter of war in Iraq. Eclipses affected the Sun in each of the three country's charts in July 2000, and the Iraq War was most intense as Mars later transited those previous eclipses (in March and April of 2003).

To find the people and things emphasized by coming eclipses, refer to table 4. To find the raw power rating of any eclipse, refer to table 1. That table also gives the dates of planetary stimulation to the eclipse, which may closely coincide with notable events traceable to the eclipse. See more definition of future eclipses in the Catalog of Annotated Eclipse Charts. Chart data source: Stephen Erlewine, *The Circle Book of Charts* (Tempe, AZ: American Federation of Astrologers, 1991), p. 261. Chart by Charles E. O. Carter.

Eclipses of Emphasis for the United Kingdom through 2011

July 1, 2000, Solar Eclipse emphasizes—The Sun and Midheaven

Jan. 9, 2001, Lunar Eclipse emphasizes—The Moon

Dec. 30, 2001, Lunar Eclipse emphasizes—The Sun and Midheaven

May 26, 2002, Lunar Eclipse emphasizes—Chiron (Wounded Healer)

June 10, 2002, Solar Eclipse emphasizes—Mercury

Nov. 8, 2003, Lunar Eclipse emphasizes—Neptune

Oct. 3, 2005, Solar Eclipse emphasizes—The Ascendant

March 29, 2006, Solar Eclipse emphasizes—The Ascendant

Aug. 28, 2007, Lunar Eclipse emphasizes—Pluto

Feb. 6, 2008, Solar Eclipse emphasizes—Venus

Feb. 20, 2008, Lunar Eclipse emphasizes—Pluto

Aug. 16, 2008, Lunar Eclipse emphasizes—Saturn

Feb. 9, 2009, Lunar Eclipse emphasizes—Saturn

July 21, 2009, Solar Eclipse emphasizes—Jupiter

Aug. 5, 2009, Lunar Eclipse emphasizes—Venus

Dec. 31, 2009, Lunar Eclipse emphasizes—The Sun and Midheaven

July 11, 2010, Solar Eclipse emphasizes—The Moon

July 1, 2011, Solar Eclipse emphasizes—The Sun and Midheaven

Dec. 10, 2011, Lunar Eclipse emphasizes—Mercury

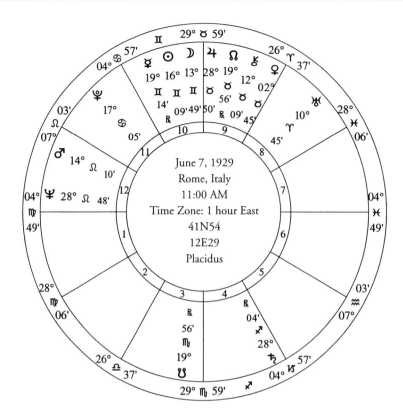

Vatican City, Rome

The restoration of the Vatican as an independent state, granted by Mussolini in 1929, came on a New Moon day. Pope John Paul II, born on the day of a Solar eclipse in Taurus in 1920, had his Sun falling on the Vatican City's Jupiter, truly a benevolent cosmic connection. His Sun also fell on the Midheaven, a powerful tie that binded him and the city together as far as recognition and status. The MC near the famed degree associated with the "weeping sisters" is truly symbolic of the Vatican. Eclipses falling prominently on planets in the Vatican City nativity indicate an eclipse process of some importance for the Vatican. For example, in 2002 an eclipse fell on Jupiter and the Moon, harkening to issues of justice and questioning the honorable actions of Catholic clergy. With the Moon involved, the eclipse told of fluctuations of public reactions toward the Church.

Sadly, as this goes to print, it is noted that with multiple eclipses falling over Venus in 2004 and early 2005, the Pope became ill and passed on. He was buried coincident with an eclipse, just as he'd been born with one. Venus rules loved ones, and he was much loved.

To find the people and things emphasized by coming eclipses, refer to table 4. To find the raw power rating of any eclipse, refer to table 1. That table also gives the dates of planetary stimulation to the eclipse, which may closely coincide with notable events traceable to the eclipse. See more definition of coming eclipses in the Catalog of Annotated Eclipse Charts. Chart data source: Maggie Hyde, "Tomorrow's News," *American Astrology* (May 2002): p. 56.

Eclipse Emphasis for Vatican City through 2011

    Jan. 9, 2001, Lunar Eclipse emphasizes—Pluto

    June 21, 2001, Solar Eclipse emphasizes—Saturn

    June 10, 2002, Solar Eclipse emphasizes—Mercury

    Nov. 19, 2002, Lunar Eclipse emphasizes—Jupiter

    Dec. 4, 2002, Solar Eclipse emphasizes—The Moon

    Nov. 23, 2003, Solar Eclipse emphasizes—The Midheaven

    April 19, 2004, Solar Eclipse emphasizes—Venus

    May 4 2004, Lunar Eclipse emphasizes—Chiron (Wounded Healer)

    Oct. 27, 2004, Lunar Eclipse emphasizes—Venus

    April 24, 2005, Lunar Eclipse emphasizes—Venus

    Oct. 3, 2005, Solar Eclipse emphasizes—Uranus

    March 29, 2006, Solar Eclipse emphasizes—Uranus

    Aug. 28, 2007, Lunar Eclipse emphasizes—The Ascendant

    July 7, 2009, Lunar Eclipse emphasizes—Pluto

    Aug. 5, 2009, Lunar Eclipse emphasizes—Mars

    July 11, 2010, Solar Eclipse emphasizes—Pluto

    Dec. 21, 2010, Lunar Eclipse emphasizes—Saturn

    June 1, 2011, Solar Eclipse emphasizes—The Moon

    Dec. 10, 2011, Lunar Eclipse emphasizes—The Sun and Mercury

    May 20, 2012, Solar Eclipse emphasizes—The Midheaven

Table 4: Planetary Keys

An eclipse brings emphasis, change, and impact to the people and things represented by the planet receiving the eclipse stimulus. The hidden power of an eclipse is that it has delayed manifestations. The keywords below describe things and people represented by the planets. If things have been going poorly in regard to the things signified, an eclipse may indicate improving conditions. If things have been going well, an eclipse may precede a reevaluation. An eclipse may amplify and/or distort planetary functioning.

For Nations & Cities

Sun ☉

King, Supreme Authority, President, Head Executive, Noble Characters, Central Figures.
Vitality, Individuality, Creative Will, Power, Ego.

Moon ☽

Common People, Public Attitude, Women, Crowds, Lower Class, Water, Liquids, Sailors, Ocean, Noted Women, Home, Family.
Fluctuation, Instinctual, Nourishing, Responsive, Domestics, Catering, Fertility.

Mercury ☿

Intelligence Gathering, Communications, News and Transport, Vehicles, Education, Post Office, General Trade Meetings.
Books, Speech, Writers, Authors, Merchants, Students, Teachers, Expression, Intellect, Adaptability, Perception, Movement, Learning, Logic, Reason, Craftsmanship, Borders, Near Neighbors.

Venus ♀

Banks/Finance, Social Affairs, Social Harmony, Young Women, Wives, Sweethearts, Art, Finery, Jewels, Luxury, Money, Festivities.
Tranquility, Cohesion, Pleasure, Affections, Love, Sharing, Decoration, Gifts, Beauty, Flowers, Perfume, Cosmetics, Confections, Dance, Song, Ladies' Interests.

Mars ♂

Young Men, Police, Firefighters, Armed Forces, Weapons, Engineers, Athletes, Surgeons, Agitators, Crime, Fever, Infection.
Sharp Tools, Users of Sharp Instruments, Fighting Spirit, Passion, Action, Hero, Initiative, Courage, Assertion, Aggression, Enterprise, Ammunition.

Jupiter ♃

Law, Courts, Judiciary, Clergymen, Religion, Distant Travelers/ET, Ceremonies, Assemblies, Universities, Publishing.
Expansion, Abundance, Honor, Respectable, Philosophy, Vision, Truth, Optimism, Generosity, Benevolence, Production, Lotteries, Gambling, Republicans.

Saturn ♄

Older People, Serious People, Farmers, Builders, Widows and Widowers, Hermits, Misers, Debts, Karma, Justice, History, Time.

Contraction, Restriction, Limitations, Boundaries, Tradition, Discipline, Restraint, Organization, Framework, Prudence, Chiropractic, Bereavement, Civil Workers, Democrats.

Uranus ♅

Chief Authority, Prime Minister, Inventors, Electricity, Pioneers, Discoverers, Antiquarians, Aeronautics, Spacecraft, Liberation.

Revolutionary, Erratic, Explosive, Unexpected, Eccentricity, Progressive, Advanced Technology, Compulsion, Nonconformity, Physics, X-ray, Storms, Lightning, Riots, Uprisings.

Neptune ♆

Social Movements, Marines, Navy, Alcohol, Drugs, Oil, Chemicals, Gas, Hospitals, Aid, Welfare, Prisons, Dance, Film, Actors, Pilots.

Assassins, Treason, Deceptions, Poisons, Photography, Addicts, Anesthetics, Antiseptics, Compassion, Glamour, Imagination, Dissolve, Collapse, Confusion, Sea, Drowning, Liquids, Recluses.

Pluto ♇

Psychologists, Healers, Reform Leaders, Miners, Refuse, Sewage Workers, Uniformed Workers, FBI, Mortuaries, Underworld.

Nuclear Energy, Transformation, Purge, Destroy, Renew, Demolition, Domination, Coercion, Plots, Atomic Science, Abduction, Riot, Crime, Ambush, Abortion, Rape, Cremation, Strength, Force.

For Businesses, Companies & Other Entities or Enterprises

Sun ☉

Leaders, Central Issues Affecting Success, President, Father, Spirit, Men, Gold.
Vitality, Individuality, Ego, Will, Power, Fame, Virility, Creativity.

Moon ☽

Public Vacillation, Sensitive Matters, Functions, Families, Home/Mother, Women, Pregnancies, Silver.
Trends, Fluctuation, Instinctual, Nourishing, Responsive, Domestics, Feminine Principle, Receptive.

Mercury ☿

Communications, Mail, Computers, Advertising, Bookkeeping, Transport, Vehicles, Documents, Licenses, Training.

Expression, Intellect, Adaptability, Perception, Dexterity, Logic, Reason, Movement, Craftsmanship, News, Rumors, Gossip, Young People, Name in Print.

Venus ♀

Banks, Finance, Luxury, Money, Safety Deposit Box, Young Ladies, Marriage, Lover, Art, Artists, Finery, Dance, Song, Garden, Parties, Vacations.

Harmony, Attraction, Cohesion, Ease, Love, Sharing, Affection, Decoration, Gifts, Beauty, Those Catering to Pursuits of Pleasure, Tranquility.

Mars ♂

Machinery, Mechanics, Young Men, Contests, Competition, Criminals, Accidents, Arson, Guns, Fire, Fever, Surgery.

Conflict, Disputes, Passion, Action, Anger, Ego, Energy, Initiative, Courage, Sexual Drive, Enterprise, Violence, Fighting Spirit, Infection.

Jupiter ♃

Legal Matters, Religion, Higher Education, Travel, Travelers, Abundance, Affluence, Beliefs, Celebrations, Ceremonies.

Honor, Badge, Expansion, Propaganda, Vision, Luck, Optimism, Prosperity, Generosity, Benevolence, Exaggeration, Overproduction, Gambling.

Saturn ♄

Administrators, Authority Figures, Employers, Older People, Debts, Karma, Delay, Misers, Discipline, Judgments, Ailments.

Ambition, Contraction, Restriction, Arthritic, Limitations, Tradition, Discipline, Organization, Framework, Prudence, Boundaries.

Uranus ♅

Chief Authority, Group Speaker, Inventors, Rebels, Humanists, Antiquarians, Astrologers, Friends, Auras, Electricity.

Originality, Unique, Unexpected, Shocking, Eccentricity, Disruption, Progressive, Discovery, Electronics, New Technology, Nonconformity, Bohemian.

Neptune ♆

Hospitals, Alcohol, Drugs, Poisons, Chemicals, Oil, Photography, Mystics, Films, Actors, Addicts, Painters, Blackmail, Deceptions, Embezzling.

Footwear, Intuition, Dreams, Illusion, Phobias, Dance, Inspiration, Dissolve, Confusion, Cloud, Fog, Annulments, Nursing Homes, Asylums, Astral Entities.

Pluto ♇

Reform Leaders, Detectives, Healers, Psychologists, Sex, Taxes, Riots, Crime, Crisis, Scandal, Demolition, Viruses, Terrorists.

Underworld, Transformation, Mutation, Regeneration, Destruction, Domination, Obsessive-Compulsive, Coercion, Exploitation, Organized Prostitution.

Extra Points

Ascendant

Doorway to Entity, Physical Structure or Body, General Situation, Attitude of Public or Personnel, Stockholders, Relations with Other Organizations and Competitors.

Midheaven

Status of Entity, Stability of Foundation, Respectability, Reputation, Professional Profile, Chairman of the Board, Governing Authority, President

Chiron ⚷

Associated with the Wounded Healer. Healing experience achieved by confronting/acknowledging painful wounds. Bringing healing to others. More research needed on eclipse meaning.

Dragon's Head ☊

Karmic Connections, Earthly Participation, Materialism, Ambitions Amplified. If positive, wisdom leads to new achievement. If negative, ambitions distorted, inaccurate perceptions, compulsion, lustful desires.

Dragon's Tail ☋

Karmic Connections, Time Continuum, Immortality, Sense of Vulnerability Amplified. If positive, selfless service, compassion, transcending. If negative, weakness, insecurity, powerless, loss of control.

The Dragon's Head and Tail are connected. The Dragon's Head breathes fire, and the Dragon's Tail inhales smoke.

Table 5: Eclipse Dates for 1900–2054

The following table provides eclipse dates from 1900 to 2054. They will allow you to locate your prenatal eclipses as discussed in part 3.

Rounded to the nearest degree, the eclipses listed here are labeled with an "S" or "L" to indicate a Solar or Lunar eclipse, and defined further according to Nicholas de Vore's *Encyclopedia of Astrology:*

A = Annular: Refers to a Solar eclipse in which the Moon is at such a distance from the earth that the apex of its shadow falls short of the earth's surface. In this case, the Moon's body will not entirely obliterate the Sun and a narrow rim of light will surround the dark body of the Moon.

T = Total: Refers to a Solar eclipse in which the apex of the Moon's shadow approaches the equatorial regions. This and the Annular are Umbral Eclipses, meaning that the Moon's disk is fully contained within that of the Sun. Where there is an appreciable separation in latitude, the result is a partial eclipse. In the table, these partial eclipses have no further definition following the S.

U = Umbral: Refers to a Lunar eclipse in which the Moon definitely enters the earth's shadow.

P = Penumbral: Refers to eclipses of the Moon in which the Moon approaches closely enough to the earth's shadow to cause an appreciable diminution of light though it does not directly touch it. Not technically classified as eclipses, the conditions present closely resemble those of an eclipse, and the phenomenon often produces similar effects to an actual eclipse.

Date	Degree/Sign	Eclipse Type	Date	Degree/Sign	Eclipse Type
05-28-1900	07 ♊	S—T	12-23-1908	01 ♑	S—T
06-12-1900	22 ♐	L—p	06-03-1909	13 ♐	L—U
11-22-1900	00 ♐	S—A	06-17-1909	26 ♊	S—T
12-06-1900	14 ♊	L—p	11-27-1909	04 ♊	L—U
05-03-1900	13 ♏	L—p	12-12-1909	20 ♐	S
05-18-1901	27 ♉	S—T	05-08-1910	18 ♉	S—T
10-27-1901	04 ♉	L—U	05-23-1910	02 ♐	L—U
11-11-1901	18 ♏	S—A	11-01-1910	09 ♏	S
04-08-1902	18 ♈	S	11-16-1910	24 ♉	L—U
04-22-1902	02 ♏	L—U	04-28-1911	07 ♉	S—T
05-07-1902	16 ♉	S	05-12-1911	21 ♏	L—p
10-16-1902	23 ♈	L—U	10-21-1911	28 ♎	S—A
10-31-1902	07 ♏	S	11-06-1911	13 ♉	L—p
03-28-1903	07 ♈	S—A	04-01-1912	12 ♎	L—U
04-11-1903	21 ♎	L—U	04-17-1912	27 ♈	S—T
09-20-1903	27 ♍	S—T	09-26-1912	03 ♈	L—U
10-06-1903	12 ♈	L—U	10-10-1912	17 ♎	S—T
03-01-1904	11 ♍	L—p	03-22-1913	01 ♎	L—U
03-16-1904	26 ♓	S—A	04-06-1913	16 ♈	S
03-31-1904	10 ♎	L—p	08-31-1913	08 ♍	S
09-09-1904	17 ♍	S—T	09-15-1913	22 ♓	L—U
09-24-1904	01 ♈	L—p	09-29-1913	06 ♎	S
02-19-1905	00 ♍	L—U	02-24-1914	06 ♓	S—A
03-05-1905	15 ♓	S—A	03-11-1914	21 ♍	L—U
08-14-1905	22 ♒	L—U	08-21-1914	28 ♌	S—T
08-30-1905	06 ♍	S—T	09-04-1914	11 ♓	L—U
02-09-1906	20 ♌	L—U	02-13-1915	24 ♒	S—A
02-23-1906	04 ♓	S	03-01-1915	10 ♍	L—p
07-21-1906	28 ♋	S	07-26-1915	02 ♒	L—p
08-04-1906	11 ♒	L—U	08-10-1915	17 ♌	S—A
08-19-1906	26 ♌	S	08-24-1915	00 ♓	L—p
01-13-1907	23 ♑	S—T	01-20-1916	29 ♋	L—U
01-29-1907	08 ♌	L—U	02-03-1916	14 ♒	S—T
07-10-1907	17 ♋	S—A	07-14-1916	22 ♑	L—U
07-24-1907	01 ♒	L—U	07-29-1916	07 ♌	S—A
01-03-1908	12 ♑	S—T	12-24-1916	03 ♑	S
01-18-1908	27 ♋	L—p	01-08-1917	18 ♋	L—U
06-14-1908	23 ♐	L—p	01-23-1917	22 ♑	S
06-28-1908	07 ♋	S—A	06-19-1917	28 ♊	S
07-13-1908	21 ♑	L—p	07-04-1917	12 ♑	L—U
12 07-1908	15 ♊	L—p	07-18-1917	26 ♋	S

Date	Degree/Sign	Eclipse Type	Date	Degree/Sign	Eclipse Type
12-14-1917	22 ♐	S—A	07-24 1926	01 ♒	L—p
12-28-1917	06 ♋	L—U	12-18-1926	27 ♊	L—p
06-08-1918	17 ♊	S—T	01-03-1927	12 ♑	S—A
06-24-1918	02 ♑	L—U	06-15-1927	23 ♐	L—U
12-03-1918	11 ♐	S—A	06-28-1927	07 ♋	S—T
12-17-1918	25 ♊	L—p	12-08-1927	16 ♊	L—U
05-14-1919	23 ♏	L—p	12-23-1927	01 ♑	S
05-29-1919	07 ♊	S—T	05-19-1928	28 ♉	S—T
11-07-1919	14 ♊	L—U	06-03-1928	13 ♐	L—U
11-22-1919	29 ♏	S—A	06-17-1928	26 ♊	S
04-18-1920	28 ♈	S	11-12-1928	20 ♏	S
05-02-1920	12 ♏	L—U	11-27-1928	04 ♊	L—U
05-17-1920	27 ♉	S	05-08-1929	18 ♉	S—T
10-27-1920	04 ♉	L—U	05-23-1929	02 ♐	L—p
11-10-1920	18 ♏	S	11-01-1929	09 ♏	S—A
04-08-1921	18 ♈	S—A	11-16-1929	24 ♉	L—p
04-22-1921	02 ♏	L—U	04-12-1930	23 ♎	L—U
10-01-1921	08 ♎	S—T	04-28-1930	08 ♉	S—T
10-16-1921	23 ♈	L—U	10-07-1930	14 ♈	L—U
03-13-1922	22 ♍	L—p	10-21-1930	28 ♎	S—T
03-28-1922	07 ♈	S—A	04-02-1931	12 ♎	L—U
04-11-1922	21 ♎	L—p	04-17-1931	27 ♈	S
09-20-1922	27 ♍	S—T	09-11-1931	18 ♍	S
10-05-1922	12 ♈	L—p	09-26-1931	03 ♈	L—U
03-02-1923	12 ♍	L—U	10-11-1931	17 ♎	S
03-17-1923	26 ♓	S—A	03-07-1932	17 ♓	S—A
08-26-1923	02 ♓	L—U	03-22-1932	02 ♎	L—U
09-10-1923	17 ♍	S—T	08-31-1932	08 ♍	S—T
02-20-1924	01 ♍	L—U	09-14-1932	22 ♓	L—U
03-05-1924	15 ♓	S	02-24-1933	05 ♓	S—A
07-31-1924	08 ♌	S	03-11-1933	21 ♍	L—p
08-14-1924	22 ♒	L—U	08-05-1933	13 ♒	L—p
08-30-1924	07 ♍	S	08-20-1933	28 ♌	S—A
01-24-1925	04 ♒	S—T	09-03-1933	11 ♓	L—p
02-08-1925	20 ♌	L -U	01-30-1934	10 ♌	L—U
07-20-1925	28 ♋	S—A	02-14-1934	25 ♒	S—T
08-04-1925	12 ♒	L—U	07-26-1934	03 ♒	L—U
01-13-1926	23 ♑	S—T	08-10-1934	17 ♌	S—A
01-28-1926	08 ♌	L—p	01-04-1935	14 ♑	S
06-25-1926	03 ♑	L—p	01-19-1935	29 ♋	L—U
07-09-1926	17 ♋	S—A	02-03-1935	14 ♒	S

Date	Degree/Sign	Eclipse Type	Date	Degree/Sign	Eclipse Type
06-30-1935	08 ♋	S	07-05-1944	14 ♑	L—p
07-16-1935	23 ♑	L—U	07-19-1944	28 ♋	S—A
07-30-1935	07 ♌	S	08-04-1944	12 ♒	L—p
12-25-1935	03 ♑	S—A	12-29-1944	08 ♋	L—p
01-08-1936	18 ♋	L—U	01-13-1945	24 ♑	S—A
06-18-1936	28 ♊	S—T	06-25-1945	04 ♑	L—U
07-04-1936	12 ♑	L—U	07-09-1945	17 ♋	S—T
12-13-1936	22 ♐	S—A	12-18-1945	27 ♊	L—U
12-27-1936	06 ♋	L—p	01-03-1946	13 ♑	S
05-25 1937	04 ♐	L—p	05-30-1946	09 ♊	S
06-08-1937	18 ♊	S—T	06-14-1946	23 ♐	L—U
11-18-1937	26 ♉	L—U	06-28-1046	07 ♋	S
12-02-1937	10 ♐	S—A	11-23-1946	01 ♐	S
05-14-1938	23 ♏	L—U	12-08-1946	16 ♊	L—U
05-29-1938	08 ♊	S—T	05-20-1947	29 ♉	S—T
11-07-1938	15 ♉	L—U	06-03-1947	12 ♐	L—U
11-21-1938	29 ♏	S	11-12-1947	20 ♏	S—A
04-19-1939	29 ♈	S—A	11-28-1947	05 ♊	L—p
05-03-1939	12 ♏	L—U	04-23-1948	03 ♏	L—U
10-12-1939	19 ♎	S—T	05-08-1948	18 ♉	S—T
10-27-1939	04 ♉	L—U	10-17-1948	25 ♈	L—p
03-23-1940	03 ♎	L—p	10-31-1948	09 ♏	S—T
04-07-1940	18 ♈	S—A	04-12-1949	23 ♎	L—U
04-21-1940	02 ♏	L—p	04-28-1949	08 ♉	S
10-01-1940	08 ♎	S—T	10-06-1949	14 ♈	L—U
10-16-1940	23 ♈	L—p	10-21-1949	28 ♎	S
03-13-1941	22 ♍	L—U	03-18-1950	28 ♓	S—A
03-27-1941	07 ♈	S—A	04-02-1950	13 ♎	L—U
09-05-1941	13 ♓	L—U	09-11-1950	19 ♍	S—T
09-20-1941	28 ♍	S—T	09-25-1950	03 ♈	L—U
03-02-1942	12 ♍	L—U	03-07-1951	17 ♓	S—A
03-16-1942	26 ♓	S	03-23 1951	02 ♎	L—p
08-11-1942	19 ♌	S	08-16-1951	23 ♒	L—p
08-25-1942	02 ♓	L—U	09-01-1951	08 ♍	S—A
09-10-1942	17 ♍	S	09-15 1951	22 ♓	L—p
02-04-1943	15 ♒	S—T	02-10-1952	21 ♌	L—U
02-19-1943	01 ♍	L—U	02-25-1952	06 ♓	S—T
07-31-1943	08 ♌	S—A	08-05-1952	13 ♒	L—U
08-15-1943	22 ♒	L—U	08-20-1952	28 ♌	S—A
01-25-1944	05 ♒	S—T	01-15-1953	25 ♑	S
02-08-1944	19 ♌	L—p	01-29-1051	10 ♌	L—U

Date	Degree/Sign	Eclipse Type	Date	Degree/Sign	Eclipse Type
02-13-1953	25 ♒	S	07-17-1962	24 ♑	L—p
07-10-1953	18 ♋	S	07-31-1962	08 ♌	S—A
07-26-1953	03 ♒	L—U	08-15-1962	22 ♒	L—p
08-09-1953	17 ♌	S	01-09-1963	19 ♋	L—p
01-04-1954	14 ♑	S—A	01-25-1963	05 ♒	S—A
01-18-1954	28 ♋	L—U	07-06-1963	14 ♑	L—U
06-30-1954	08 ♋	S—T	07-20-1963	28 ♋	S—T
07-15-1954	23 ♑	L—U	12-30-1963	08 ♋	L—U
12-25-1954	03 ♑	S—A	01-14-1964	24 ♑	S
01-08-1955	17 ♋	L—p	06-09-1964	19 ♊	S
06-05-1955	14 ♐	L—p	06-24-1964	04 ♑	L—U
06-19-1955	28 ♊	S—T	07-09-1964	17 ♋	S
11-29-1955	07 ♊	L—U	12-03-1964	12 ♐	S
12-14-1955	22 ♐	S—A	12-18-1964	27 ♊	L—U
05-24-1956	03 ♐	L—U	05-30-1965	09 ♊	S—T
06-08-1956	18 ♊	S—T	06-13-1965	23 ♐	L—U
11-17-1956	26 ♉	L—U	11-22-1965	01 ♐	S—A
12-02-1956	10 ♐	S	12-08-1965	16 ♊	L—p
04-29-1957	09 ♉	S	05-04-1966	14 ♏	L—p
05-13-1057	23 ♏	L—U	05-20-1966	29 ♉	S—A
10-22-1957	00 ♏	S	10-29-1966	06 ♉	L—p
11-07-1957	15 ♉	L—U	11-12-1966	20 ♏	S—T
04-03-1958	14 ♎	L—p	04-24-1967	04 ♏	L—U
04-18-1958	29 ♈	S—A	05-09-1967	18 ♉	S
05-03-1958	13 ♏	L—U	10-18-1967	24 ♈	L—U
10-12-1958	19 ♎	S—T	11-01-1967	09 ♏	S—T
10-27-1958	04 ♉	L—p	03-28-1968	08 ♈	S
03-24-1959	03 ♎	L—U	04-12-1968	23 ♎	L—U
04-07-1959	18 ♈	S—A	09-22-1968	29 ♍	S—T
09-16-1959	23 ♓	L—p	10-06-1968	13 ♈	L—U
10-02-1959	09 ♎	S—T	03-17-1969	27 ♓	S—A
03-13-1960	23 ♍	L—U	04-02-1969	13 ♎	L—p
03-27-1960	07 ♈	S	08-27-1969	04 ♓	L—p
09-05-1960	13 ♓	L—U	09-11-1969	19 ♍	S—A
09-20-1060	28 ♍	S	09-25-1969	03 ♈	L—p
02-15-1961	27 ♒	S—T	02-21-1970	02 ♍	L—U
03-02-1961	12 ♍	L—U	03-07-1970	17 ♓	S—T
08-11-1961	19 ♌	S—A	08-16-1970	24 ♒	L—U
08-25-1961	03 ♓	L—U	08-31-1970	08 ♍	S—A
02-04-1962	16 ♒	S—T	01-29-1971	06 ♒	S
02-19-1962	00 ♍	L—p	02-10-1971	21 ♌	L—U

Date	Degree/Sign	Eclipse Type	Date	Degree/Sign	Eclipse Type
02-25-1971	06 ♓	S	07-27-1980	05 ♒	L—p
07-22-1971	29 ♋	S	08-10-1980	18 ♌	S—A
08-06-1971	14 ♒	L—U	08-25-1980	03 ♓	L—p
08-20-1971	27 ♌	S	01-20-1981	00 ♌	L—p
01-16-1972	25 ♑	S—A	02-04-1981	16 ♒	S—A
01-30-1972	10 ♌	L—U	07-16-1981	25 ♑	L—U
07-10-1972	19 ♋	S—T	07-30-1981	08 ♌	S—T
07-26-1972	03 ♒	L—U	01-09-1982	19 ♋	L—U
01-04-1973	14 ♑	S—A	01-24-1982	05 ♒	S
01-18-1973	29 ♋	L—p	06-21-1982	29 ♊	S
06-15-1973	25 ♐	L—p	07-06-1982	14 ♑	L—U
06-30-1973	08 ♋	S—T	07-20-1982	28 ♋	S
07-15-1973	23 ♑	L—p	12-15-1982	23 ♐	S
12-09-1973	18 ♊	L—U	12-30-1982	08 ♋	L—U
12-24-1973	03 ♑	S—A	06-10-1983	20 ♊	S—T
06-04-1974	14 ♐	L—U	06-25-1983	04 ♑	L—U
06-19-1974	28 ♊	S—T	12-04-1983	12 ♐	S—A
11-29-1974	07 ♊	L—U	12-19-1983	28 ♊	L—p
12-13-1974	21 ♐	S	05-14-1984	24 ♏	L—p
05-11-1975	20 ♉	S	05-30-1984	09 ♊	S—A
05-24-1975	03 ♐	L—U	06-13-1984	23 ♐	L—p
11-03-1975	10 ♏	S	11-08-1984	16 ♉	L—p
11-18-1975	26 ♉	L—U	11-22-1984	01 ♐	S—T
04-29-1976	09 ♉	S—A	05-04-1985	14 ♏	L—U
05-13-1976	23 ♏	L—U	05-19-1985	28 ♉	S
10-22-1976	00 ♏	S—T	10-28-1985	05 ♉	L—U
11-06-1976	15 ♉	L—p	11-12-1985	20 ♏	S—T
04-03-1977	14 ♎	L—U	04-08-1986	19 ♈	S
04-18-1977	28 ♈	S—A	04-24-1986	04 ♏	L—U
09-27-1977	04 ♈	L—p	10-03-1986	10 ♎	S—T
10-12-1977	19 ♎	S—T	10-17-1986	24 ♈	L—U
03-24-1978	04 ♎	L—U	03-29-1987	08 ♈	S—T
04-07-1978	17 ♈	S	04-13-1987	24 ♎	L—p
09-16-1978	24 ♓	L—U	09-22-1987	00 ♎	S—A
10-01-1978	09 ♎	S	10-06-1987	13 ♈	L—U
02-26-1979	07 ♓	S	03-03-1988	13 ♍	L—p
03-13-1979	23 ♍	L—U	03-17-1988	28 ♓	S—T
08-22-1979	29 ♌	S—A	08-27-1988	04 ♓	L—U
09-06-1979	13 ♓	L—U	09-10-1988	19 ♍	S—A
02-16-1980	27 ♒	S—T	02-20-1989	02 ♍	L—U
03-01-1980	11 ♍	L—p	03-07-1989	17 ♓	S

Date	Degree/Sign	Eclipse Type	Date	Degree/Sign	Eclipse Type
08-16-1989	24 ♒	L—U	09-06-1998	14 ♓	L—p
08-30-1989	08 ♍	S	01-31-1999	11 ♌	L—p
01-26-1990	07 ♒	S—A	02-15-1999	27 ♒	S—A
02-09-1990	21 ♌	L—U	07-28-1999	05 ♒	L—U
07-21-1990	29 ♋	S—T	08-11-1999	18 ♌	S—T
08-06-1990	14 ♒	L—U	01-20-2000	01 ♌	L—U
01-15-1991	25 ♑	S—A	02-05-2000	16 ♒	S
01-29-1991	10 ♌	L—p	07-01-2000	10 ♋	S
06-26-1991	05 ♑	L—p	07-16-2000	24 ♑	L—U
07-11-1991	19 ♋	S—T	07-30-2000	08 ♌	S
07-26-1991	03 ♒	L—p	12-25-2000	04 ♑	S
12-21-1991	29 ♊	L—U	01-09-2001	20 ♋	L—U
01-04-1992	14 ♑	S—A	06-21-2001	00 ♋	S—T
06-14-1992	24 ♐	L—U	07-05-2001	14 ♑	L—U
06-30-1992	09 ♋	S—T	12-14-2001	23 ♐	S—A
12-09-1992	18 ♊	L—U	12-30-2001	09 ♋	L—p
12-23-1992	02 ♑	S	05-26-2002	05 ♐	L—p
05-21-1993	01 ♊	S	06-10-2002	20 ♊	S—A
06-04-1993	14 ♐	L—U	06-24-2002	03 ♑	L—p
11-13-1993	21 ♏	S	11-19-2002	28 ♉	L—p
11-29-1993	07 ♊	L—U	12-04-2002	12 ♐	S—T
05-10-1994	20 ♉	S—A	05-15-2003	25 ♏	L—U
05-25-1994	04 ♐	L—U	05-30-2003	09 ♊	S—A
11-03-1994	11 ♏	S—T	11-08-2003	16 ♉	L—U
11-17-1994	26 ♉	L—p	11-23-2003	01 ♐	S—T
04-15-1995	25 ♎	L—U	04-19-2004	30 ♈	S
04-29-1995	09 ♉	S—A	05-04-2004	15 ♏	L—U
10-08-1995	15 ♈	L—p	10-13-2004	21 ♎	S
10-23-1995	00 ♏	S—T	10-27-2004	05 ♉	L—U
04-03-1996	15 ♎	L—U	04-08-2005	19 ♈	S—T
04-17-1996	28 ♈	S	04-24-2005	04 ♏	L—p
09-26-1996	04 ♈	L—U	10-03-2005	10 ♎	S—A
10-12-1996	20 ♎	S	10-17-2005	24 ♈	L—U
03-09-1997	19 ♓	S—T	03-14-2006	24 ♍	L—p
03-23-1997	04 ♎	L—U	03-29-2006	09 ♈	S—T
09-01-1997	10 ♍	S	09-07-2006	15 ♓	L—U
09-16-1997	24 ♓	L—U	09-22-2006	29 ♍	S—A
02-26-1998	08 ♓	S—T	03-03-2007	13 ♍	L—U
03-12-1998	22 ♍	L—p	03-18-2007	28 ♓	S
08-07-1998	15 ♒	L—p	08-28-2007	05 ♓	L—U
08-21-1998	29 ♌	S—A	09-11-2007	18 ♍	S

Date	Degree/Sign	Eclipse Type	Date	Degree/Sign	Eclipse Type
02-06-2008	18 ♒	S—A	09-16-2016	24 ♓	L—p
02-20-2008	02 ♍	L—U	02-10-2017	22 ♌	L—p
08-01-2008	10 ♌	S—T	02-26-2017	08 ♓	S—A
08-16-2008	24 ♒	L—U	08-07-2017	15 ♒	L—U
01-26-2009	06 ♒	S—A	08-21-2017	29 ♌	S—T
02-09-2009	21 ♌	L—p	01-31-2018	11 ♌	L—U
07-07-2009	15 ♑	L—p	02-15-2018	27 ♒	S
07-21-2009	29 ♋	S—T	07-12-2018	21 ♋	S
08-05-2009	14 ♒	L—p	07-27-2018	05 ♒	L—U
12-31-2009	10 ♋	L—U	08-11-2018	19 ♌	S
01-15-2010	25 ♑	S—A	01-05-2019	15 ♑	S
06-26-2010	05 ♑	L—U	01-20-2019	01 ♌	L—U
07-11-2010	19 ♋	S—T	07-02-2019	11 ♋	S—T
12-21-2010	29 ♊	L—U	07-16-2019	24 ♑	L—U
01-04-2011	14 ♑	S	12-25-2019	04 ♑	S—A
06-01-2011	11 ♊	S	01-10-2020	20 ♋	L—p
06-15-2011	24 ♐	L—U	06-05-2020	16 ♐	L—p
07-01-2011	09 ♋	S	06-20-2020	00 ♋	S—A
11-24-2011	03 ♐	S	07-04-2020	14 ♑	L—p
12-10-2011	18 ♊	L—U	11-30-2020	09 ♊	L—p
05-20-2012	00 ♊	S—A	12-14-2020	23 ♐	S—T
06-04-2012	14 ♐	L—U	05-26-2021	05 ♐	L—U
11-13-2012	22 ♏	S—T	06-10-2021	20 ♊	S—A
11-28-2012	07 ♊	L—p	11-19-2021	27 ♉	L—U
04-25-2013	06 ♏	L—U	12-04-2021	12 ♐	S—T
05-09-2013	20 ♉	S—A	04-30-2022	10 ♉	S
05-24-2013	04 ♐	L—p	05-15-2022	25 ♏	L—U
10-18-2013	26 ♈	L—p	10-25-2022	02 ♏	S
11-03-2013	11 ♏	S—T	11-08-2022	16 ♉	L—U
04-15-2014	25 ♎	L—U	04-19-2023	30 ♈	S—T
04-28-2014	09 ♉	S—A	05-05-2023	15 ♏	L—p
10-08-2014	15 ♈	L—U	10-14-2023	21 ♎	S—A
10-23-2014	00 ♏	S	10-28-2023	05 ♉	L—U
03-20-2015	29 ♓	S—T	03-25-2024	05 ♎	L—p
04-04-2015	14 ♎	L—U	04-08-2024	19 ♈	S—T
09-12-2015	20 ♍	S	09-17-2024	26 ♓	L—U
09-27-2015	05 ♈	L—U	10-02-2024	10 ♎	S—A
03-08-2016	19 ♓	S—T	03-13-2025	24 ♍	L—U
03-23-2016	03 ♎	L—p	03-29-2025	09 ♈	S
08-18-2016	25 ♒	L—p	09-07-2025	15 ♓	L—U
09-01-2016	09 ♍	S—A	09-21-2025	29 ♍	S

Date	Degree/Sign	Eclipse Type	Date	Degree/Sign	Eclipse Type
02-17-2026	29 ♒	S—A	03-09-2035	19 ♓	S—A
03-03-2026	13 ♍	L—U	08-18-2035	26 ♒	L—U
08-12-2026	20 ♌	S—T	09-01-2035	09 ♍	S—T
08-27-2026	05 ♓	L—U	02-11-2036	23 ♌	L—U
02-06-2027	18 ♒	S—A	02-26-2036	08 ♓	S
02-20-2027	02 ♍	L—p	07-23-2036	01 ♌	S
08-02-2027	10 ♌	S—T	08-06-2036	15 ♒	L—U
08-17-2027	24 ♒	L—p	08-21-2036	29 ♌	S
01-11-2028	21 ♋	L—U	01-16-2037	27 ♑	S
01-26-2028	06 ♒	S—A	01-31-2037	12 ♌	L—U
07-06-2028	15 ♑	L—U	07-12-2037	21 ♋	S—T
07-21-2028	30 ♋	S—T	07-26-2037	04 ♒	L—U
12-31-2028	11 ♋	L—U	01-05-2038	15 ♑	S—A
01-14-2029	25 ♑	S	01-20-2038	01 ♌	L—p
06-11-2029	21 ♊	S	06-16-2038	26 ♐	L—p
06-25-2029	05 ♑	L—U	07-02-2038	11 ♋	S—A
07-11-2029	20 ♋	S	07-16-2038	24 ♑	L—p
12-05-2029	14 ♐	S	12-11-2038	20 ♊	L—p
12-20-2029	29 ♊	L—U	12-25-2038	04 ♑	S—T
05-31-2030	11 ♊	S—A	06-06-2039	16 ♐	L—U
06-15-2030	25 ♐	L—U	06-21-2039	00 ♋	S—A
11-24-2030	03 ♐	S—T	11-30-2039	08 ♊	L—U
12-09-2030	18 ♊	L—p	12-15-2039	24 ♐	S—T
05-06-2031	16 ♏	L—p	05-10-2040	21 ♉	S
05-21-2031	00 ♊	S—A	05-26-2040	06 ♐	L—U
06-05-2031	14 ♐	L—p	11-04-2040	13 ♏	S
10-30-2031	07 ♉	L—p	11-18-2040	27 ♉	L—U
11-14-2031	22 ♏	S—T	04-30-2041	10 ♉	S—T
04-25-2032	06 ♏	L—U	05-15-2041	26 ♏	L—U
05-09-2032	19 ♉	S—A	10-24-2041	02 ♏	S—A
10-18-2032	26 ♈	L—U	11-07-2041	16 ♉	L—U
11-02-2032	11 ♏	S	04-05-2042	16 ♎	L—p
03-30-2033	10 ♈	S—T	04-19-2042	00 ♉	S—T
04-14-2033	25 ♎	L—U	09-29-2042	06 ♈	L—p
09-23-2033	01 ♎	S	10-13-2042	21 ♎	S—A
10-08-2033	15 ♈	L—U	10-28-2042	06 ♉	L—p
03-20-2034	30 ♓	S—T	03-25-2043	05 ♎	L—U
04-03-2034	14 ♎	L—p	04-09-2043	20 ♈	S
09-12-2034	20 ♍	S—A	09-18-2043	26 ♓	L—U
09-27-2034	05 ♈	L—U	10-02-2043	10 ♎	S
02-22-2035	04 ♍	L—p	02-28-2044	10 ♓	S

Date	Degree/Sign	Eclipse Type
03-13-2044	24 ♍	L—U
08-22-2044	01 ♍	S—T
09-07-2044	15 ♓	L—U
02-16-2045	29 ♒	S—A
03-03-2045	13 ♍	L—p
08-12-2045	20 ♌	S—T
08-27-2045	05 ♓	L—p
01-22-2046	03 ♌	L—U
02-05-2046	17 ♒	S—A
07-17-2046	26 ♑	L—U
08-02-2046	10 ♌	S—T
01-11-2047	22 ♋	L—U
01-25-2047	06 ♒	S
06-23-2047	02 ♋	S
07-07-2047	15 ♑	L—U
07-22-2047	00 ♌	S
12-16-2047	25 ♐	S
12-31-2047	11 ♋	L—U
06-11-2048	21 ♊	S—A
06-25-2048	05 ♑	L—U
12-05-2048	14 ♐	S—T
12-19-2048	29 ♊	L—p
05-17-2049	27 ♏	L—p
05-31-2049	11 ♊	S—A
06-15-2049	25 ♐	L—p
11-09-2049	18 ♉	L—p
11-24-2049	03 ♐	S—T
05-06-2050	17 ♏	L—U
05-20-2050	00 ♊	S—T
10-29-2050	07 ♉	L—U
11-14-2050	22 ♏	S

Glossary

Air signs: Gemini, Libra, and Aquarius. See chapter 2.

angles, the: The cusps of the First, Fourth, Seventh, and Tenth Houses.

Aries Point degrees: The opening degree, or zero degree, of the signs Aries, Cancer, Libra, and Capricorn, which represent the beginning of each season. These points are indicative of dynamic energy. There is frequently an involvement with the world at large. Those with a planet in one of these degrees in the natal chart often have an influence in worldly affairs or at some point they come into public view. These degrees are also associated with fame.

Ascendant: The degree and sign located on the First House cusp. It describes the physical body, personality, and attitude. The Ascendant is sometimes called the Rising Sign.

aspect: The relationship of two planets to one another. The relationship may be "easy" or "difficult." Squares and oppositions represent challenges. The sextile and trine aspects are opportunistic but undemanding. Conjunctions may be either easy or difficult according to the nature of the two planets and of the relationship that the conjoined planets form with other planets.

astrology: The science of the planets: their movements and relationships to one another as they affect the affairs of persons on earth. Also called an art or an art science because of the necessity to blend a great number of factors into one seamless picture. As knowledge and understanding of the laws of astrology increase, the student becomes more adept at picking up the images lent by the planetary configurations, appearing similar to an intuitive process.

astronomy: The science of the physical attributes and locations of the planets in the celestial sphere. Astronomy does not take into account the planets' effects in the affairs of people.

benefic: Jupiter and Venus are planets of fortune and benefits, and are therefore called benefic. The Sun can usually be deemed a benefic planet as well.

benevolent: Kindly.

birth chart: A picture of the heavens and heavenly bodies at your birth as seen in your horoscope figure that is calculated according to your date of birth, location of birth, and time of birth. This is the life blueprint and map that can be utilized to navigate the life journey.

birth map: See entry for *horoscope* or *birth chart.*

cardinal signs: Aries, Cancer, Libra, and Capricorn. Also referred to as seasonal signs.

conjunction: When two or more planets occupy the same degree, or space, in the zodiac, they are said to be in conjunction. During a Solar eclipse, the Sun and Moon are in conjunction. When a transiting planet moves into the degree of the zodiac where an eclipse has occurred, this is also called a conjunction, a placement from where it may stimulate potential happenings associated with that eclipse.

critical degrees: The critical degrees are 0, 13, and 26 degrees of cardinal signs (Aries, Cancer, Libra, Capricorn); 9 and 21 degrees of fixed signs (Taurus, Leo, Scorpio, Aquarius); and 4 and 17 degrees of mutable signs (Gemini, Virgo, Sagittarius, Pisces). When a critical degree falls on a house cusp, it shows stress and climax. The matters of the houses ruled and occupied by a planet in one of the critical degrees are grave, serious, and climactic. See also *Aries Point degrees.*

cusp: The line that divides one house from the next in a horoscope.

Descendant: The cusp of the Seventh House is called the Descendant. It is a point of interaction or partnership with others.

Dragon's Head: A point of intake or gain. Usually considered to be auspicious and beneficial. Associated with participation in earthly matters and material acquisition. The Dragon's Head is said to breathe fire. In the personal chart, it shows where an individual is going in life—the spiritual calling.

Dragon's Tail: A point associated with the release of accumulated energy. It is sometimes connected to sacrifice or selfless compassion. The Dragon's Tail is said to inhale smoke. It is without ego, transcends time, and draws us to things everlasting. In the personal horoscope, it shows qualities mastered in previous lifetimes.

Earth signs: Taurus, Virgo, and Capricorn. See chapter 2.

eclipse: A celestial mechanism that ensures constant cosmic balance, prevents stagnant conditions, and calls us to our destiny. The definition of eclipse is to dim; to hide or conceal; to render invisible by an elimination of light. See *Lunar eclipse* and *Solar eclipse.*

ecliptic: The apparent yearly path of the Sun as the earth orbits the Sun.

elements: The four elements are Fire, Earth, Air, and Water. See chapter 2.

epoch: An interval of time or a series of years.

era: A period of time.

Fire signs: Aries, Leo, and Sagittarius. See chapter 2.

fixed stars: Our Sun is a fixed star, one that is very close to us. There are many fixed stars further away. Each has a name and a reputation for being prominent during certain kinds of events. Astrologers use their significance to clarify a chart reading.

Greater Fortune: Jupiter is called the Greater Fortune, known for bringing spiritual or material benefits and expansion.

horoscope: A map or figure erected from the time and location of birth as the sky appeared at that moment from that location on earth. It reflects the precise planetary configurations at birth. Also called a nativity or birth chart.

house: A particular area of experience in the life. The horoscope contains twelve houses, or twelve departments of life. See part 3 for what each house governs.

karma: The laws of cause and effect. To every action there is an equal and opposite reaction, as noted by Sir Isaac Newton.

Lesser Fortune: Venus is the Lesser Fortune, known for bringing favors, gifts, and material benefits. It is also prominent during happy occasions.

Lord: The planet ruling an eclipse is said to be Lord of the eclipse. See chapter 2.

luminaries: The Sun and Moon are luminaries but are often called "planets."

Lunar eclipse: Two or three times a year, all conditions are right for a Lunar eclipse to take place. As the Sun, Moon, and earth align themselves in a straight line, the earth comes between the Sun and Moon, causing an eclipse of the Moon as it loses its reflected light from the Sun. This can occur only at the time of a Full Moon; however, all Full Moons are not eclipses.

Lunar Nodes: The points of intersection of two orbits that pierce the celestial sphere; in this case, the Moon's orbit with that of the ecliptic (the apparent yearly path of the Sun through the celestial sphere as the earth orbits the Sun) as the Moon circles the earth. Occurring twice a month, there is a pair of Nodes opposite one another—the North Node and the South Node.

lunation: A New Moon or a Full Moon. An astrological chart of the lunation portends coming events, especially if the lunation is also an eclipse.

malefic: Mars and Saturn were traditionally termed malefic because they are so frequently prominent when troublesome situations occur. Pluto is similar in nature to Mars. Uranus sometimes acts in a malefic manner, as does Neptune, although perhaps less often.

MC: The highest point in the chart, reflecting public reputation and recognition. The Midheaven.

Midheaven: Tenth House cusp. Point of professional status and reputation. The MC.

mundane astrology: An interpretation of astrology in terms of world trends and the destinies of nations and large groups of individuals, based on an analysis of the effects of equinoxes, solstices, New Moons, eclipses, planetary conjunctions, and similar celestial phenomena; as distinguished from natal astrology, specifically applicable to an individual birth horoscope. This definition comes from Nicholas de Vore's *Encyclopedia of Astrology.*

mutable: The signs Gemini, Virgo, Sagittarius, and Pisces are called mutable signs, or changeable signs.

mutual reception: When two planets occupy each other's signs they are said to be in mutual reception. Uranus in Pisces and Neptune in Aquarius are in a long-lasting mutual reception from 2003 to 2010. This condition means that each of the two planets is treated as if it falls in two places in the chart—the actual position and the same degree in the sign of the planet's rule.

natal: Usually refers to the birth placements of planets or luminaries.

nativity: The horoscope or birth chart is sometimes referred to as the nativity.

Node: The intersections of two circles or spheres. They show connections in time and space. The Lunar Nodes are discussed herein.

opposition: When two planets are directly opposite one another in the zodiac, they are said to be in opposition. They are 180 degrees apart in the horoscope wheel. During a Lunar eclipse, the Sun and Moon are in opposition. When a transiting planet moves through the degree opposite a previous eclipse, it is in opposition, from where it can stimulate the eclipse potential.

orb: An orb is the number of degrees of separation from exact aspect that is allowed. An exact conjunction is when two planets are zero degrees apart. An exact opposition is when two planets are 180 degrees apart. The orb used herein for planetary stimulation to an eclipse is +/- 3 degrees of exact. The same orb is recommended for an eclipse falling on a natal planet or point.

penumbral: Eclipses of the Moon in which the Moon approaches closely enough to the earth's shadow to cause an appreciable diminution of light, though it does not directly touch it.

progressed: See *secondary progressions.*

progressions: See *secondary progressions.*

rectification: A process of correcting a horoscope to precision based on astrological laws and a study of events that match up experiences with planetary prominence at the time of the event. It is used when there is no known birth time or only an approximate birth time is known.

retrograde: Applies to the apparent backward motion of planets from our earth-centered perspective at certain times of the year. Mercury retrogrades three or four times a year for three weeks at a time; Venus retrogrades once every eighteen months; and Mars once every two years. Jupiter, Saturn, Uranus, Neptune, and Pluto spend several months each year in retrograde motion. The Sun and Moon are never retrograde.

Rising Sign: This is the sign located on the First House cusp of a horoscope. For most people, this sign is different from the Sun sign and gives a description of the personality as distinct from ego characteristics, which are described by the Sun sign.

rising degree: Also called the Ascendant. It is the degree and sign located on the cusp of the First House. In a chart, it reflects and describes the physical body and attitude.

Saros series: Each single eclipse belongs to a larger family of eclipses. The family consists of up to seventy eclipses and covers a span of some 1,260 years. Starting at the top or bottom of the globe, the family series spirals downward or upward until reaching the opposite pole. As one series nears its demise, another takes over, resulting in an increase of yearly eclipses. That was the case in the year 2000. Each of the nineteen eclipse families is identified by a number and belongs to a specific series. Historians study these eclipse series for events dating before the birth of Christ.

Some astrologers study the effects of a later eclipse by the parent eclipse, or the first eclipse, of the series. In his book *Interpreting the Eclipses*, Carl Jansky says the original eclipse in a Saros series is of importance in delineating a later eclipse from that series. In this exercise, it is the sign of the original eclipse in a series that holds information regarding later eclipses of that series. Bernadette Brady concurs and goes a step further in her book *The Eagle and the Lark*, providing excellent short delineations for the first eclipse in each series. Although this cannot replace a study of the current eclipse features, it does add insight to note the nature of the parent eclipse.

secondary progressions: A technique that's used to get an up-to-date view of how a person is progressing in life. It shows the current potential. This is discussed in my book *Identifying Planetary Triggers*, published by Llewellyn in 2000.

Solar eclipse: A couple of times a year, conditions are right for a Solar eclipse to occur. As the Sun, Moon, and earth align in a straight line, the Moon comes directly between the earth and Sun, shutting off the light of the Sun temporarily; hence the Solar eclipse. A

Solar eclipse can occur only at the time of a New Moon; however, all New Moons are not eclipses.

square: A stressful relationship between two planets that forces events. Planets in square are 90 degrees apart. An aspect that requires great effort.

taskmaster: Saturn is said to be the taskmaster. It brings the result of situations by the passage of time and is associated with maturity.

transits: The daily movements of the planets.

trine: A flowing relationship between two planets but one that is undemanding of action. It is sometimes called lucky and effortless. Planets in trine are 120 degrees apart.

umbral: A Lunar eclipse in which the Moon definitely enters the earth's shadow.

Vertex: A point in the horoscope that is associated with encounters of a fateful nature, either with people or experiences. Researched originally by Canadian astrologer L. Edward Johndro.

warrior planet: Mars is called the warrior planet. It often reflects conflict.

Water signs: Cancer, Scorpio, and Pisces. See chapter 2.

Bibliography

Adams, Evangeline. *The Bowl of Heaven*. 1926. Reprint, Santa Fe, NM: Sun Publishing Co., 1995.

Allan, Herbert S. *John Hancock: Patriot in Purple*. New York: Macmillan Co., 1940.

Billington, Ray Allen, Bert James Loewenborg, and Samuel Hugh Brockunier. *The United States*. New York: Rinehart and Co., 1947.

Bonatus, Guido, and Jerom Cardan. *The Astrologer's Guide: Anima Astrologle*. 1675. Reprint, Montana, USA: Kessinger Publishing Co., 1886, ISBN: 1-56459-960-4.

Brady, Bernadette. *The Eagle and the Lark: A Textbook of Predictive Astrology*. York Beach, ME: Samuel Weiser, 1992.

Brands, H. W. *The First American: The Life and Times of Benjamin Franklin*. New York: Doubleday, 2000.

Campion, Nicholas. *The Book of World Horoscopes*. Bristol, England: Cinnabar Books, 1999.

de Vore, Nicholas. *Encyclopedia of Astrology*. New York: Philosophical Library, 1947.

Erlewine, Stephen. *The Circle Book of Charts*. Tempe, AZ: American Federation of Astrologers, 1991.

Freidel, Frank, and William Pencak, eds. *The White House: The First Two Hundred Years*. Boston, MA: Northeastern University Press, 1994.

Goodavage, Joseph F. *Write Your Own Horoscope*. New York: New American Library, 1968.

Green, H. S., Raphael, and C.E.O. Carter. *Mundane Astrology*. Three books in one volume. Abingdon, MD: Astrology Classics, 2003.

Jansky, Robert Carl. *Interpreting the Eclipses*. San Diego, CA: ACS Publications, 1979.

Louis, Anthony. *Horary Astrology Plain & Simple*. St. Paul, MN: Llewellyn Publishing, 1998.

Lupiano, Vincent dePaul, and Ken W. Sayers. *It Was a Very Good Year*. Holbrook, MA: B. Adams Inc., 1994.

Moore, Thomas. *Care of the Soul*. New York: HarperCollins, 1992.

Oken, Alan. *As Above, So Below*. New York: Bantam Books, 1973.

Penfield, Marc. *Horoscopes of the Western Hemisphere*. San Diego, CA: ACS Publications. 1984.

Robson, Vivian E. *The Fixed Stars and Constellations in Astrology*. 1923. Reprint, Santa Fe, NM: Sun Publishing Co., 1995.

Schulman, Martin. *Karmic Astrology: The Moon's Nodes & Reincarnation: Volume I*. New York: Samuel Weiser, 1975.

Teal, Celeste. *Identifying Planetary Triggers*. St. Paul, MN: Llewellyn Publishing, 2000.

————. *Predicting Events with Astrology*. St. Paul, MN: Llewellyn Publishing, 1999.

Zolar. *The Encyclopedia of Ancient and Forbidden Knowledge*. Los Angeles, CA: Nash Publishing, 1970.

————. *The History of Astrology*. New York: Arco Publishing, 1972.

Web Site Resources

The following is a list of Internet astrology resources. There are several links where you can acquire either a free or fee-based copy of your horoscope just by entering your birth data, including date, time, and location. Along with the date and city of your birth, having an accurate birth time produces an accurate chart. Check your birth certificate for your exact birth time. Omit the time entirely if you are unsure of your exact birth time. This will produce a sunrise chart, and the Sun will be seen on your First House cusp (the Ascendant). This produces a logical house sequence and planetary placements, whereas an inaccurate time only confuses things. When entering your birth time, be sure to enter a.m. or p.m.

If you are obtaining a birth chart for your company or business enterprise to stay abreast of how future eclipses will affect it, use the most official record you have that established the beginning of the enterprise. The birth of a business is generally based on its incorporation date and time, or the time of its official opening, when it is both an operating entity in the world and operating within legal boundaries. If you have the date but don't recall the time, use 12 noon. A noontime chart works very well for companies without an accurate birth time.

All new enterprises, from a company to a Web site, have a birth time, which is dependant upon the moment it is up and functioning and able to receive visitors.

Eclipses falling on prominent places in an enterprise chart signal similar types of transitions for the company as for an individual in a natal chart. For example, an eclipse falling on one of the chart angles may be followed by relocation, changes in structural appearance, or a change of personnel.

All of the following Web site links have informative articles, and some also provide free or fee-based software to create your own charts.

www.alabe.com

www.astrology-numerology.com

www.astro-horoscopes.com

www.astrology-search.com

www.astrologyhouse.com

www.astrodatabank.com

www.llewellyn.com

www.astro.com

www.astrologers.com

www.stariq.com

www.mountainastrologer.com

www.moonvalleyastrologer.com

www.astrologysoftware.com

www.astrolog.org

www.nickcampion.com

Index

To Write to the Author

If you wish to contact the author or would like more information about this book, please write to the author in care of Llewellyn Worldwide and we will forward your request. Both the author and publisher appreciate hearing from you and learning of your enjoyment of this book and how it has helped you. Llewellyn Worldwide cannot guarantee that every letter written to the author can be answered, but all will be forwarded. Please write to:

Celeste Teal
℅ Llewellyn Worldwide
2143 Wooddale Drive, Dept. 0-7387-0771-6
Woodbury, Minnesota 55125-2989, U.S.A.

Please enclose a self-addressed stamped envelope for reply,
or $1.00 to cover costs. If outside U.S.A., enclose
international postal reply coupon.

Many of Llewellyn's authors have websites with additional information and resources. For more information, please visit our website at http://www.llewellyn.com.